时文速递

云图英语

让/阅/读/更/具/时/事/感

完形填空 | 阅读理解 | 任务型阅读 | 短文填空

云图分级阅读研究院·编著

冲刺篇

本书编委

编者（按姓氏音序排列）

陈郅　李如　刘倩倩　刘雪
杨元元　张欢

编审

侯琳

北京理工大学出版社
BEIJING INSTITUTE OF TECHNOLOGY PRESS

版权专有　侵权必究

图书在版编目（CIP）数据

云图英语时文速递．冲刺篇／云图分级阅读研究院编著．—北京：北京理工大学出版社，2021.6（2022.6重印）
ISBN 978-7-5682-9883-4

Ⅰ.①云… Ⅱ.①云… Ⅲ.①英语—阅读教学—初中—升学参考资料 Ⅳ.①G634.413

中国版本图书馆CIP数据核字（2021）第102215号

出版发行 /	北京理工大学出版社有限责任公司
社　　址 /	北京市海淀区中关村南大街5号
邮　　编 /	100081
电　　话 /	（010）68914775（总编室）
	（010）82562903（教材售后服务热线）
	（010）68944723（其他图书服务热线）
网　　址 /	http://www.bitpress.com.cn
经　　销 /	全国各地新华书店
印　　刷 /	三河市文阁印刷有限公司
开　　本 /	889毫米×1194毫米　1/16
印　　张 /	12.25
字　　数 /	353千字
版　　次 /	2021年6月第1版　2022年6月第3次印刷
定　　价 /	36.00元

责任编辑／王晓莉
文案编辑／王晓莉
责任校对／周瑞红
责任印制／李志强

图书出现印装质量问题，请拨打售后服务热线，本社负责调换

作者的话

一直以来，阅读理解都是中考英语分数占比较高的题型。2022年4月出台的《义务教育英语课程标准（2022年版）》（以下简称"新课标"）中，对阅读"理解性技能"的要求进行了升级，在原来"能理解段落中各句子之间的逻辑关系"的基础上增加了"理解语篇中显性或隐性的逻辑关系"。另外，新课标从"语言能力""文化意识""思维品质""学习能力"四个方面明确了英语学习的目标，其中强调了"对中外文化的理解和对优秀文化的鉴赏"。由此可见，对于阅读理解题型，相比于生硬的解题技巧，学生在新时代表现出的逻辑思维能力以及跨文化认知、态度和行为选择将变得更为重要。

时文阅读作为一种非常有意义的新型阅读模式，不仅可以帮助学生增加阅读量，扩展阅读范围，还能引导学生关注国内外社会热点，关注人类命运和地球家园，帮助学生形成跨文化交际的意识，培养学生跨文化交际的能力，从而进一步拓宽学生的国际视野。现在，越来越多的英语教师选择将英语时文引进课堂教学，让学生接触原汁原味的英文，在培养学生语言能力的同时，还为学生营造了一种英语本土的教学氛围，加深了学生对英语知识、外国文化和风土人情的理解，帮助学生在跨文化交际中克服由于文化背景、交际习惯和思维模式的差异导致的阅读障碍。因此，初中阶段渗透时文阅读具有重要意义。

为了满足广大师生的需求与期望，《云图英语时文速递》在一线名师的共同努力下应运而生。作者精选时文材料，准确把握难易度。全套书共分为基础篇、强化篇和冲刺篇3册，每册设置了14周的阅读内容，每周包括6篇阅读理解题和1篇新闻速递，能满足学生一学期的学习需求。全套书主要包括以下显著特点：

1. 选材新颖，体裁多样

作者依据新课标三大"主题"——人与自我、人与社会、人与自然，从知名新闻网站、杂志刊物广泛选取有关不同国家热点事件的文章，并进一步细分为14个"主题群"，涵盖生活成长、家庭教育、健康饮食、社会人际、文化风俗、科学技术、环境保护等话题。文章结合中学生生活实际情境进行选段，是学生了解国内外信息、提升英语阅读能力的不二之选。同时应用文、记叙文、说明文、议论文等常见文章体裁能让学生着眼于不同体裁文章的思路结构，把握不同文本特点。

2. 贴合学情考情，科学系统设题

本书以新课标为依据，题目设置紧密契合中考要求。题型丰富，既有传统的阅读理解题，

也有符合各地区不同需求的完形填空、任务型阅读与短文填空等题型。因此，本书适用于人教版、仁爱版、外研版、北师大版等多版本初中教材使用者，能满足各地区学生中考阅读的需求。

难度的把控是同类书共同的难点。作者在编写本书时，充分考虑并准确把握词汇的丰富度、用语的精准度、句型结构的多样性以及时文的篇幅和词汇量等。全书难度符合新课标7至9年级的目标要求以及初中三个年级学生的认知水平，对学校平时的测验命题也有一定的可借鉴性。

3. 紧跟潮流，时事风向我知道

本书除每周6篇阅读练习外，另新增一篇新闻速递拓展阅读。新闻均出自知名网站与刊物，包括英国广播公司（BBC）、美国之音广播电台（VOA）、《中国日报国际版》《科学美国人》《卫报》《时代周刊》《美国国家地理》《环球时报》。精选最新季度发布且贴合中学生认知兴趣的新闻，同时在改编过程中保留原文特点与风格，帮助学生在掌握新闻类文章阅读技巧的同时，了解国内外最新热点事件，拓宽阅读面。

4. 特色栏目配置，360度全方位攻克阅读

文前小标签给出了词数、难度和建议用时等信息，方便学生进行自我评估。

"答案解析"梳理思路，解答清晰。

"词汇碎片"积累核心词汇。

"重难句讲解"梳理句式，沉淀语法。

"参考译文"单独成册，实现逐句对照精读。

作者期望通过最新的热点和最优质的题文设计，为学生打开探寻国内外热点讯息的一个小小的窗口；作者期望能帮助家长和老师一起把握中考动态，为学生提供训练素材；作者期望能让学生在做题的过程中，有效提高阅读理解能力，并逐渐了解国内外社会动态发展趋势，打开国际视野，把握时代脉搏。

ENGLISH READING

Contents 目录

人与自我

Week One — 生活成长 / 兴趣爱好 — 主题

- 001 Monday　A 完形填空　湄洲岛少年开设螃蟹博物馆
- 002 Tuesday　B 阅读理解　少年在天文摄影大赛中获奖
- 003 Wednesday　C 阅读理解　走在科技前沿的年轻人们
- 004 Thursday　D 阅读理解　岩坎香：不能做职业球员，那就成就别人
- 005 Friday　E 任务型阅读　冬奥会激发人们对冬季运动项目的热爱
- 006 Saturday　F 短文填空　疫情时的爱好成为一种痴迷

Week Two — 校园生活 — 主题

- 007 Monday　A 完形填空　探索宇宙：中国山区学生成功制造微型火箭
- 008 Tuesday　B 阅读理解　教育质量的提高有助于打破贫困循环
- 009 Wednesday　C 阅读理解　融合教育：为更多残疾儿童提供九年义务教育
- 010 Thursday　D 任务型阅读　学校允许学生在期末考试中携带"小抄"
- 011 Friday　E 短文填空　校园推广冰雪运动，增强学生体魄，促进性格发展
- 012 Saturday　F 短文填空　年轻的时装设计师在校园茁壮成长

Week Three — 家庭教育 — 主题

- 013 Monday　A 完形填空　偏爱一个孩子真的是一件坏事吗？
- 014 Tuesday　B 阅读理解　一份情人节亲子活动邀请函
- 015 Wednesday　C 阅读理解　父母应该在孩子面前争论吗？
- 016 Thursday　D 任务型阅读　言传身教：让每一个孩子都成为"改变世界的人"
- 017 Friday　E 短文填空　关于疫情期间家长帮助孩子在家学习的建议
- 018 Saturday　F 短文填空　父子搭档：用善良助力成功

Week Four — 健康饮食 — 主题

编号	星期	题型	主题
019	Monday	A 完形填空	总是忍不住想喝汽水？当心汽水成瘾
020	Tuesday	B 阅读理解	"绿色巴士"蔬菜餐厅
021	Wednesday	C 阅读理解	关于帮助有心理健康问题的人，你需要知道这些
022	Thursday	D 阅读理解	有助于缓解焦虑的食物
023	Friday	E 任务型阅读	米饼属于健康食品吗？
024	Saturday	F 短文填空	旅行者腹泻：闹心的"水土不服"

人与社会

Week Five — 社会人际 — 主题

编号	星期	题型	主题
025	Monday	A 完形填空	真人秀节目《奇遇·人间角落》的意义
026	Tuesday	B 阅读理解	女性在时尚界的影响力与责任
027	Wednesday	C 短文填空	美国"乒乓外交"亲历者讲述访华之旅
028	Thursday	D 任务型阅读	宁波"00后时光修复师"为烈士修复遗物
029	Friday	E 任务型阅读	女航天员进行舱外活动的独特优势
030	Saturday	F 短文填空	疫情期间，地铁清洁工们超高标准的清洁工作

Week Six — 文学/艺术/体育 — 主题

编号	星期	题型	主题
031	Monday	A 完形填空	《我们北京见》欢迎世界各国共享体育盛事
032	Tuesday	B 阅读理解	充满年味的北京艺术展
033	Wednesday	C 阅读理解	冬季运动未来在中国年轻一代中的发展潜力巨大
034	Thursday	D 任务型阅读	第六届中欧国际文学节：女性写作具有非凡价值
035	Friday	E 任务型阅读	艺术项目用音乐抚慰新冠肺炎患者
036	Saturday	F 短文填空	《中国潮音》：以时尚的方式呈现传统音乐

Week Seven 历史地理 主题

- 037 Monday   A 完形填空   延续古籍生命，让文字"活"起来
- 038 Tuesday   B 阅读理解   探秘中轴线，品读北京城
- 039 Wednesday C 任务型阅读 西藏考古发现实证民族文化交流历史
- 040 Thursday   D 任务型阅读 太子城遗址——考古发现的第一座金朝行宫
- 041 Friday   E 短文填空   西安西汉古墓确定墓主人身份
- 042 Saturday   F 短文填空   广东鲜为人知的历史

Week Eight 文化风俗 主题

- 043 Monday   A 完形填空   奥运五环的象征意义是什么？
- 044 Tuesday   B 阅读理解   讲述无数传奇的光影戏剧——皮影戏
- 045 Wednesday C 阅读理解   少数民族服饰：历史传统与艺术的融合
- 046 Thursday   D 任务型阅读 为什么玫瑰在情人节大受欢迎？
- 047 Friday   E 任务型阅读 拥有光明未来的古老艺术——醴陵陶瓷
- 048 Saturday   F 短文填空   为什么四叶草被认为能带来好运？

Week Nine 科学技术 主题

- 049 Monday   A 完形填空   高效杀菌空气消毒机助力科技抗疫
- 050 Tuesday   B 阅读理解   无人驾驶汽车传递火炬，点亮智能驾驶的未来
- 051 Wednesday C 阅读理解   未来的"飞行汽车"等待起飞许可
- 052 Thursday   D 阅读理解   世界首条仿生机器鲸鲨惊艳亮相上海
- 053 Friday   E 短文填空   嫦娥五号取得月球上有水的实证
- 054 Saturday   F 短文填空   金属3D打印如何发展以适应极端的太空条件？

Week Ten　人物传奇　　主题

055	Monday	A 完形填空	"最飒女保镖"张美丽
056	Tuesday	B 阅读理解	2022年北京冬奥会：中国设计师们书写时尚新篇章
057	Wednesday	C 阅读理解	"打树花"艺术家和其伤痕背后的匠人精神
058	Thursday	D 阅读理解	倪沈键：让蓝印花布染色技艺流传于世
059	Friday	E 阅读理解	《构建一朵雪花》编舞者——王媛媛
060	Saturday	F 任务型阅读	黄杨伟：为黎族织锦编织一个光明的未来

Week Eleven　旅行交通　　主题

061	Monday	A 完形填空	2022年春运开始，预计客运量达11.8亿人次
062	Tuesday	B 阅读理解	不能错过的中老铁路中国段沿线景点
063	Wednesday	C 阅读理解	冬奥会热带动旅游热潮
064	Thursday	D 阅读理解	深圳湾公园——摄影者的天堂
065	Friday	E 任务型阅读	北京环球度假区日游客量或超上海迪士尼
066	Saturday	F 短文填空	北京公布冬奥会交通管理细节：优先保障冬奥交通

Week Twelve　异国风情　　主题

067	Monday	A 完形填空	印度孔通村：名字是一首歌的地方
068	Tuesday	B 阅读理解	斯凯岛：苏格兰盖尔语复兴的地方
069	Wednesday	C 阅读理解	让初到挪威的人瞠目的社交准则
070	Thursday	D 阅读理解	拉茶：马来西亚的国民饮料
071	Friday	E 任务型阅读	夏威夷羽毛花环：一种表达感恩的最高仪式
072	Saturday	F 短文填空	的里雅斯特：令人震惊的意大利咖啡之都

人与自然

Week Thirteen   自然生态   主题

073	Monday	A 完形填空	在"海底大草原"上"种草",赋予海洋新的生命力
074	Tuesday	B 阅读理解	蝙蝠幼崽像人类婴儿一样咿呀学语
075	Wednesday	C 阅读理解	蜂房中的秘密
076	Thursday	D 任务型阅读	大兴安岭重现野生东北虎踪迹
077	Friday	E 任务型阅读	中国研究人员发现野生兰科植物新品种
078	Saturday	F 短文填空	39头野生亚洲象在中国云南"聚餐"

Week Fourteen   环境保护   主题

079	Monday	A 完形填空	冬奥会期间,北京PM 2.5浓度创历史新低
080	Tuesday	B 阅读理解	来自护鸟摄影师的一封信
081	Wednesday	C 阅读理解	环保与浪漫交织的冬奥烟花秀
082	Thursday	D 任务型阅读	中国出台首部湿地保护法,守护"地球之肾"
083	Friday	E 短文填空	上海致力于改善空气和水质
084	Saturday	F 短文填空	世界顶尖科学家齐聚上海讨论双碳治理

答案解析   085

Week One 生活成长/兴趣爱好

Monday A 完形填空

体 裁	记叙文	题 材	兴趣爱好	正确率	___/10	词 数	293
难 度	★★★☆☆	建议用时	10分钟	实际用时		答案页码	085

原创题

The World Crab Museum on Meizhou Island, Putian, Fujian Province, is drawing enthusiasts (爱好者) from across China. Covering over 1,000 square meters, this museum is home to more than 323 species of __1__.

"More than 90 percent of the collections here are rarely seen crabs, and a dozen of those on display are endangered (濒临灭绝的) species, __2__ the six-legged giant crab," said Liu Cheng-hung, the museum's owner and manager.

Born in an island county, Liu has felt __3__ to the ocean since he was very young. Most of his memories of his hometown are about gentle breezes (微风) in spring, heat waves in summer and the vast ocean year-round.

"I feel familiar with the ocean. I have been interested in water sports and ocean activities __4__ a young age," he said. His __5__ crabs and ocean creatures has been deeply influenced by his family. "My grandfather started collecting crabs out of interest. My father joined him and __6__ making crab specimens (标本). They gained lots of experience and professional knowledge," Liu said.

After graduating in 2017, when he was in his 20s, Liu decided to __7__ to Penghu, his hometown, and work in the local travel industry. In 2019, he __8__ a temporary (临时的，暂时的) crab museum in Xiamen, Fujian, to make his debut (首次亮相) and test the market, closing it in December that year. Last year, Liu opened the World Crab Museum in Meizhou. __9__ the number of crabs the family collected grew, Liu learned about the diversity (多样性) of the natural world and of ocean creatures. As a result, his hobby __10__ became his career.

Since it opened, the museum has received 100,000 public visits. Liu hopes to collect many more specimens so he can open more museums nationwide.

1. A. trees   B. animals
   C. crabs   D. flowers
2. A. except for   B. such as
   C. let alone   D. more than
3. A. connected   B. similar
   C. harmful   D. useful
4. A. in   B. on
   C. of   D. from
5. A. fear of   B. love for
   C. hatred for   D. worry about
6. A. refused   B. forgot
   C. stopped   D. started
7. A. keep   B. invite
   C. return   D. compare
8. A. joined   B. opened
   C. discovered   D. entered
9. A. Before   B. If
   C. As   D. Unless
10. A. gradually   B. recently
    C. hardly   D. suddenly

词汇碎片

manager n. 经营者；经理   creature n. 生物；动物   collect v. 收集   professional adj. 专业的

重难句讲解

After graduating in 2017, when he was in his 20s, Liu decided to return to Penghu, his hometown, and work in the local travel industry. 2017年大学毕业后，20多岁的柳政鸿决定回到家乡——澎湖，在当地的旅游行业工作。

本句是复合句。介词短语 After... 和 when 引导的状语从句均表示时间，his hometown 是 Penghu 的同位语。

Tuesday B 阅读理解

Wang Zhipu, a student at Yongtai No. 1 High School, taught himself astrophotography (天体摄影术) by reading books and by searching online.

Recently, his efforts were rewarded (奖励) when he won the title of "Young Astronomy Photographer of the Year 2021" in the Royal Observatory Greenwich's annual astrophotography competition.

The event, jointly organized by the Royal Observatory Greenwich in London and the BBC's *Sky at Night* magazine, is the world's biggest astrophotography competition. This year the competition attracted (吸引) over 4,500 entries from 75 countries. Wang's photo took first prize in the Young Competition category, an award for photographers aged 15 and under.

Following the online awards ceremony (典礼) in September, some of the shortlisted (入围的) and prizewinning photos have been put on display at the National Maritime Museum, which is part of the Royal Museums Greenwich in London.

Wang worked on the photo for some time. During last year's summer vacation, he took photos of Saturn, Venus and Jupiter. Last October, he shot the moon, the Sun, Uranus and Neptune and earlier this year, he tried three times to take a satisfactory shot of Mercury.

He chose one photo of each planet from the numerous ones he'd taken, and then created a single, composite (合成的) image using computer software. Busy with his studies, Wang made use of every spare moment, getting up at dawn (黎明), sleeping early to wake up at midnight, and even taking time off from evening classes when necessary.

His passion (热情) touched the jury (裁判委员会). One of the judges said, "As a planetary scientist, I applaud the work that has gone into creating this photo."

1. How did Wang Zhipu learn about astrophotography?
   A. Learning from his teachers.
   B. Learning from his parents.
   C. Learning from his classmates.
   D. Learning by himself.

2. What is the condition for entering the Young Competition category?
   A. Aged 15 and under.
   B. Aged 15 and over.
   C. Living in London.
   D. Living outside London.

3. What can we know about Wang Zhipu?
   A. He is from a wealthy family.
   B. His studies are unsatisfactory.
   C. He works hard on taking photos.
   D. He spends lots of money taking photos.

词汇碎片

search v. 搜索；搜寻   competition n. 比赛   display n. 展示，陈列   touch v. 感动，触动

重难句讲解

Following the online awards ceremony in September, some of the shortlisted and prizewinning photos have been put on display at the National Maritime Museum, which is part of the Royal Museums Greenwich in London. 在9月的线上颁奖典礼之后，一些入围和获奖的照片已在英国国家海事博物馆展出，该博物馆是伦敦格林尼治皇家博物馆的一部分。

本句是复合句。其中 which 引导非限制性定语从句，修饰 the National Maritime Museum。

Dear John,

　　I'm writing to share with you the story of four young people who are quite popular online for their achievements in the fields they are interested in. They are Lingshiqi, Zhihuijun, Hetongxue and Liu Shang.

　　When Lingshiqi had too many bags to carry, instead of asking someone for help, the then 18-year-old spent 200 days addressing the problem. He built a robot, which can follow him wherever he goes, and upon which he can ride. The robot's name is Devil.

　　Tech influencer Zhihuijun is already a household (家喻户晓的) name. A 16-minute video clip features the 28-year-old Huawei engineer designing and creating a robotic arm. Powered by Huawei's 5G technology, it can be remotely (远程地) controlled to do the most precise (精确的；准确的) activity.

　　After hearing that Apple canceled its AirPower wireless charging mat in 2019, Hetongxue was inspired (鼓舞，激励) and invented his own wireless charging desk, which can fill the batteries of three devices at the same time. The 22-year-old graduate (大学毕业生) from the Beijing University of Posts and Telecommunications posted a 7-minute video in October, which has been viewed more than 17 million times.

　　As if these <u>feats</u> were not surprising enough, the self-built model rocket launch of another young man, Liu Shang, may actually push the boundaries (边界) to a new horizon. The aerospace (航空航天) engineering sophomore's (大二学生) 10-minute video, posted last month, shows how Liu built a 4.5-kilogram, 1.1-meter-tall rocket. In the conclusion of the video, viewers see it take off to a height of 300 meters, before deploying (利用；调动) a parachute (降落伞) and gently touching back down.

　　All of them brought about great innovation out of interest, so I wish you could follow your heart and choose a job you are interested in.

　　　　　　　　　　　　　　　　　　　　　Sincerely yours,
　　　　　　　　　　　　　　　　　　　　　Lisa

1. What can the robot Devil do?
   A. Cleaning the house.
   B. Washing the dishes.
   C. Carrying bags.
   D. Writing letters.
2. What did Zhihuijun do?
   A. He built a robotic arm.
   B. He created a robot.
   C. He invented a wireless charging mat.
   D. He built a rocket.
3. What can we know about Hetongxue's video?
   A. It features him building a rocket.
   B. It is a 10-minute video.
   C. It was made and posted by his parents.
   D. It was very popular online.
4. What does the underlined word "feats" in Paragraph 5 mean in Chinese?
   A. 盛宴
   B. 成就
   C. 命运
   D. 冲动

field n. 领域　　feature v. 由……主演　　cancel v. 取消　　viewer n. 观众

Thursday D 阅读理解

Ai Kanxiang is about to finish his first semester at college, where he is working hard to make his dream come true. A physical education major, he hopes to become a PE teacher and train China's future soccer players. Two years ago, though, his dream was even bigger. Ai hoped to join the men's national soccer team, but the 20-year-old has experienced twists and changed his dream.

Born and raised in a small village in the Xishuangbanna Dai Autonomous Prefecture (西双版纳傣族自治州) in Southwest China's Yunnan Province, Ai drew public attention last year after videos of him playing soccer in a river went viral. Demonstrating (展示) creativity, such as the way to do a precise bicycle kick in the water, he became an online celebrity (名人), with some fans even saying that he was "better than professional players".

Some of those professional players, like Liu Yang and Wei Shihao, recorded videos to encourage Ai, and he later received an offer to train with a professional team in Kunming, further boosting his confidence. He then made up his mind to develop his skills, setting the goal of joining the national team someday. But when Ai finally played with the team, he was humbled. He was barely (几乎不) able to keep up. His skills were not as strong as he had imagined, and he had little awareness of teamwork.

The setback (挫折；阻碍) cooled his enthusiasm (热情). Ai realized he had bitten off more than he could chew. He needed more experience. So he set a new and more practical goal—to apply (申请) to university and become a PE teacher. In August, Ai was accepted at the Yunnan Minzu University in Kunming to major in physical education.

He said that his experiences as a high schooler will help him understand his future students better, as well as bringing him closer to his dream.

1. What was Ai Kanxiang's dream at first?
   A. To become a PE teacher.
   B. To become a math teacher.
   C. To become a soccer player.
   D. To become a baseball player.

2. What does the underlined phrase "went viral" in Paragraph 2 mean in Chinese?
   A. 走红   B. 消失
   C. 增加   D. 失败

3. Which of the following is NOT the reason for Ai Kanxiang to change his dream?
   A. He was lack of awareness of teamwork.
   B. His teammates were not friendly to him.
   C. His skills were not good enough.
   D. He found it hard to keep up with the team.

4. Why did Ai Kanxiang apply to university?
   A. To get into the men's national soccer team.
   B. To gain more experience for being a PE teacher.
   C. To earn more money after graduation (毕业).
   D. To make more friends in college.

5. What might be the best title for this passage?
   A. A Student Hopes to Become a Soccer Player
   B. A Student's Soccer Dream Failed
   C. A Student's Soccer Dream Came True
   D. A Student Hopes to Train Future Athletes

semester n. 学期   receive v. 收到；接受   major in 以……为专业

Some of those professional players, like Liu Yang and Wei Shihao, recorded videos to encourage Ai, and he later received an offer to train with a professional team in Kunming, further boosting his confidence. 一些职业球员，如刘洋和韦世豪，录制了视频鼓励岩坎香，后来他收到了去昆明与职业球队一起训练的邀请，这进一步增强了他的信心。

本句为and连接的并列句。like Liu Yang and Wei Shihao 为插入语，further boosting his confidence 是现在分词短语作结果状语。

Friday E 任务型阅读

| 体 裁 | 记叙文 | 题 材 | 兴趣爱好 | 正确率 | ___/5 | 词 数 | 329 |
| 难 度 | ★★★★☆ | 建议用时 | 7分钟 | 实际用时 | ___ | 答案页码 | 087 |

Fourth grader Xu Depei has been skating a couple of times over the winter holidays. "I've had a lot of fun on the ice. It wasn't cold, and exercising makes me strong and warm," the 10-year-old said.

Thanks to the Beijing 2022 Olympic and Paralympic Winter Games, many Beijing residents like Xu and her family have been able to enjoy winter sports-related activities and to get to know more about them.

Beijing has done a lot to promote (促进，推广) winter sports. According to Beijing's cultural and tourism bureau, the capital will be organizing 8,266 city activities to encourage residents to engage (使融入) with the Games and promote winter sports during the Olympics. Sixteen Winter Olympic squares have been set up in 15 districts, mostly in parks and open public spaces.

"Information about the Games is everywhere these days, and it's making people excited about winter sports," said Zhang Chao, adding that he's now more interested in taking up winter sports as a result. "I'd heard of some winter sports before, but I didn't pay them much attention. The Winter Olympic Games actually makes me want to participate (参加) more," he said, adding that he planned to go skating the following day.

Wei Yurong said that he enjoys figure skating (花样滑冰) the most. <u>Born and raised in Northeast China's Heilongjiang Province—the coldest province in the country—the 70-year-old has enjoyed winter sports since he was young.</u> But he said that because of the Winter Olympics, even he has learned about a few new sports, like curling.

"Compared to my hometown, Beijing was less passionate (狂热的，热诚的) about winter sports before. But in recent years, especially this year, they have started trending (成为热门话题), thanks to the Games," he said, adding that his granddaughter is learning ice hockey. "My son took my granddaughter skiing several times this winter," he said.

将下面两个句子补充完整。
1. I've enjoyed my time on the ice. I don't feel cold, and skating ___
2. ___ Beijing residents to enjoy winter sports-related activities.

找出并写下第三段的主题句。
3. ___

简要回答下面这个问题。
4. When did Zhang Chao plan to go skating?
___

将文中画线的句子译成汉语。
5. ___

词汇碎片

thanks to 由于，幸亏   resident n. 居民   capital n. 首都   compare v. 比较

重难句讲解

According to Beijing's cultural and tourism bureau, the capital will be organizing 8,266 city activities to encourage residents to engage with the Games and promote winter sports during the Olympics. 据北京市文化和旅游局介绍，北京将组织8 266场城市活动，鼓励市民融入冬奥会，并在冬奥会期间推广冬季运动。

本句是简单句。主干为 the capital will be organizing 8,266 city activities。According to... 作状语，to encourage... and promote... 为目的状语。

Saturday F 短文填空

This long-running pandemic (流行病) has turned many of us, locked in our homes, from unskilled (1) _____ expert. When there's nothing to do, you just have to find something to do. The lockdown (行动限制) taught (2) _____ (I) a thing or two about orchids (兰花).

Back home in New Jersey, I've got pots (盆) of these pretty houseplants in the kitchen, the (3) _____ (live) room and the home office. They're basically put there for aesthetics (美学，美感) but also to have some form of nature breathing life inside our house.

When we (4) _____ (come) to live in Beijing, I found out how inexpensive orchids are. A potted orchid costs around 100 yuan ($14) through the online shopping platform Taobao. Something similar would have cost at least $30 in (5) _____ Jersey store. I was instantly thrilled.

I bought a couple of plants to liven (使活跃) up our Beijing apartment and also to re-create the feel of home. (6) _____ (sad), after a couple of months, my orchids started dying. From YouTube, I learned to prune stems (修剪花茎), use banana leaves as fertilizer (肥料，化肥) (7) _____ just use a little more water to prolong (延长) their lives. I learned that US orchids and Beijing orchids are raised under (8) _____ (difference) growing conditions, therefore cared for in different ways.

My orchids and I get along fine these days. I have one pot by the kitchen window, two pots by the altar table and one by the living room. I (9) _____ love to have two more by the night stand, until my husband stopped me. He said the apartment is starting to look (10) _____ a funeral parlor (殡仪馆)! Funny how this little hobby has become an obsession (痴迷).

阅读短文，在短文空缺处填入适当的单词，或用括号内所给单词的适当形式填空。

(1) _____
(2) _____
(3) _____
(4) _____
(5) _____
(6) _____
(7) _____
(8) _____
(9) _____
(10) _____

词汇碎片
expert n. 专家 pretty adj. 漂亮的 form n. 形式，形态 husband n. 丈夫

重难句讲解
I learned that US orchids and Beijing orchids are raised under different growing conditions, therefore cared for in different ways.
我了解到，美国兰花和北京兰花是在不同的生长条件下培养的，因此照料的方式也有所不同。
本句是复合句。主句主干为 I learned that...，that 引导宾语从句。under... conditions 和 in... ways 为介词短语作状语。

Week Two 校园生活

Monday　A 完形填空

体　裁	记叙文	题　材	校园生活	正确率	／15	词　数	298
难　度	★★★☆☆	建议用时	15分钟	实际用时		答案页码	088

In southwest China's wild mountains, a small rocket took off. It wasn't an official rocket, __1__ an edutainment (寓教于乐) experiment by two software engineers from the __2__ coast and 200 children at a rural elementary school. The mini rocket was named "Lead Mine School No.1" and it was 1.37 meters __3__.

"I wish in the future I could __4__ in a rocket to see whether Mercury (水星) can spray (喷) water and whether Mars can breathe flames," a boy said when asked what he was __5__ upon seeing the rocket take off.

Last October, __6__ the students watched the livestream for the launch (发射) of the Shenzhou-13 crewed spaceship at school, they were so __7__. Days later, two software engineers from the east __8__ to give online classes to the students.

During the classes, the children __9__ many questions. "Why is there no water on Mars?" "Why are there so many craters (坑) on the Moon?" "Will the Sun collide (碰撞) with the Earth in thousands of years?" The two men __10__ them one by one until one student asked, "Can we make a rocket?" After hesitating (犹豫) for a few seconds, they said, "Okay, let's give it a __11__." Then an amateur (业余的) rocket team was born.

But designing and building a rocket was much more __12__. For three months, the two men spent every weekend building the rocket. Day by day, they made all the 100-odd parts needed to build a small rocket. In early December, they __13__ tested the engines (引擎).

On January 5, the mini rocket was __14__ for launch. Students wrote their __15__ on the rocket. "I want to be an astronaut when I grow up," a boy wrote.

1. A. and　　　　B. so
   C. but　　　　D. or
2. A. south　　　B. north
   C. west　　　　D. east
3. A. long　　　 B. big
   C. deep　　　　D. far
4. A. fly　　　　B. live
   C. call　　　　D. move
5. A. caring about　　B. thinking about
   C. worrying about　D. talking about
6. A. though　　B. when
   C. since　　　D. until
7. A. relaxed　　B. afraid
   C. bored　　　D. excited
8. A. discussed　B. expected
   C. volunteered D. regretted
9. A. agreed　　B. raised
   C. realized　D. expressed
10. A. answered　B. forced
    C. examined　D. promised
11. A. share　　B. smile
    C. try　　　D. turn
12. A. dangerous　B. interesting
    C. challenging D. satisfying
13. A. successfully B. seriously
    C. easily　　　D. secretly
14. A. sudden　　B. ready
    C. special　　D. sure
15. A. steps　　 B. stories
    C. predictions D. dreams

词汇碎片

take off 起飞　　experiment n. 实验；试验　　elementary adj. 初级的；基础的

重难句讲解

Day by day, they made all the 100-odd parts needed to build a small rocket. 日子一天天过去，制造一枚小型火箭所需的100多个零件全部备齐。

本句是简单句。主语是 they，谓语是 made，宾语是 all the 100-odd parts。过去分词短语 needed to build a small rocket 修饰宾语 all the 100-odd parts。odd 有"大约；略多"之意。

Tuesday B 阅读理解

China has lifted about eight hundred million people out of absolute poverty (绝对贫困) within 40 years. A very important effort in achieving this goal (目标) was improving the quality of education for those living in poor rural areas.

Our reporter today takes us to southwest China's Sichuan Province, to a middle school in the Liangshan Yi Autonomous Prefecture (凉山彝族自治州), which used to be one of the poorest areas in China.

Wenggu Wushamo	Student, Xide Middle School "I'm in junior high school. My dream is to get into a senior high school, and then into a college. My sister is a college student. She told me that the college life is so colorful that I can do many things to improve myself."
Lei Yousheng	Teacher, Xide Middle School "I think education plays a key role in fighting poverty. So we encourage students to work hard and get good grades. What we're doing here, is to bring positive changes to a student, to a family, an ethnic (民族的) group and even a whole nation."
Lege Watie	Principal (校长), Xide Middle School "We've piloted a program of sending some of our students to middle schools in more developed areas, where they have better chances of going to colleges. It allows them to realize an education gap (差距), and encourages them to work even harder. When they return, they could contribute (贡献) more to local communities."
Puti Aji	Xide Resident (居民) "I've never attended schools in my life, but I wish that all my children receive high-quality education. I really hope that I could read Chinese characters, speak the language well, and experience more new things."

1. Xide Middle School is in _____ Province.
   A. Hunan   B. Sichuan
   C. Shanxi   D. Shandong
2. What can we know about Wenggu Wushamo?
   A. She is a college student.
   B. She has a sister.
   C. Her school life is colorful.
   D. Her dream has come true.
3. Who is Lei Yousheng?
   A. He is the principal of Xide Middle School.
   B. He is a student of Xide Middle School.
   C. He is a teacher of Xide Middle School.
   D. He is a local farmer in Xide.
4. Why are some students of Xide Middle School sent to other middle schools?
   A. To receive better education.
   B. To compete with other students.
   C. To experience college life.
   D. To work in more developed areas.
5. Where can we probably find this passage?
   A. In a diary.
   B. In a history book.
   C. In a science magazine.
   D. In a newspaper.

quality n. 质量   key adj. 关键的；主要的   pilot v. 试点，试行   character n. 文字

Our reporter today takes us to southwest China's Sichuan Province, to a middle school in the Liangshan Yi Autonomous Prefecture, which used to be one of the poorest areas in China. 今天，我们的记者带领我们走进中国西南部的四川省，走进凉山彝族自治州的一所中学。凉山彝族自治州曾是中国最贫穷的地区之一。

本句是复合句。which引导的定语从句修饰the Liangshan Yi Autonomous Prefecture。used to do sth. 表示"过去常常做某事"；"one of the + 形容词最高级 + 可数名词复数"表示"……中最……之一"。

Wednesday C 阅读理解

体 裁	记叙文	题 材	校园生活	正确率	___/5	词 数	251
难 度	★★★☆☆	建议用时	6 分钟	实际用时	___	答案页码	089

More than 97 percent of China's disabled children will receive schooling from first to ninth grade by 2025, according to a new plan designed to make sure such children have equal (平等的) access to education and the opportunity to shine.

The average government expenditure (开支) on disabled children in compulsory education (义务教育) will be raised to 7,000 yuan per student per year by 2025, it said. The plan also called for more efforts to develop preschool education, vocational education (职业教育), higher education and adult education for disabled people.

Special education is one of the most urgent (急迫的) needs for children with disabilities, and the level of special education shows the development and civilization (文明) of society.

Internationally, integrated education (融合教育) is the main approach (方式) to achieving the high-quality development of special education, as integrating children with special needs in regular schools helps them fully achieve their potential (潜力) and fit into society.

Qi Yonggang, the father of a 10-year-old girl with autism (自闭症) in Beijing, said hiring a teacher for his daughter cost the family up to 15,000 yuan a month. Qi said he was not willing to send his daughter to a special education school because he wants her to experience regular schooling, believing that will help her learn skills and abilities that can be used in everyday life.

He said he was glad to see the government pay more attention to integrated education for children with autism, and he wants to send his daughter to a secondary vocational school, so that she can find a job.

1. Why did the authority design the new plan according to Paragraph 1?
   A. To make sure all the children receive education.
   B. To help every student shine.
   C. To help disabled children find a job.
   D. To protect disabled children's right to receive education.

2. The government is doing a lot to help disabled children except _____.
   A. offering jobs to them
   B. raising the expenditure on them
   C. providing special education for them
   D. helping them receive higher education

3. According to Paragraph 4, "integrated education" means _____ study together.
   A. students from different countries
   B. students in different health conditions
   C. students of all ages
   D. students of different majors

4. How did Qi Yonggang's daughter receive education?
   A. By having a teacher at home.
   B. By going to a special education school.
   C. By going to a vocational school.
   D. By taking online classes.

5. What is the best title for the text?
   A. Special Education in China
   B. The Important Integrated Education
   C. A Plan for Disabled Kids
   D. Children with Autism

词汇碎片

shine v. 出色，出类拔萃；发光　　call for 提倡；要求　　special adj. 特殊的；特别的

重难句讲解

Qi said he was not willing to send his daughter to a special education school because he wants her to experience regular schooling, believing that will help her learn skills and abilities that can be used in everyday life. 齐永刚说他不愿意把女儿送到特殊教育学校，因为他想让女儿体验常规的学校教育，他相信这将有助于她学习日常生活中使用的技能和能力。

本句是复合句。主句为主谓宾结构，宾语是省略了引导词 that 的宾语从句 (that) he was not willing to... schooling，be willing to do sth. 意为"愿意做某事"。because 引导原因状语从句。现在分词短语 believing that will... everyday life 作状语，其中 that can be used in everyday life 是定语从句，修饰名词短语 skills and abilities。

Students of Yuanling Primary School were allowed to bring "crib notes (小抄)" in the final exams. In this case, "crib notes" were not something students cheat with in exams, but a summary (总结) of how well students mastered the knowledge. __1__.

It answered the call of the country's "burden-reducing policies" (减负政策). __2__ and they were aimed to ease (减轻) the burden on students during the period of compulsory education.

__3__. The first and second graders were examined by playing games connected to the subject. Each student in the third to the sixth grades could bring a piece of A4 paper with their summaries of the key points of knowledge and the parts of knowledge that he or she has not fully mastered.

The vice principal (副校长) of Yuanling Primary School said, "__4__. A student who can summarize knowledge on a piece of A4 paper can understand the knowledge and increase his or her thinking ability, and such a student can deal with different subjects in the future."

In terms of school reports, students only received their grading levels instead of specific scores. __5__: subject awareness (意识), subject competence, class performance, after-school performance, and final assessment. The final assessment of the subject was determined (决定) by the number of A grades earned in the five aspects. "We hope this move could bring change in education," the vice principal said.

阅读短文，从下列选项中选出能填入文中空白处的最佳选项。

A. The final exams in the school were taken in different forms

B. This move was a part of the school's "5A Academic Assessment"

C. Each subject was assessed (评估) by five aspects (方面)

D. These policies were introduced by Chinese authorities

E. We value students' learning abilities more than their scores

Friday E 短文填空

| 体裁 | 记叙文 | 题材 | 校园生活 | 正确率 | ___/10 | 词数 | 264 |
| 难度 | ★★★☆☆ | 建议用时 | 10分钟 | 实际用时 | | 答案页码 | 090 |

In midafternoon, a group of students from Yanqing No. 2 Primary School in Beijing went to a nearby ice rink (溜冰场).

Among them, a student (1) _____ people's eyes for her deft (灵巧的) moves on the ice. "My daughter loves skating," the student's mother said. "It has been two and a half years since she started going to an ice rink for practice about four (2) _____ a week." "We hope that every student from our school will be able to master at (3) _____ one ice and snow sport," the vice principal of the school said.

At Beijing Guangqumen Middle School, floor hockey (地板曲棍球) is in the curriculum (课程). A student said she became interested (4) _____ floor hockey in her second year at the junior middle-school division. "We were given a lot of opportunities for (5) _____ in classes and our school has also offered optional (选修的) (6) _____, including skating and skiing. Thus, I've gained a better understanding of ice and snow sports," she said.

The Beijing Education Commission (北京市教育委员会) has held a series of promotional (推广的) events citywide (7) _____ 2017, encouraging ice and snow sports into campuses. Data from the commission show that Beijing is home to 200 schools featuring ice and snow sports and 200 Olympic education demonstration schools. The (8) _____ of the annual event's participants (参与者) has grown from some 500 before to more (9) _____ 1,700, and the period has extended from one month to nearly two months.

Promoting ice and snow sports at school (10) _____ students to build their strength and develop a strong character.

阅读短文，从方框中选择合适的单词并用其正确形式填空，使短文通顺、意思完整。每空限填一词，每词限用一次。

practice
little
time
than
catch
help
in
since
course
number

词汇碎片

a group of 一群；一组   nearby adj. 附近的；邻近的   skating n. 溜冰，滑冰   skiing n. 滑雪

重难句讲解

Data from the commission show that Beijing is home to 200 schools featuring ice and snow sports and 200 Olympic education demonstration schools. 来自该委员会的数据显示，北京市拥有200所以冰雪运动为特色的学校和200所奥林匹克教育示范学校。

本句是复合句。主句的主干是 Data show that...，为主谓宾结构，其中宾语是 that 引导的宾语从句。介词短语 from the commission 作后置定语，修饰 Data。现在分词短语 featuring ice and snow sports 修饰 200 schools，feature 作动词时可表示"以……为特色"。

Saturday F 短文填空

体裁: 记叙文　题材: 校园生活　正确率: ___/10　词数: 262
难度: ★★★☆☆　建议用时: 10分钟　实际用时: ___　答案页码: 090

Unlike traditional fine art (美术) courses where kids learn drawing and painting, a practical art course given (1)_____ Longhua District No. 3 Experimental School teaches students to design and make their own dresses. Starting this month, all students in Longhua can take the course online.

After having a basic understanding of traditional Hakka (客家) clothes, students in pairs spent (2)_____ hour drawing, cutting and making their prototype (雏形) dresses during a fashion design class.

In each group, two students posed as a client (客户) and a fashion (3)_____, and discussed every detail of the dresses they were going to make. (4)_____ some trial and error (反复试验), the young designers finally turned a piece of fabric (布料) into a dress. Then, they displayed their work and received comments from fellow students (5)_____ the tutor.

The idea to start a fashion designing course appeared (6)_____ 2019, as the fine arts teachers at the school decided (7)_____ combine the local cultural traditions with their teaching. The school is located in the heartland of Longhua, a district with a large Hakka population.

Starting with painting patterns, the teachers guided (8)_____ step by step to learn the basics of fashion design. The effort aims to bring out students' creativity and nurture (培养) in them a love for the Hakka culture. There (9)_____ two student manuals (手册) for the course, teaching about the history of the Hakka people and their clothes.

The school also organized field trips to nearby museums and galleries, (10)_____ students saw Hakka clothes from the past and sat through lectures (讲座) by established designers on how to find inspiration (灵感) for new creations.

阅读短文，在短文空缺处填入适当的单词，使短文通顺、意思完整。

(1)_____
(2)_____
(3)_____
(4)_____
(5)_____
(6)_____
(7)_____
(8)_____
(9)_____
(10)_____

词汇碎片
design v. 设计　　basic adj. 基本的；基础的　　turn... into... 使……变成……　　comment n. 评论

重难句讲解
The effort aims to bring out students' creativity and nurture in them a love for the Hakka culture. 这一活动旨在激发学生的创造力，培养学生对客家文化的喜爱。

本句是简单句。不定式短语 to bring out... the Hakka culture 中包含两个并列的动宾结构 bring out students' creativity 和 nurture in them a love for the Hakka culture。aim to do sth. 意为"旨在做某事"，bring out 意为"激发"。

Week Three 家庭教育

Monday A 完形填空

体裁: 议论文　题材: 家庭教育　正确率: ___/10　词数: 303
难度: ★★★☆☆　建议用时: 10分钟　实际用时: ___　答案页码: 091

Although it may be uncomfortable to admit (承认), many parents have their favourites among their children. Is that "bad" parenting?

Joanna knew she had a favourite child from the __1__ her second son was born. The Kent, UK-based mum says she __2__ both of her children, but her youngest child just "gets" her in a way that her first-born doesn't.

When Joanna's first baby was born, he was __3__ from her right away because of a health problem, and she couldn't see him for 24 hours. Missing this __4__ bonding (建立关系) period was, she believes, the start of a long-lasting preference for her __5__ son, whom she was able to spend time with immediately after he was born.

Though she battled (与……斗争) her feelings for years, Joanna says now she has __6__ it. "I could write a book on why I love one more than the other," she says. "It has been hard, but I haven't got any guilt (内疚)."

Unlike Joanna, most parents' favouritism is hard to __7__ and goes undiscussed. Having a favourite child might be the greatest taboo (禁忌) of parenthood, __8__ research shows that most parents do indeed have a favourite.

With plenty of evidence (证据) to show that being the least-favoured child can fundamentally (根本地) shape the personality and lead to intense sibling rivalries (激烈的手足之争), it's no wonder that parents might __9__ letting their preferences be seen. Yet research also shows that most kids can't tell who their parents' favourite child really is. And evidence shows that unless preferential treatment is very extreme (极端的), most children are not influenced by being the least favourite child. The real __10__, then, is how parents manage their children's perception (感知) of favouritism.

1. A. chance　　B. reason
   C. moment　　D. process
2. A. gives　　　B. loves
   C. makes　　　D. offers
3. A. turned away　B. thrown away
   C. put away　　D. taken away
4. A. valuable　　B. funny
   C. hard　　　　D. difficult
5. A. first　　　　B. second
   C. third　　　　D. fourth
6. A. accepted　　B. discovered
   C. brought　　　D. protected
7. A. afford　　　B. encourage
   C. notice　　　D. leave
8. A. and　　　　B. but
   C. or　　　　　D. so
9. A. talk about　B. lie about
   C. think about　D. worry about
10. A. decision　　B. accident
    C. problem　　D. dream

词汇碎片

period *n.* 时期；一段时间　　preference *n.* 偏爱　　immediately *adv.* 立即地　　shape *v.* 塑造

重难句讲解

And evidence shows that unless preferential treatment is very extreme, most children are not influenced by being the least favourite child. 而且有证据表明，除非偏爱对待的行为非常极端，否则大多数孩子不会因为成为最不受喜爱的孩子而受到影响。

本句是复合句。that引导宾语从句，其中又包含一个unless引导的条件状语从句。

Tuesday B 阅读理解

Valentine's Day (情人节) is coming! I'm preparing for a big party which will be held on February 14 from 15:00 to 18:00 in my garden. All parents of children aged 3 to 6 years are welcomed. During the party, plenty of games will be played. You can choose from the following games:

Cupid Arrow Toss (投掷) Game

This is a tossing game that kids love which lets you have much fun creating the game pieces with your kids using some basic materials such as construction paper, paper plates, and straws (吸管), all in valentine themed colors.

Valentine Memory Matching Game

Memory is a family favorite when it comes to games. Finding a match for adorable (可爱的) pictures displaying love in different forms makes it even sweeter. You can play the game together with your children as you draw a few pictures with images such as families, hearts, hugs, and more. Cut them into two to four pieces and have your child match them.

Candy Hearts Tower Game

This is an excellent choice for kids who love STEM (science, technology, engineering, mathematics) activities. Building towers using estimation (估算), measurement (测量), and some engineering skills makes it a fun learning activity, and kids love to eat the props (道具) after.

Unwrap (拆开……的包装) the Hearts Relay Race (接力赛)

Relay races are exciting ways for kids to work together as a team. It's even more exciting when candy is involved. Simply create relay race teams and have each child wear a pair of mittens (连指手套). They will take turns racing up to a table where they have a heart-shaped candy to fully unwrap. The first team to complete the tasks wins!

Please call me a day before the party if you can't come.

Your neighbor from Building 101

Tel: 12345678

1. How long will the party last?
   A. 1 hour.
   B. 2 hours.
   C. 3 hours.
   D. 4 hours.

2. You might need the following to play the Cupid Arrow Toss Game except _____.
   A. construction paper
   B. paper plates
   C. straws
   D. candies

3. Which game needs to be played in teams?
   A. Cupid Arrow Toss Game.
   B. Valentine Memory Matching Game.
   C. Candy Hearts Tower Game.
   D. Unwrap the Hearts Relay Race.

4. If you can't go to the party, you can call the host on _____.
   A. February 13
   B. February 14
   C. February 15
   D. February 16

5. You most probably receive the invitation in _____.
   A. a company
   B. a community
   C. a gym
   D. a mall

词汇碎片

prepare v. 准备，预备 material n. 材料 when it comes to 当提到；就……而论 display v. 表现；显露

重难句讲解

This is a tossing game that kids love which lets you have much fun creating the game pieces with your kids using some basic materials such as construction paper, paper plates, and straws, all in valentine themed colors. 这是一个孩子们喜欢的投掷游戏，你可以和你的孩子一起用一些涂有情人节主题颜色的基本材料，如彩色美术纸、纸盘和吸管，来创作游戏作品，从而让你获得许多乐趣。

本句是复合句。that 引导定语从句，which 也引导定语从句，两个定语从句都修饰 a tossing game。

Wednesday C 阅读理解

I have friends that have said, "My parents never argued in front of us." Still, some others have been traumatized (使受精神创伤) by fights and disagreements. But perhaps there's another choice. The problem with the former (前者的), children may think there's something wrong with their parent's relationship when they argue if they've never seen it done properly. The latter (后者的) can leave lasting scars that can cause relationship problems for kids for years to come.

There are some differences between fighting and arguing. Fighting usually involves (包含) hurtful words, name-calling, raised voices, and more. These kinds of fights are unproductive, can harm marriage and has negative effects on children. On the other hand, arguing is a difference of opinion. It can include a heated yet controlled discussion, difference of opinion, and an underlying (潜在的) desire to find a place of agreement.

I think that the latter is something we should do in front of our children. And here's the reason, in life, we will disagree with others. Kids will grow up and face conflicts (冲突) with family members, teachers, bosses, and in relationships of their own.

As role models for kids, showing them how to resolve (解决) marriage conflicts in a mature, healthy way will leave an impact (巨大影响) on them far beyond childhood. Setting an example for our children about how to disagree or argue respectfully (尊敬地), is a valued life skill that some have not been taught.

It would be impossible to live life without disagreeing or arguing. This is not among couples only, but also coworkers, supervisors, and other relationships as well. Along with how to properly load the dishwasher and how to cook a basic meal, let's send our kids into their futures with how to deal with a disagreement.

1. What might cause relationship problems for kids in the future?
   A. Never arguing.
   B. Fights and disagreements.
   C. Too much housework.
   D. Controlled discussion.

2. The underlined word "unproductive" in Paragraph 2 probably means "_____" in Chinese.
   A. 无关紧要的
   B. 不合情理的
   C. 无益的
   D. 效率低的

3. What might be involved when people argue?
   A. Hurtful words.
   B. Raised voices.
   C. Name-calling.
   D. Heated discussion.

4. According to the passage, conflicts _____.
   A. can be predicted
   B. can be taught
   C. are everywhere
   D. are valuable

5. What does the passage mainly tell us?
   A. Parents shouldn't fight at all.
   B. Parents shouldn't argue at all.
   C. Parents should fight properly.
   D. Parents should argue properly.

---

argue v. 争论；争辩　　disagreement n. 意见不一，分歧　　relationship n. 关系

词汇碎片

Setting an example for our children about how to disagree or argue respectfully, is a valued life skill that some have not been taught. 为我们的孩子树立榜样，告诉他们如何以尊重他人的方式提出异议或争论，这是一项宝贵的生活技能，有些人还没有学过这项技能。

本句是复合句。Setting... respectfully 是动名词短语作主语，其中 how to disagree or argue respectfully 是"疑问词+动词不定式"的结构，作介词 about 的宾语；that 引导定语从句，修饰 skill。set an example for sb. 意为"为某人树立榜样"。

重难句讲解

Dave: Welcome to "People Making a Difference". I'm Dave. Welcome, Daisy!

Daisy: Thank you. Happy to be here.

Dave: Daisy, I heard you founded an organization (组织) named Including You. __1__

Daisy: Yes, it is.

Dave: __2__

Daisy: It is an organization set up for kids to mentor (指导) other kids who experience learning or physical disabilities (身体残疾).

Dave: Are you doing it all by yourself?

Daisy: Of course not! My mom has always been helping me.

Dave: What specifically does your mother help you with?

Daisy: __3__ For example, she helps me deal with emails or buy anything that will be needed to help other kids.

Dave: I can see she has been very helpful. Daisy, what motivates (激励) you to help others?

Daisy: Well, __4__ They've instilled (逐渐灌输) in me a sense of responsibility to our community. Part of that responsibility means not to sit out when we see others in need. And it's really hard for me to see someone suffering (受苦), experiencing unkindness. __5__ So if I know I have the power to help, I'll try and assist.

Dave: I've learned a lot from you. What you are doing takes a special kind of courage. OK, audiences, if you want to learn more about Daisy's efforts, go to IncludingYou.org. You've been listening to "People Making a Difference", and we will be back in a minute.

阅读对话,从下列选项中选出能填入文中空白处的最佳选项,选项中有两项为多余选项。

A. Tell us more about it.

B. I want to do something about that.

C. Is that real?

D. That's wonderful.

E. She has been supporting me in any way that she can.

F. I think it comes a lot from my parents.

G. So how does that make you feel?

Friday E 短文填空

| 体 裁 | 说明文 | 题 材 | 家庭教育 | 正 确 率 | ___/10 | 词 数 | 304 |
| 难 度 | ★★★★☆ | 建议用时 | 11分钟 | 实际用时 | ___ | 答案页码 | 092 |

As the new Omicron variant (变体) spreads across the globe, many parents are worried about whether schools will close again. Many kids have been facing less time out with (1)_____ and online learning because of the pandemic (流行病). Here are some ways you can support kids and their schooling during the pandemic.

Set a Routine (常规) for Home Learning

Distance learning comes with its own set of challenges for both parents and (2)_____. Their usual school day has a structure, which includes particular (3)_____ during specific times of the day. Establishing a new routine at home will be extremely (4)_____ because then your child will know exactly what to expect. This can give them a sense of normalcy (常态) until they go back to school.

Make Home Learning Fun with Educational Activities

(5)_____ doesn't have to stop when school is over. Show your children that learning can be turned into (转变为) super fun (6)_____ that you can do together. Take a break from textbooks to do some crafts (手工) and creative projects with your kids. Things like (7)_____ educational posters or dioramas (透视画) can help your kids learn about history. Going on a nature walk through the woods can be a great way for kids to learn about their surroundings, and pick up some basic life (8)_____.

Have a Designated (指定的) Area for Online Learning

Just like you can't do your job your best (9)_____ in your bed, kids need to create a special space for school and learning. Bedrooms (10)_____ too many distracting (分散注意力的) toys and electronics. If you have a home office, you may be able to set up a quiet workspace for them there. If not, you can use the kitchen or dining room table or a desk in another room in your home. A specific space for school can make a big difference.

阅读短文，从方框中选择合适的单词或短语并用其正确形式填空，使短文通顺、意思完整。

learn

subject

skill

be full of

friend

activity

lie

child

create

help

词汇碎片

support v. 帮助；支持   take a break 休息一下   electronics n. 电子产品

重难句讲解

Show your children that learning can be turned into super fun activities that you can do together. 要让你的孩子知道，学习可以转变为你们一起做的超级有趣的活动。

本句是复合句。主句是 Show your children that..., 为祈使句。第一个 that 引导宾语从句，作 Show 的直接宾语，其中又包括了一个 that 引导的定语从句，修饰 activities。

Saturday F 短文填空

| 体 裁 | 记叙文 | 题 材 | 家庭教育 | 正确率 | ___/10 | 词 数 | 274 |
| 难 度 | ★★★★☆ | 建议用时 | 11分钟 | 实际用时 | ___ | 答案页码 | 093 |

阅读短文，根据首字母提示，在短文空缺处填入适当的单词，使短文通顺、意思完整。

Thor Hendrickson Jr., age 16, turned a passion (热情) for helping others into a successful landscaping (对……做景观美化) and snow removal (清除) business in the north of New York.

You probably won't (1) f_____ the secret sauce (秘诀) of T and Sons Property Management LLC in a Harvard Business School textbook. But maybe it should be. The cornerstone (基石) of this small business in Mechanicville, New York, is kindness.

About five years ago, young Thor Hendrickson Jr. started helping out a (2) n_____, whom he saw doing yard work with a cast (石膏) on her arm. He volunteered to help. That single act (3) t_____ into cutting the lawn, moving furniture, and shoveling (铲) snow for her. No charge.

(4) L_____ a hand to other neighbors soon led to paid landscaping and snow removal jobs for Thor. "I'm not a sit inside kind of person. I (5) l_____ to go out and help people with their yards and stuff," the 16-year-old said. "And if they don't want to (6) p_____ me, it's OK."

In the past year, Thor persuaded (说服) his dad to (7) b_____ a snow plow (犁) for his pickup truck, so they could help more people, together. Word spread. Their new father-and-son landscaping and snow removal business keeps (8) g_____.

"I wouldn't be doing what I'm doing with my son if it wasn't for his inspiration (鼓舞)," Thor Hendrickson Sr. said. Growing up, his son was labeled as having a learning disability, Mr. Hendrickson added, but that (9) n_____ stopped him.

It sure looks like the son is (10) t_____ the father how the currency (流行；流传) of kindness can fuel (给……提供燃料) success.

(1) _____
(2) _____
(3) _____
(4) _____
(5) _____
(6) _____
(7) _____
(8) _____
(9) _____
(10) _____

词汇碎片
business n. 业务；企业　　volunteer v. 自愿做；无偿做　　spread v. 传播；散布

重难句讲解
"I wouldn't be doing what I'm doing with my son if it wasn't for his inspiration," Thor Hendrickson Sr. said. 如果不是受我儿子鼓舞，我不会和他一起做现在所做的事情。老托尔·亨德里克森说。

本句是复合句。引号内的直接引语中，what I'm doing 为宾语从句，作第一个 doing 的宾语；if 引导状语从句，表示条件。此句使用了虚拟语气。

Week Four 健康饮食

Monday A 完形填空

体 裁	说明文	题 材	健康饮食	正确率	/15	词 数	309
难 度	★★★★☆	建议用时	16分钟	实际用时		答案页码	095

Do you often find yourself wanting a soda (汽水)? Do you need a soda to wash down a meal? Do you drink soda every day, sometimes more than once a day? If so, it's __1__ that you have a soda addiction (上瘾).

A soda addiction refers to a person's __2__ to drink plenty of soda every day. Marney White, a doctor at Yale Medicine, explains that __3__ a soda addiction isn't a formal health condition in medical field, people can __4__ an addiction to caffeine (咖啡因) or the sugar in soda.

According to Dr. White, some of the signs of a soda addiction may be __5__ to the symptoms (症状) of a drug addiction. She says you may have symptoms like being hungry for soda, __6__ control, headache and so on if you are unable to get a soda. Addictive ingredients (成分) (like caffeine and sugar), unhealthy eating __7__ (drinking a soda while eating meals) and personal preferences (偏好) are the possible __8__ of a soda addiction.

A soda addiction is __9__ because it has been linked __10__ several serious health __11__, such as heart disease, high blood pressure and tooth decay (蛀牙). If you think that you drink too much soda __12__ that you might have a soda addiction, it's a good idea to try and reduce drinking soda.

For example, Dr. White suggests you can __13__ reduce the number of sodas you drink in a(n) __14__. You can set goals such as two sodas per day this week; one soda per day next week; half a soda per day the week after, and so on. It also can be helpful to drink __15__ as much water as you drink soda every time. So, if you're drinking one cup of soda, you should drink at least one cup of water along with it.

1. A. boring   B. lucky
   C. possible D. different
2. A. shame   B. pride
   C. satisfaction D. need
3. A. because   B. although
   C. unless   D. if
4. A. waste   B. steal
   C. develop   D. refuse
5. A. friendly B. afraid
   C. popular   D. similar
6. A. getting out of   B. taking care of
   C. looking out of   D. running out of
7. A. habits   B. methods
   C. hobbies   D. choices
8. A. tasks   B. causes
   C. results   D. lessons
9. A. good   B. harmful
   C. successful D. special
10. A. from   B. for
    C. over   D. to
11. A. pictures B. behaviors
    C. problems D. skills
12. A. or   B. and
    C. but   D. so
13. A. sadly   B. closely
    C. amazingly D. gradually
14. A. year   B. month
    C. day   D. hour
15. A. at least B. at most
    C. at present D. at all

词汇碎片

plenty of 许多，大量   explain v. 解释；说明   condition n. 状况；条件   reduce v. 减少

重难句讲解

If you think that you drink too much soda or that you might have a soda addiction, it's a good idea to try and reduce drinking soda. 如果你认为自己喝了太多汽水，或者你可能已经对汽水上瘾，那么尝试减少汽水的饮用量是一个好办法。

本句是复合句。If引导条件状语从句，其中or表示选择，连接两个并列的that宾语从句作think的宾语。

Green Bus

Are you a vegetable lover? Are you trying to find something healthy to eat? Here is an ideal restaurant for you!

- Opening hours: 11:30 am-8:30 pm from Tuesday to Sunday
- Address: 1/F Smith Shopping Center, 334 Victor Road
- Tel: 6000-0006

The menu of Green Bus offers all kinds of choices from different plant-based ingredients (食材). Each dish is created with balanced flavor (风味) and color. You can start from the classic Green Bus warm salad based on your choice of ingredients from pickled (腌制的), smoked or roasted (烘烤的) vegetables to special plant-based crab or meatballs and other special sauces.

- Green Bus warm salad $18
- Daily soup $13
- 4 plant-based meatballs $12
- Lemon Green tea $10

Green Bus uses different cooking methods for different plant-based ingredients. Low temperature baking is important to keep nutrition (营养) in the food, and fermentation (发酵) is used for preservation (保存) in a process that produces lactic acid (乳酸) found in sour foods.

It focuses on not only the nutrition of each meal, but also environmental protection. Nothing is wasted in the kitchen. Seven kinds of sauces are prepared using the remaining ingredients like tomatoes, strawberries and apples.

Welcome to Green Bus to try more dishes!

1. When can you go to the restaurant for a meal?
   A. 8:00 pm on Monday.
   B. 1:00 pm on Tuesday.
   C. 9:30 am on Friday.
   D. 10:00 pm on Sunday.
2. Where is the restaurant?
   A. On Smith Road.
   B. On Victor Road.
   C. Near a hotel.
   D. Behind a bookstore.
3. You should pay _____ if you want to have a warm salad and a bowl of soup.
   A. $28
   B. $22
   C. $30
   D. $31
4. Which of the following is TRUE?
   A. The ingredients of this restaurant are meat.
   B. Low temperature baking is a way to cook.
   C. Environmental protection is the only focus.
   D. The remaining tomatoes are thrown away.
5. The text is _____.
   A. a story
   B. a diary
   C. a postcard
   D. an advertisement

Wednesday C 阅读理解

体 裁	说明文	题 材	健康饮食	正确率	___/5	词 数	327
难 度	★★★★☆	建议用时	7分钟	实际用时		答案页码	096

Mental health problems are common. Whether it's depression (抑郁), anxiety or another of the many mental health problems, all of these can influence someone's life. Here, several mental health professionals offer their tips for how best to support a friend or anyone who's struggling with (与……做斗争) any kind of mental health problems.

● Start a conversation

Showing an interest in a conversation is the first step in creating a safe space for those who might be struggling with mental health problems.

● Listen

While listening, be sure to avoid giving advice or fixing things quickly, or it will make the person sharing their experience feel worse. When you are listening rather than lecturing, people with mental health problems are more likely to feel understood, which opens the door to them receiving more help.

● Support

You can offer support by focusing on concrete (具体的) and specific tasks. Sometimes asking "what can I do to help" isn't enough, as it places the burden (责任；负担) back on the person with the condition to tell you what they need. In some cases, it's better just to provide support without waiting for an invitation. Bringing over a meal or inviting the person to the movies can all be good starting points to give needed support.

● Avoid labeling (贴标签)

You should avoid labeling others with "you're depressed" or "you're anxious", and choose to use language such as "it seems like you've been distracted (心烦意乱的) lately, would you like to talk about it".

● Be patient

Mental health problems can take a long time to relieve (缓解), and it may also take your friend a while to accept professional help when needed. But you need to avoid pushing them before they're comfortable moving forward. Pushing people to seek help before they're ready is not helpful because it can often create resistance (抵抗) to seeking help.

1. The first step to help a person with mental health problems is to _____.
   A. open up a conversation   B. try to listen
   C. give your support   D. avoid labeling

2. Why is listening needed for someone with mental health problems?
   A. Because he doesn't need advice.
   B. Because he has no one to talk to.
   C. Because it makes him feel understood.
   D. Because he wants to have a discussion.

3. Which of the following is TRUE according to "Support"?
   A. You should give support only by asking "What can I do to help".
   B. Providing support by focusing on a clear task is helpful.
   C. You shouldn't offer support unless you receive an invitation.
   D. Seeing a movie is not helpful.

4. According to this passage, we know that _____ is "labeling".
   A. little Mark receiving birthday gifts from his friends
   B. little Mark brushing his teeth after getting up
   C. little Mark being told "You are a loser" when losing a game
   D. little Mark getting the highest test scores in his class

5. The passage is written to tell us _____.
   A. how to start a conversation with a friend
   B. why we need to help a friend in need
   C. how to help a person with mental health problems
   D. when we should support a person with mental health problems

词汇碎片

mental adj. 精神的   anxiety n. 焦虑   support v. & n. 支持   show an interest in 对……表现出兴趣

重难句讲解

Whether it's depression, anxiety or another of the many mental health problems, all of these can influence someone's life. 无论是抑郁、焦虑还是其他许多心理健康问题中的一个，都会影响人的生活。

本句是复合句。Whether 引导让步状语从句，Whether it's... or... 意为"无论（不管）是……还是……"。

Sometimes asking "what can I do to help" isn't enough, as it places the burden back on the person with the condition to tell you what they need. 有时问"我能做些什么来帮助你"是不够的，因为这又把告诉你他们需要什么的责任推回给了患者。

本句是复合句。主句是 Sometimes asking "what can I do to help" isn't enough, as 引导原因状语从句，第二个 what 引导宾语从句，作 tell 的直接宾语。

Thursday D 阅读理解

Overall, more than 40 million US adults—a little more than 19%—feel anxious, according to a mental illness organization in the US.

While no food or beverage (饮料) is a silver bullet for anxiety or depression, what you eat and drink can influence your level of calm. Here are several foods and beverages that may help you stay away from anxiety.

Raw (生的) fruits and vegetables	A study in 2018 suggested that raw fruits and vegetables could lead to positive moods (情绪) and life satisfaction among young adults. Top raw foods linked to better mood are bananas, apples, carrots and lettuce (生菜).
Foods high in vitamin C	Research suggests that foods rich in vitamin C can reduce symptoms (症状) of anxiety. Fruits and vegetables high in vitamin C include broccoli, green and red peppers, kiwi fruit (猕猴桃) and tomatoes.
Whole grains (全谷物)	Eating whole grains can have a calming effect. That's because it's believed that they can increase the amount of serotonin (血清素) in your brain, which can improve feelings of peace of mind. Ways to take in more whole grains include eating breads made from whole wheat flour (面粉), brown rice, oatmeal and millet.
Different types of milk	Some research suggests that vitamin D may be helpful in improving mood and sleep. Milk can be a good source of vitamin D, and the types of milk to choose from include cow's milk, oat milk, coconut milk and almond milk.

1. Over 19% of American adults are _____.
   A. busy   B. fat
   C. calm   D. nervous

2. What does the underlined phrase "silver bullet" in the second paragraph probably mean?
   A. 毒药   B. 良方
   C. 检测剂 D. 反应物

3. Top raw fruits and vegetables don't include _____.
   A. bananas   B. apples
   C. lettuce   D. broccoli

4. According to this passage, which of the following is FALSE?
   A. Tomatoes are rich in vitamin C.
   B. Whole grains can increase serotonin.
   C. Brown rice is rich in vitamin D.
   D. Milk is helpful for sleep.

5. The best title for this passage can be _____.
   A. Why Are American People Anxious
   B. Foods and Drinks for Better Mood
   C. Raw Fruits and Vegetables Are Popular
   D. Milk: Rich in Vitamin D and Vitamin C

---

organization n. 组织；机构   influence v. 影响   positive adj. 积极的

That's because it's believed that they can increase the amount of serotonin in your brain, which can improve feelings of peace of mind. 这是因为人们认为全谷物可以提升大脑内血清素的含量，而这有助于平复心情。

本句是复合句。because 引导表语从句，it's believed that... 意为"人们认为……"。which 引导非限制性定语从句，修饰前面的句子 they can increase... your brain。

Friday E 任务型阅读

Rice cakes are a popular snack, especially for those looking to maintain a healthy weight, as they can be low in calories (卡路里) and carbohydrates (碳水化合物). Why? Because a rice cake is basically pieces of puffed (膨化的) rice pressed together to form a patty (小馅饼).

But are these crunchy (松脆的) snacks really good for your health? __1__ It's best to avoid flavored rice cakes, which have higher amounts of sugar, sodium (钠), and other artificial (人工的) ingredients. You should also refuse those made from refined (精炼的) white rice.

__2__ Research has found that whole grains, including brown rice (糙米), can control blood sugar levels in people. That's because whole grains contain high amounts of fiber (纤维), which the body cannot break down and absorb for energy. __3__

Rice cakes can help you keep a healthy weight if they replace (取代) high-calorie, high-carbohydrate foods in your diet. For example, eating one plain bagel with two brown rice cakes cuts out 130 calories and 21g of carbohydrates. __4__

Rice is easy to digest (消化), and that's true for plain brown rice cakes as well. In addition, since brown rice is naturally gluten-free (无麸质的), rice cakes made from brown rice are a great option for people with celiac (腹腔的) disease.

__5__ Just watch out for flavored varieties which can be high in sodium and sugar.

阅读短文，从下列选项中选出能填入文中空白处的最佳选项，选项中有两项为多余选项。

A. In general, rice cakes are a healthy snack.
B. Here are some benefits of rice cakes.
C. Eating rice cakes can help you to lose weight.
D. Therefore, they don't cause an increase in blood sugar.
E. Rice cakes made from white rice are another good choice.
F. In fact, whether rice cakes are healthy or not depends on the type of rice cakes you buy.
G. Making that three times a week could result in nearly six pounds of weight loss over a year.

Saturday F 短文填空

Vacation should be a time of rest and relaxation, but a case of travelers' diarrhea (腹泻) can turn your trip into a terrible (1) _____. According to the Centers for Disease Control and Prevention (CDC), travelers' diarrhea is the most common travel-related illness; CDC data suggests it can (2) _____ 30%-70% of travelers, depending on the destination (目的地) and season. It can occur (发生) anywhere in the world, (3) _____ it's more common in high-risk destinations in parts of the Middle East, Africa, Mexico, and Central and South America.

Here, experts explain what causes travelers' diarrhea and how best to treat it, so you can enjoy as much of your vacation as (4) _____. The most common cause is bacteria (细菌), which may make up about 80%-90% of illnesses. Poor hygiene (卫生) practices in vacation destination restaurants are a big risk factor for travelers' diarrhea caused by bacteria—that's largely due to the water supply in underdeveloped nations. Even in developed nations, people can pick up travelers' diarrhea because (5) _____ poor food preparation conditions and lack of proper hand-washing.

It can be (6) _____ to avoid travelers' diarrhea, especially when traveling abroad. The best way to (7) _____ travelers' diarrhea is to be careful of what you eat and drink. Firstly, you'll need to avoid undercooked (未煮熟的) meats and seafood, like sushi (寿司) made with raw fish. Fried foods are your safest choice while traveling anywhere (8) _____ you're unsure about how safe the food is. While fruits or things you don't have to cook might seem like a safe enough choice, they also carry risk, since they could have been washed in polluted water. In that case, fruit that you can peel (like bananas or oranges) may be a safer choice.

Secondly, paying (9) _____ to what you drink is key to preventing travelers' diarrhea, too. Alcohol is considered safe, because it can (10) _____ bacteria; bottled soda, bottled water, bottled juice are also considered safe. If those choices aren't available, boiled water is your next safest choice.

阅读短文，从方框中选择合适的单词填空，使短文通顺、意思完整。每空限填一词，每词限用一次。

influence

possible

attention

kill

where

prevent

difficult

of

but

experience

词汇碎片

relaxation *n.* 放松；休息　　common *adj.* 常见的；共同的　　treat *v.* 治疗；对待

重难句讲解

While fruits or things you don't have to cook might seem like a safe enough choice, they also carry risk, since they could have been washed in polluted water. 虽然水果或无须烹饪的东西看起来是足够安全的选择，但它们也有风险，因为它们可能是在受污染的水中洗过的。

本句是复合句。主句是they also carry risk，While引导让步状语从句，since引导原因状语从句，polluted意为"受污染的"。

Week Five 社会人际

Monday A 完形填空

体裁	记叙文	题材	社会人际	正确率	___/8	词数	229
难度	★★★☆☆	建议用时	8分钟	实际用时		答案页码	098

The Vicinity, a reality show, hopes to rekindle (重新点燃) the sense of community that shaped the nation's ethos (民族精神) by bringing together people from very different lifestyles. Among those living a modern city life, many may not even know who their __1__ are. However, for director Zhao Qi, warmth between people is not gone, it just needs to be rekindled.

This documentary-style reality show premiered (首次公演) __2__ Nov. 8 online through Tencent. The __3__ looks for the subtle (不易察觉的) and sentimental (情感的) moments which reflect the simple, but sincere interpersonal relationships found in often neglected (被忽视的) corners.

In each of the seven episodes (一集), two popular celebrities (名人) will spend days working with locals, whether it's a group of errand (跑腿) runners who shuttle (频繁往来) around the city __4__ people with day-to-day tasks or a herding family of the Kazak ethnic group.

Being taken out of their comfort zones, the self-exploration of the celebrities will enrich (使丰富) __5__ their own understanding of life, but also that of the audience (观众).

"You can feel the general ethos of __6__ Chinese people," Zhao explains. "Wherever you go, people are kind, hard-working, and willing __7__ help each other." "Some people (in the show) may work under difficult __8__, they may complain," he continues. "But they don't give up. They present vitality (活力), and that's deeply touching."

1. A. fathers B. neighbors C. friends
2. A. on B. in C. at
3. A. doctor B. teacher C. director
4. A. helping B. taking C. asking
5. A. even if B. not only C. in spite of
6. A. simple B. ancient C. modern
7. A. of B. to C. for
8. A. conditions B. purposes C. promises

词汇碎片
sense *n.* 意识；感觉　community *n.* 共享，共有；社区　reflect *v.* 表达；反映　continue *v.* 继续说（或做）

重难句讲解
The director looks for the subtle and sentimental moments which reflect the simple, but sincere interpersonal relationships found in often neglected corners. 导演在那些常常被忽视的角落里寻找那些不易被人察觉的动人时刻，这些时刻展现了人与人之间简单而真挚的关系。

本句是包含定语从句的复合句。主句的主干是 The director looks for moments，为主谓宾结构。which reflect the simple, but sincere interpersonal relationships... 是 which 引导的定语从句，修饰 moments；found in often neglected corners 是过去分词短语作后置定语，修饰 relationships。

Tuesday B 阅读理解

体 裁	记叙文	题 材	社会人际	正确率	___/5	词 数	243
难 度	★★★★☆	建议用时	7分钟	实际用时	___	答案页码	098

Women's power has had a profound (深远的) influence on the country and the economy with the improvement in career (职业) development and social position. This is especially so in the fashion industry, where women's power is becoming more and more dazzling (耀眼的), said Zhen Yan, former vice-president of the All-China Women's Federation (联合会), in a forum (讨论会) that was held at Fosun Foundation in Shanghai during the Shanghai Fashion Week.

Titled Her Power Fashion Dialogue and held by the Shanghai Fashion Week Organizing Committee, the forum used speeches and roundtable discussions to explore (探讨) women's power and responsibilities through fashion with officials, artists and celebrities. As the main speaker, Zhen shared information about the public welfare (福利) fashion events that were launched jointly (共同地) by the federation and Shanghai Fashion Week since April 2021, including Genius Mom and Dongxiang Embroidery (刺绣).

According to Zhen, these fashion events helped women embroiderers from underdeveloped areas display and sell their intangible cultural heritage (非物质文化遗产) handicrafts (手工艺品) to cities, helping to improve their living conditions. "Half a year later, we came to Shanghai Fashion Week again. We saw more and more women playing leadership roles and showing their creativity. They resolutely (坚决地) pursue progress, devote themselves to public welfare, and use their own strength to help more women realize their self-worth," Zhen says. "Cross-disciplinary (跨领域的) cooperation (合作), as well as today's dialogue, are beneficial attempts at public welfare to join hands with fashion industry resources," she adds.

1. Where was the forum held?
   A. In Beijing.
   B. In Shanghai.
   C. In Shenzhen.
2. How did the forum Her Power Fashion Dialogue explore women's power and responsibilities?
   A. Through speeches and roundtable discussions.
   B. Through discussions about officials and artists.
   C. Through information sharing with the public.
3. The underlined word "launched" in Paragraph 2 means "____" in Chinese.
   A. 设置　　B. 举办　　C. 经历
4. What is the purpose of helping women embroiderers in underdeveloped areas sell their intangible cultural heritage handicrafts to cities?
   A. To improve their living conditions.
   B. To teach them more skills.
   C. To help them become rich.
5. According to Zhen Yan, is cross-disciplinary cooperation good for public welfare?
   A. Not mentioned.
   B. No, it isn't.
   C. Yes, it is.

词汇碎片

development *n.* 发展　　industry *n.* 行业　　share *v.* 分享

重难句讲解

This is especially so in the fashion industry, where women's power is becoming more and more dazzling, said Zhen Yan, former vice-president of the All-China Women's Federation, in a forum that was held at Fosun Foundation in Shanghai during the Shanghai Fashion Week. 在上海时装周期间，中华全国妇女联合会前副主席甄砚在上海复星艺术中心举办的讨论会上提到，这在时尚行业尤其如此，女性的力量正变得越来越耀眼。

本句是包含宾语从句和定语从句的复合句。主句是 ...said Zhen Yan, 为主谓宾结构，主语是 Zhen Yan, 谓语是 said, 宾语是前面整个宾语从句，宾语从句中还嵌套了一个由 where 引导的定语从句。former vice-president of the All-China Women's Federation 是同位语，对 Zhen Yan 进行补充说明。in a forum 是地点状语，后面还有一个 that 引导的定语从句。

Wednesday C 短文填空

体 裁	记叙文	题 材	社会人际	正确率	___/5	词 数	271
难 度	★★★☆☆	建议用时	6分钟	实际用时		答案页码	099

阅读短文，在短文空缺处填入适当的单词，使短文通顺、意思完整。

"Everything was new; everything was amazing," said Judy Hoarfrost, a former American ping-pong player, when telling Xinhua about her team's historic visit to China half a century ago, a trip that would become known as "Ping-Pong Diplomacy (外交)".

The 66-year-old remembers almost every detail about that eight-day journey, which she called "a great adventure (冒险)", (1) _____ the Chinese phrases she learned, the (2) _____ she ate and the places she toured. "Everything was impressive… but if I had to pick one thing, it would be going to the Great Hall of the People and meeting Premier Zhou Enlai, because that was a great honor. It was maybe the most influential thing that our team did during that trip," said Hoarfrost.

In 2016, Hoarfrost led her team to open a full-time table tennis club in (3) _____ to make the sport more accessible (可接近的) to people. She hopes that players at her club would have more opportunities to visit China and (4) _____ with top ping-pong players there.

Hoarfrost has been to China eight times, with several trips related to celebrating the anniversaries (周年纪念日) of Ping-Pong Diplomacy. "It's incredible (难以置信的) that people are still interested in the Ping-Pong Diplomacy," she said. "It's important, but it's even more (5) _____ that we need to carry the torch (火炬) to the next generation." The most important legacy (遗产) of the diplomacy is the power that a sport like table tennis can play in bringing people together, and the power of people-to-people exchange in breaking down barriers and creating bridges to understanding.

(1) _____
(2) _____
(3) _____
(4) _____
(5) _____

词汇碎片
historic *adj.* 历史上著名（或重要）的　　century *n.* 世纪；百年　　impressive *adj.* 令人难忘的

重难句讲解
The most important legacy of the diplomacy is the power that a sport like table tennis can play in bringing people together, and the power of people-to-people exchange in breaking down barriers and creating bridges to understanding. 乒乓外交最重要的遗产是像乒乓球这样的运动所发挥的把人们团结在一起的力量，以及人与人之间的交流在打破障碍、建立理解的桥梁方面的力量。

本句是包含定语从句的复合句。主句的主干是 The legacy is the power and the power，为主系表结构，表语是由 and 连接的两个 the power。that a sport like table tennis can play in bringing people together 为定语从句，修饰第一个 the power。of people-to-people exchange... 为介词短语作后置定语，修饰第二个 the power。

"After taking off the tape and glue and smoothing out the creases (折痕) across the pages, the near hundred-year-old letters and martyr's certificate (烈士证) were revitalized (使恢复生机)," said Chen Hezhen, __1__. On Nov. 13, she received the restored (修复) memorial papers left by her father, who sacrificed (牺牲) his life on the battlefield when she was only 1 year old. She was grateful to a group of college students from Ningbo University of Finance & Economics (NUFE), who helped bring her precious memory to life.

Repairing relics (遗物) left by veterans (老兵) and martyrs is a part of NUFE's social practice project. Since June, __2__ and returned them to families of revolutionary (革命的) martyrs. "When we visited martyrs' families, we heard many inspiring stories and were touched by those late soldiers," said Wang Yiqun, 21, the project's leader. "__3__. But we've found that those objects have different degrees of damage, so we want to do something to help them."

However, __4__. Pan Yi, 22, one young restorer, stared at a damaged page of a martyr's letter with adhesive tape. For days, she worked to separate the tape and paper safely. "I need to be especially careful and patient because __5__," said Pan. "What encourages us is our faith (信念)—those old papers carrying the spirit of undaunted (无畏的) heroes and the feelings of mourning (哀悼) that their family members endure. We need to repair them as they were before."

Now, these students are preparing to hold an exhibition of restored relics, sharing their stories with more people.

阅读短文，从下列选项中选出能填入文中空白处的最佳选项，选项中有一项为多余选项。

A. Their family members have saved their letters in memory of them
B. it isn't easy to restore these relics
C. a 71-year-old grandmother from Ningbo, Zhejiang
D. these young people have helped restore letters and other documents
E. Pan carefully checked the holes and worn-out margins
F. the process can take a few weeks just to repair a single page

Friday E 任务型阅读

体裁	记叙文	题材	社会人际	正确率	___/5	词数	239
难度	★★★☆☆	建议用时	6分钟	实际用时		答案页码	099

On Nov. 8, Wang Yaping, a female (女性的) taikonaut (中国航天员) of Shenzhou XIII mission (任务), became China's first and the world's 16th female spacewalker. The expected six-month journey in space has left many curious about the differences between male (男性的) and female astronauts, especially in terms of performing extravehicular (太空船外的) activities (EVAs). Despite physical challenges, female astronauts have unique (独特的) advantages.

Mutual (相互的) understanding between astronauts is very important for carrying out EVAs, which is based on excellent communication skills. Women are superior (更好的) in communication and language expression, and this helps female astronauts perform extravehicular activities.

Female astronauts' strong communication skills and energy also help the crew maintain high morale (士气) throughout their stay, according to Pang Zhihao, a spaceflight researcher in Beijing. Men and women are different in body size, which also gives women unique advantages for spacewalks. <u>Their generally smaller size is an advantage, as women will be able to control their weight better and thus perform more tasks, Pang told China Daily.</u> Women in general weigh less, eat less food, consume (消耗) less oxygen (氧气), and therefore require less fuel (燃料) to get into space. A taikonaut must weigh between 55 kilograms and 70 kilograms to fit in the cabin of spacecraft and consume less fuel, according to CGTN.

According to Pang, many studies have found that female astronauts are well adapted to executing (执行) space missions, and have advantages over male astronauts in qualities such as attention to detail and thinking comprehensively.

阅读短文，回答下面1~5小题。

1. Before Wang Yaping, how many female astronauts in the world finished spacewalk?
   _____
   _____

2. According to Paragraph 2, what are the advantages of female astronauts?
   _____
   _____

3. Please translate the underlined sentence into Chinese.
   _____
   _____

4. If Tom weighs 80 kilograms, can he get into the cabin of spacecraft according to the passage?
   _____
   _____

5. What have you learned from this passage?
   _____
   _____

词汇碎片

journey *n.* 旅行   especially *adv.* 尤其，特别   challenge *n.* 挑战   language *n.* 语言

重难句讲解

Men and women are different in body size, which also gives women unique advantages for spacewalks. 男性和女性的体型不同，这也赋予了女性进行太空行走的独特优势。

本句是包含定语从句的复合句。主句的主干是 Men and women are different，为主系表结构。which 引导非限制性定语从句，修饰整个主句。

Saturday F 短文填空

After a day's operation of the Shanghai Metro (地铁) trains, some people start their night work to make sure that the trains are clean and safe for passengers the (1) _____ morning. Among them are the train cleaners who since late January last year have got an additional (额外的) task in their routine—a COVID-19 pandemic control measure of spraying (喷洒) disinfectants (消毒剂) in the trains.

Yang Wenqing, 49, is a (2) _____ of the No. 2 Train Cleaning Department of Shanghai Metro Property Management Co. A total of 82 workers on her team work at nine subway stations (3) _____ the city. The staff (4) _____ to work around 9 pm and often work until 3 am the next morning. Yang and two of her fellow managers also work at night to coordinate (协调) and inspect (检查) the (5) _____ of their work.

"Train cleaning is a demanding (要求高的) job (6) _____ all work has to be completed within a certain time," Yang said. "When we are short of hands, some workers need to do overtime." The workers, most of them aged (7) _____ 40 and 55, have become increasingly efficient in the disinfection work, according to Yang. Yang herself started working for Shanghai Metro as a cleaning worker in 1999 and has (8) _____ in stations on lines 1, 2 and 3.

"Our company has been implementing (执行) high standards for cleaning work, and the establishment of the train cleaning department proves that," she said. Yang has spent a lot of holidays on her post in the past 20 years, and it is the same for many of her co-workers. "Our job seems to be minute (微小的), (9) _____ we take it as our responsibility to ensure a safe riding experience for (10) _____," she said.

阅读短文，从方框中选择合适的单词并用其正确形式填空，使短文通顺、意思完整。每空限填一词，每词限用一次。（其中有两项为多余选项。）

around
quality
go
manager
passenger
work
but
help
to
because
between
next

Week Six 文学／艺术／体育

Monday A 完形填空

| 体　裁 | 记叙文 | 题　材 | 艺术 | 正确率 | ____/10 | 词　数 | 332 |
| 难　度 | ★★★☆☆ | 建议用时 | 10分钟 | 实际用时 | | 答案页码 | 101 |

　　See You in Beijing, a Chinese song which was released (发布) to mark the 100-day countdown (倒计时) to the Beijing 2022 Winter Olympic Games, was sung by a number of Chinese famous singers, actors and athletes during a great gala (庆典) held at the Tianqiao Performing Arts Center in Beijing on Thursday. The gala __1__ the 22nd Meet in Beijing International Arts Festival and Meet in Beijing Olympic Culture Festival.

　　The song was first released __2__ October last year and on Dec. 26, a music video of the song was released. The video featured 55 Chinese athletes.

　　The song, with lyrics (歌词) __3__ by Wang Pingjiu and music made by Chang Shilei, expresses greetings and a(n) __4__ message to all the people who will take part in the coming Beijing 2022 Winter Olympics and the Winter Paralympics.

　　Chang is a pop singer-songwriter and is __5__ for writing the theme song of the 2008 Beijing Olympics, You and Me, which was __6__ at the opening ceremony by Chinese singer Liu Huan and British singer Sarah Brightman.

　　Wang, an experienced songwriter, __7__ the creative team behind the song, Beijing Welcomes You, which was released in April 2008, marking the 100-day countdown of that year's Beijing Olympic Games.

　　"I am glad __8__ the song, Beijing Welcomes You, is still enjoyed by many people now. When we planned to release this new song, See You in Beijing, we wanted to __9__ people the same warmth and pleasure as the song Beijing Welcomes You did," said Wang in an interview with *Beijing Evening News*.

　　In the interview, Wang __10__ that it took him a long time to give the new song a name.

　　"Despite the difficulties presented by the COVID-19 pandemic, people from all over the world will gather in Beijing for the Olympic Games, which are about friendship, peace and trust. The name of the song, See You in Beijing, like the song's lyrics, is very simple and sincere," Wang said.

1. A. cut　　　　B. opened
   C. connected
2. A. on　　　　B. to
   C. in
3. A. sung　　　B. written
   C. drawn
4. A. welcoming　B. interesting
   C. missing
5. A. heard　　　B. said
   C. known
6. A. found　　　B. performed
   C. developed
7. A. led　　　　B. took
   C. ended
8. A. which　　　B. when
   C. that
9. A. lend　　　　B. bring
   C. pay
10. A. remembered　B. forgot
    C. expected

词汇碎片

mark *v.* 庆贺；纪念　　message *n.* 信息　　pleasure *n.* 快乐；满足

重难句讲解

See You in Beijing, a Chinese song which was released to mark the 100-day countdown to the Beijing 2022 Winter Olympic Games, was sung by a number of Chinese famous singers, actors and athletes during a great gala held at the Tianqiao Performing Arts Center in Beijing on Thursday.《我们北京见》这首中文歌曲是为了庆祝北京2022年冬奥会倒计时100天而发布的，周四在北京天桥艺术中心举行的盛典上，数位中国著名歌手、演员和运动员演唱了该曲目。

本句是复合句。a Chinese song... Olympic Games 为同位语，补充说明《我们北京见》这首歌的信息。该同位语中包含一个 which 引导的定语从句，修饰 song。held at... on Thursday 为后置定语，修饰 gala。

Tuesday B 阅读理解

体裁	说明文	题材	艺术	正确率	___/3	词数	244
难度	★★★☆☆	建议用时	5分钟	实际用时		答案页码	101

All kinds of exhibitions are held in the capital city to celebrate the new year.

National Museum of China
People visit a tiger-themed exhibition at the National Museum of China in Beijing, the capital of China, Jan. 19, 2022. 2022 is the Year of Tiger. *The Tiger as Talisman* (护身符): *2022 Chinese New Year Exhibition*, with a number of artworks showing tigers in Chinese culture, opened to the public here on Wednesday.

China National Academy of Painting
Harmony (和谐) *with People and Earth*, an exhibition at the art museum of China National Academy of Painting, shows paintings, sculptures (雕塑) and calligraphic (书法的) works presenting scenes of the Olympic Games and people taking part in sports. The exhibition ends on Feb. 10.

The Art Museum of the Beijing Fine Art Academy
It is showing some of Qi Baishi's ink-color paintings and calligraphic scrolls (卷轴) in its collection to celebrate the Chinese New Year.
Works on show include *Sui Zhao Tu*, a scroll painting which has a particular style of classical (古典的) Chinese artwork. The style of *Sui Zhao Tu* paintings, made to celebrate the Spring Festival, became popular in Song Dynasty (朝代).
The paintings present blooming plants in anticipation (预期) of spring as well as cultural objects, such as incense burners (香炉), catering to the tastes of aristocrats (贵族) and intellectuals (知识分子). Qi Baishi changed the style to make it easier to be accepted by ordinary people by painting everyday objects such as red lanterns, fireworks and cabbages. The exhibition ends on April 5.

1. The tiger-themed exhibition opened to the public on _____.
 A. Jan. 19
 B. Feb. 10
 C. Feb. 11
 D. April 5

2. _____ was held at the art museum of China National Academy of Painting.
 A. A tiger-themed exhibition
 B. An exhibition about harmony
 C. An exhibition of ink-color paintings
 D. An exhibition of the Spring Festival

3. The style of *Sui Zhao Tu* paintings was made _____.
 A. to please ordinary people
 B. to celebrate the birthday of the emperor of Song Dynasty
 C. in memory of Qi Baishi's teacher
 D. to celebrate the Spring Festival

词汇碎片
capital *n.* 首都　　celebrate *v.* 庆祝，庆贺

重难句讲解
The paintings present blooming plants in anticipation of spring as well as cultural objects, such as incense burners, catering to the tastes of aristocrats and intellectuals. （宋朝流行的）画作不仅描绘了迎春盛开的植物，还描绘了香炉等文物，迎合了贵族和知识分子的品味。

本句是简单句。cater to 意为"迎合，满足"。catering 为现在分词表示主动意义，其逻辑主语为 The paintings。

Wednesday C 阅读理解

A survey shows that 30 percent of the 3,890 respondents (调查对象) have taken part in winter sports and more than 60 percent have a positive view on its future development among young Chinese.

Nearly 90 percent of those surveyed were aged 18 to 21, and 93.8 percent are college students, according to the survey report, which was made by Tsinghua University's Center for Development of Sports Industry and Youth.cn.

The 2022 Beijing Winter Olympics has seen 46.3 percent of respondents start to pay attention to information of winter sports, while 48.9 percent have deepened their knowledge of winter sports and 36.8 percent like the idea of taking part in winter sports.

About 81.5 percent of respondents took part in ice sports one to five times a year and 62.7 percent prefer snow sports, the report says.

As schools introduced activities of winter sports, young people become more interested in the Winter Olympics.

The report shows that 61.3 percent of respondents are likely to watch the Games on television or via the internet, and 38.4 percent would like to serve the Games as volunteers.

Social media has become the main way for young people to follow winter sports, with nearly 70 percent of respondents to the survey choosing apps such as WeChat and Douyin, while 36.6 percent follow popular bloggers (写博客的人) and winter sports stars.

Convenient and cheap equipment has become the first choice of 48 percent of respondents. So far, 88.5 percent spent less than 1,000 yuan each year on snow and ice sports, while 25.4 percent are willing to spend more.

Wang Xueli, director of the center, says, based on the survey, the report suggests cutting the price of ice and snow sports for youths. "Many resorts have offered coupons (优惠券) and free tickets to youngsters," she said.

New media platforms, which are commonly used by young people, are expected to play a bigger role in boosting the development of winter sports, she added.

1. Over _____ percent of respondents have a positive opinion on the future development of winter sports among young Chinese.
   A. 30   B. 60
   C. 90   D. 36.8

2. The survey report was made by _____.
   A. Tsinghua University's Center for Development of Sports Industry
   B. Youth.cn
   C. a company
   D. both A and B

3. Young people follow winter sports mainly by _____.
   A. social media B. television
   C. radio   D. newspaper

4. You may see this passage on _____.
   A. a history book
   B. a fashion magazine
   C. a sports newspaper
   D. a food magazine

5. Which word can be used to describe respondents' view on the Games?
   A. Hate.   B. Support.
   C. Worry.   D. Disagree.

---

take part in 参加   introduce v. 引进；实施   play a role in 在……中起作用

重难句讲解

Nearly 90 percent of those surveyed were aged 18 to 21, and 93.8 percent are college students, according to the survey report, which was made by Tsinghua University's Center for Development of Sports Industry and Youth.cn. 该调查报告由清华大学体育产业发展研究中心和中国青年网联合发布。报告显示，近90%的受访者的年龄在18岁到21岁之间，其中93.8%是大学生。

本句是复合句。which...Youth.cn 为非限制性定语从句，修饰 the survey report。

Thursday D 任务型阅读

With the theme "Through women's eyes—reading between the lines", the 6th EU-China International Literary (文学的) Festival started on Saturday.

"__1__", Nicolas Chapuis, EU ambassador (大使) to China, said at the festival's online opening ceremony (开幕式).

During the festival, 50 novelists, writers and poets from China and the European Union will discuss their works, creative ideas and so on.

"__2__, but has gradually been seen over the last century," Chapuis said.

__3__. "At this moment of social change, it is necessary for women to play a role in economic and social recovery of today's world," he said.

"Putting the spotlight on female writers this year is necessary. We would like to give people a chance to discover the excellent value of women's writing and cultural production," he said.

Portuguese (葡萄牙的) writer Lidia Jorge, one of the guest speakers for the opening ceremony, said that "our life is created through writing. We must write our own lives and the most important thing for women is to find our own views to write. __4__. But now things have changed."

"Women's writing matters to the entire human race. There have been a lot of movements (运动), in Portugal, so that women can use their own words to tell people about their own life. __5__," she said.

Another guest speaker, Chinese writer Xu Xiaobin, the author of *Crystal Wedding* and *Feathered Serpent*, said to keep creativity, woman writers should open their minds to connect with the outside world, to draw something useful from philosophy (哲学), natural sciences, art and life itself.

阅读短文，从下列选项中选出能填入文中空白处的最佳选项。

A. The true value of women's writing was out of people's sight for a long time

B. But there are still a lot of places that women have not touched and explored

C. After almost two years, the world is still fighting against the COVID-19 pandemic

D. We stress the diversity and creativity of women writers across the EU and China in this year's literary festival

E. In a long time in the past, women couldn't write

Ten years after his last show as actor and singer with the Greek (希腊) National Opera, Georgios Sochos stands confidently on the main stage of the 19th century Ziller Building of the National Theater of Greece in central Athens (雅典), practicing breathing exercises before singing, again.

In April 2021, Sochos contracted (感染) COVID-19 and was sent to hospital. Two long months later he still didn't feel well, and singing was the last thing on his mind.

"I was so tired, and there was also this sense of insecurity and fear due to the illness and being treated in hospital alone," he says. "I was affected psychologically (心理受到影响) for certain."

Sochos performed recently in a conference of Greek pulmonologists (胸腔内科医生) together with other members in a program organized by the National Theater of Greece for people being treated for COVID-19.

Inspired (启发) by a similar project run by the English National Opera in London, the National Theater of Greece started in May a free-of-charge online program developed by a team of professionals to help people who have difficulty in breathing and those who get great stress. The program uses singing to make them feel better.

Thirty patients have benefited to date, and as the program continues, thanks to the money provided by pharmaceutical (制药的) companies, the goal is to support 100 people this year, says Sofia Vienopoulou, head of the Young Peoples' Stage of the National Theater of Greece.

In the past four years, the National Theater of Greece has run all kinds of programs with the aim of treating trauma (心理创伤) through art, Vienopoulou says.

The theater invited Aggeliki Toubanaki to organize the new program. Holding a doctoral (博士的) degree in molecular (分子的) biology, Toubanaki is a singer, researcher, performer, producer and vocal educator.

During the current program, Toubanaki helps her students to use voice and the mechanism (方法) of breathing to deal with their wounds, both physical and psychological.

"All patients need to communicate their experiences, all those strong feelings that they have from their time in hospital. The purpose of this laboratory program is to connect voice, breath and body," she says.

阅读短文，回答下面1~5小题。

1. What is Georgios Sochos's job?

2. Where does the National Theater of Greece get the idea of organizing a free-of-charge online program?

3. What is the purpose of the free-of-charge online program organized by the National Theater of Greece?

4. How does Aggeliki Toubanaki help her students to deal with their wounds?

5. What should patients do in this program?

Saturday F 短文填空

| 体裁 | 记叙文 | 题材 | 艺术 | 正确率 | ___/10 | 词数 | 315 |
| 难度 | ★★★★☆ | 建议用时 | 11分钟 | 实际用时 | ___ | 答案页码 | 103 |

An online reality show *Zhongguo Chaoyin* tries to (1) _____ (display) traditional music in a fashionable way for young people.

Disco, hip-hop, rock 'n' roll and traditional Chinese cultural elements (要素) all come together in this reality show. The show caused discussion among young netizens about *guofeng*—"Chinese flavor (风味)", a popular word in entertainment for a few years. It (2) _____ (mean) the rise of traditional culture in cartoon, music and other art forms among young people.

Popular players of *pipa*, *guzheng*, *suona*, and other traditional instruments, presented their understanding of Chinese culture through music on the show. And new flavors were (3) _____ (introduce) by some bands that played avant-garde (前卫的) music, thus mixing cultures in the shows.

"This show is experimental," says Wang Chenchen, director of the program. When (4) _____ (produce) the program, he wanted to discuss with people musical aesthetics (美学) of the East on an open platform, he adds.

"Young people (5) _____ (grow) up with the internet are used to globalization (全球化), and how to express our own cultural aesthetics thus becomes a meaningful topic," Wang says.

As an (6) _____ (experience) producer (制作人) of musical reality shows, Wang has (7) _____ (try) to lead his team to accept different things.

"People may not notice traditional music in their spare time," Wang says. "But as long as (8) _____ (hear) the melodies (旋律) of flute (长笛) or *guzheng*, they'll get (9) _____ (move). That's the cultural DNA of Chinese people."

"We don't expect everyone to accept our experiment right away. But if more people become interested in it, we're close to our target."

Wu Qunda is the screenwriter (编剧) of the reality show. Wu says such a show also encourages musicians (10) _____ have a deeper understanding of traditional cultures. "If they don't have their own understanding, they're unable to easily mix their work with others."

阅读短文，在短文空缺处填入适当的单词，或用括号内所给单词的适当形式填空。

(1) _____
(2) _____
(3) _____
(4) _____
(5) _____
(6) _____
(7) _____
(8) _____
(9) _____
(10) _____

词汇碎片

traditional *adj.* 传统的　　right away 马上

重难句讲解

"Young people growing up with the internet are used to globalization, and how to express our own cultural aesthetics thus becomes a meaningful topic," Wang says. "伴随着互联网成长起来的年轻人已经习惯了全球化，因此，如何表达我们自己的文化审美就成了一个有意义的话题。" 王晨辰说。

本句的直接引语是一个并列句。growing up... internet 为现在分词作后置定语，修饰 Young people；and 连接两个并列分句。

Week Seven 历史地理

Monday — A 完形填空

| 体 裁 | 记叙文 | 题 材 | 历史地理 | 正确率 | ___/15 | 词 数 | 298 |
| 难 度 | ★★★☆☆ | 建议用时 | 15分钟 | 实际用时 | | 答案页码 | 104 |

For the hundreds of thousands of ancient Chinese books, some of them are the last remaining copies of their kind. There is almost no __1__ for us to see them with our own eyes, let alone touch or read them. They have to be __2__ in state libraries or private institutions (机构).

It is important to develop technologies to protect these books and __3__ those that have been partly damaged (损坏) for different kinds of __4__.

However, it has long been the dream of many scholars (学者) to have these ancient books replicated (复制) with the same look and feel, __5__ their original style, beautiful handwriting and the seals of those who once kept them, as well as the thoughts and feelings of ancient scholars written __6__ the lines, can be presented to __7__.

Some publishing houses (出版社) have __8__ the effort. But replicated ancient books have not been published in series (系列) and their quality can be different.

It was not __9__ *The Hundreds of Ancient Chinese Classic Books Remade* was published by Huabaozhai (China's Treasure) Studio in 2018 that the books replicated became better in quality than the originals, and many of the __10__ editions (版本) of some well-known ancient books could be read in their original form.

There are __11__ several editions of the same ancient book, and the annotations (注释，评注) by different scholars make a __12__ in their quality. So for that series, the choosing of the best edition of each of the books was __13__, as it would reflect (反映) the quality of the whole set in general. A team was organized to choose __14__ hundreds of thousands of ancient books kept in thousands of libraries.

Even after publication of the whole set, __15__ are being made all the time in terms of the edition of a particular book.

1. A. book   B. opportunity   C. money   D. risk
2. A. thrown   B. brought   C. kept   D. bought
3. A. destroy   B. repair   C. choose   D. create
4. A. times   B. reasons   C. jobs   D. dreams
5. A. as soon as   B. unless   C. even though   D. so that
6. A. between   B. without   C. on   D. for
7. A. authors   B. workers   C. managers   D. readers
8. A. sought   B. made   C. missed   D. spoken
9. A. before   B. because   C. until   D. since
10. A. smallest   B. worst   C. best   D. biggest
11. A. immediately   B. once   C. seldom   D. usually
12. A. difference   B. hole   C. guess   D. wish
13. A. pleasant   B. boring   C. easy   D. important
14. A. out   B. behind   C. of   D. from
15. A. plans   B. changes   C. mistakes   D. statements

词汇碎片

remaining *adj.* 遗留的，剩下的   original *adj.* 最初的 *n.* 原件   particular *adj.* 特定的；特殊的

重难句讲解

However, it has long been the dream of many scholars to have these ancient books replicated with the same look and feel, so that their original style, beautiful handwriting and the seals of those who once kept them, as well as the thoughts and feelings of ancient scholars written between the lines, can be presented to readers. 然而，把这些古籍以相同的外观和触感复制出来，以便将它们原本的风格、优美的字迹和曾经拥有过它们的人的印章，以及古代文人写在字里行间的思想和感情呈现给读者，一直是许多学者的梦想。

本句是复合句。主句的主干为 it has long been the dream，其中 it 为形式主语，真正的主语是后面的动词不定式 to...feel。so that 引导目的状语从句，从句主语较长，其中还嵌套了一个 who 引导的定语从句，修饰 those。

Tuesday B 阅读理解

China, even after almost 35 years, can still be a learning experience, with environment or roads fundamentally (从根本上来说) different from what I was familiar (熟悉的) with back in Scotland.

My first visit, to Beijing, in 1987 was short, and I only paid attention to large and important architectural masterpieces (建筑杰作) dating back to the Ming Dynasty. Seven years later, in 1994, I returned to Beijing, staying in a *hutong* alley (小巷) near Yonghegong. Walking daily, I started to understand a certain order about the direction of alleys, the location (位置) of buildings such as traditional *siheyuan* and how they were arranged. It was really interesting, but what of the story and history of the city, why did some of it appear as almost a chessboard (棋盘)?

With no online search possible at that time, I would look closely at any street maps I could find while also searching through the shelves at Beijing Foreign Languages Bookstore on Wangfujing. Gradually (逐渐地) I started to concentrate on how the historic Beijing was built around a big plan that envisaged (设想) a central axis (轴) line at its heart. As I looked closely at historic maps, it became very clear how the early city had been arranged to follow this in many ways.

The axis, going through the core (主要的，核心的) area of the historic city of Beijing, is the longest urban (城市的) central axis still existing in the world. Forbidden City, built during 1406-1420, sits exactly on the axis, representing its position then at the center of China.

Beijing today may become a dazzling (耀眼的；令人印象深刻的) modern city. However, at its core is a special example of historic urban design based around an axis line showing its location at the heart of China.

1. Which of the following is WRONG about the author's first visit to Beijing?
   A. It happened in 1987.
   B. It didn't last long.
   C. He only paid attention to *siheyuan*.
   D. He didn't pay attention to all buildings.

2. How did the author start to understand a certain order about the direction of alleys in Beijing?
   A. By asking people living there.
   B. By observing (观察) while walking daily.
   C. By reading history books.
   D. By studying maps.

3. According to the author, what was envisaged at its heart while planning the building of historic Beijing?
   A. A central axis line.
   B. A chessboard.
   C. A *hutong* alley.
   D. Nothing.

4. What was the aim of building the Forbidden City on the axis?
   A. To make it look better.
   B. To show its importance.
   C. To save land and money.
   D. To prevent it from falling.

词汇碎片

almost *adv.* 几乎，差不多   pay attention to 关注；重视   concentrate on 集中精力于   modern *adj.* 现代的

重难句讲解

With no online search possible at that time, I would look closely at any street maps I could find while also searching through the shelves at Beijing Foreign Languages Bookstore on Wangfujing. 那时没有互联网搜索，我就仔细查看我能找到的任何街道地图，同时在王府井的北京外文书店的书架上搜寻。

本句是复合句。With介词短语作状语；I could find 为省略了引导词的定语从句，修饰 street maps；while also...Wangfujing 为"while+现在分词短语"的结构，表示"同时……"。

Wednesday C 任务型阅读

体 裁	记叙文	题 材	历史地理	正确率	___/5	词 数	245
难 度	★★★☆☆	建议用时	6分钟	实际用时		答案页码	105

An interesting picture of ancient cultural exchange routes across the Qinghai-Tibet Plateau (青藏高原) is appearing from below ground.

Thanks to recent discoveries in Lhasa, archaeologists (考古学家) are learning more about how different ethnic (民族的) groups from the 7th to 9th centuries communicated with one another.

In 2020 and last year, archaeologists dug out 36 tombs (坟墓) from that period. For Tashi Tsering, who introduced the findings during an online conference on Jan. 13, the site (遗址) offers exciting prospects (前景). "Many of the unearthed relics (出土文物) feature typical characteristics from the plains of Central China and neighboring cultures," he said.

From the 7th to 9th centuries, the Tubo kingdom's rule spread across the Qinghai-Tibet Plateau. At the same time, to the east, the Tang Dynasty, famous for its inclusive (包容的) culture, also experienced a golden era.

As a result, communication between the two sides was certain to happen, and can be seen clearly by visiting the Damshung site.

For example, black-and-white stone pieces from the traditional Chinese board game Go, or *weiqi*, were discovered. A pair of golden ear picks (挖耳勺) with lion- and bird-shaped designs was also among the main findings.

Tashi Tsering said, "None of these things had been seen among archaeological findings in Tibet before. Go, of course, originated (起源) in Central China and was very popular during the Tang Dynasty."

"These discoveries provide important information to prove cultural exchanges between the Tang Dynasty and Tubo, explaining how different ethnic groups came together," he said.

阅读短文，回答下面 1~5 小题。

1. What is appearing from below ground?

   _____

2. Who introduced the findings of 36 tombs from the 7th to 9th centuries during an online conference?

   _____

3. How can we see the communication between the Tubo kingdom and the Tang Dynasty?

   _____

4. According to the passage, where did *weiqi* originate?

   _____

5. Why is the discovery of *weiqi* and ear picks with lion- and bird-shaped designs important?

   _____

词汇碎片

ancient *adj.* 古代的；古老的　　period *n.* 时期　　conference *n.* 会议　　prove *v.* 证明

重难句讲解

Thanks to recent discoveries in Lhasa, archaeologists are learning more about how different ethnic groups from the 7th to 9th centuries communicated with one another. 得益于最近在拉萨的发现，考古学家更多地了解了从 7 世纪到 9 世纪的不同民族是如何相互交流的。

本句是复合句。Thanks to... 为状语，表示原因；how 引导宾语从句，该从句的主干为 different ethnic groups communicated with one another，from the 7th to 9th centuries 为后置定语，修饰 ethnic groups。

Thursday D任务型阅读

体裁：记叙文　题材：历史地理　正确率：___/5　词数：234
难度：★★★☆☆　建议用时：6分钟　实际用时：___　答案页码：105

In Taizicheng of Chongli district in Zhangjiakou City, north China's Hebei Province (省), many local people say the name (A)_____ their village is from the local belief (信仰) that a member of the imperial (皇帝的) family once stayed in the area.

In the 1970s, an archaeological (考古的) find seemed to prove their rich heritage (遗产). According to the archaeological (B)study, the site, 140 kilometers from Beijing, was built (C)_____ Emperor (皇帝) Zhangzong of the Jin Dynasty in 1202. Zhangzong was the sixth emperor in the Jin period.

According to the record, (D)金章宗曾两次到访该遗址, with each visit lasting more than three months and the site was destroyed in a fire in 1209.

On Dec. 31, 2021, an exhibition showing the results of the excavation (发掘) opened at the Taizicheng site exhibition hall in Chongli.

"With the Taizicheng site at the center, we are showing society and people's lives during the Jin Dynasty, especially its nomadic hunting (游猎文化), which the site was mainly used for," said the curator (负责人) of the exhibition.

"As the first temporary palace (行宫) of the Jin Dynasty (E)discovered by archaeological excavation, (F)its importance is second only to that of the Jin capital. It is also an important Jin city site, with the largest excavation area of its kind and the most well-preserved (保存完好的) structures found in recent years," said the person who was responsible for the excavation of the site.

阅读短文，按要求作答。

1. 在文中（A）和（C）的空白处填入适当的单词：
   _____ ; _____

2. 写出文中画线部分（B）和（E）的同义词或近义词：
   _____ ; _____

3. 将文中画线部分（D）译成英语：
   _____

4. 将文中画线部分（F）改写为：
   it is only _____ important _____ the Jin capital

5. 从文中找出两个与时间有关的名词：
   _____ ; _____

词汇碎片
district n. 地区，行政区　　member n. 成员　　destroy v. 毁坏　　structure n. 结构；建筑物

重难句讲解
With the Taizicheng site at the center, we are showing society and people's lives during the Jin Dynasty, especially its nomadic hunting, which the site was mainly used for. 以太子城遗址为中心，我们展示了金朝的社会以及当时人民的生活，尤其是其游猎文化，这是该遗址的主要用途。

本句是复合句。With 介词短语作状语，we are showing society and people's lives 是主句的主干，which 引导非限制性定语从句，修饰 nomadic hunting。

Friday E 短文填空

阅读短文，用括号内所给单词的适当形式填空。

After years of study, a more than 2,000-year-old great tomb in Xi'an, the capital of Shaanxi Province, was (1) _____ (prove) to belong to a famous emperor of the Western Han Dynasty.

Liu Heng, or Emperor Wen of Han, was the (2) _____ (three) emperor of the Western Han Dynasty. He was famous for his hardwork and thriftiness (节俭).

Ancient documents showed the (3) _____ (possibly) location (位置) of Emperor Wen's mausoleum (陵墓), but its specific location remained unclear.

The newly confirmed (确认) mausoleum site was found in 2006. In 2016, some (4) _____ (area) around the site were raided (偷盗), and archaeologists started to protect it.

Based on the excavations at the tomb site since 2017, the structure and objects that (5) _____ (be) dug out have revealed who is buried (埋葬) there, according to a researcher.

"It fits the highest-level tomb of the Western Han Dynasty," the researcher said. "The idea is also supported by our investigations of the outer burial pits (外藏坑) around the tomb."

(6) _____ (many) than 110 burial pits were around the tomb. According to the researcher, though only eight burial pits have been excavated, over 1,000 pottery figurines (陶俑) that "guarded" the emperor were found.

"It showed these pits may mimic (模拟) a whole system of government," the researcher said. "The emperor wanted (7) _____ (rule) his country even in the underworld."

(1) _____
(2) _____
(3) _____
(4) _____
(5) _____
(6) _____
(7) _____

词汇碎片

capital n. 省会；首都　　belong to 属于　　specific adj. 具体的　　rule v. 统治；控制

重难句讲解

Based on the excavations at the tomb site since 2017, the structure and objects that were dug out have revealed who is buried there, according to a researcher. 一位研究人员称，根据自2017年以来在墓地的发掘工作，挖掘出的结构体和物件揭示了墓主人的身份。

本句是复合句。Based on... 为过去分词短语作状语，主句的主干为 the structure and objects have revealed who...。其中 that 引导定语从句，修饰 the structure and objects；who 引导宾语从句，作 have revealed 的宾语。

Saturday F 短文填空

Guangdong is one of the most important economic centers of modern China. However, when speaking of its (1) _____, a stereotypical (刻板印象的) idea often appears.

Compared with the (2) _____ we have that tell us of life in Central China more than 2,000 years ago, there isn't enough information and stories about Guangdong around this time. People used to believe that the development of this place only began during the reign (统治时期) of Qinshihuang.

However, archaeological findings discover a much older culture, and the area's relation with other places in present-day China is also greater (3) _____.

Yanshanzhai site, Lingnan's largest known human settlement (定居地) from the Neolithic period (新石器时代), was found on a mountain in Yingde, a city in the north of Guangdong. Since 2019, an archaeological team has dug out many tombs at the site, spreading across (4) _____ 80,000 square meters, as announced during an online conference earlier this month.

A large number of discoveries surprised the archaeologists, not only because of the beautiful jade artifacts (玉器), but also their mirroring of the social class, a key sign of an infant civilization (初期文明).

"They offer important clues (线索) in studying how an early society gets complicated (复杂的)," says Liu Suoqiang, a researcher. "In high-level tombs, there are many jade artifacts and many other kinds of objects."

"But in (5) _____ ones, only some stones and pottery (陶器) were found," Liu explains. "It clearly shows the stratification (分层) of a society."

阅读短文，从方框中选择合适的短语填空，使短文通顺、意思完整。每个短语限用一次。

than people thought

ancient history

an area of

the lower-level

rich documents

Week Eight 文化风俗

Monday A 完形填空

体 裁	说明文	题 材	文化风俗	正 确 率	___/10	词 数	278
难 度	★★★★☆	建议用时	12 分钟	实际用时		答案页码	107

The five interlocked (联结的) Olympic rings have become so well-known. But you may not give them much thought. Given what we know about the meaning of wedding rings (婚戒), you may think there's a __1__ meaning behind the Olympic rings, but it's much more than that. Here's what the Olympic rings mean and the story behind their creation (创作).

The 1912 Olympic Games were the first to __2__ athletes (运动员) from what were then considered the five continents (洲): Africa, Asia, Europe, Oceania (Australia and New Zealand), and a combination (结合体) of North and South America. Coubertin designed what would become the __3__ of the global Games: the Olympic rings. The Olympic rings have been used in every summer and winter Games __4__ 1920 and have remained relatively (相对地) unchanged.

Humans have long used rings or circles as symbols, but the Olympic rings' meaning is __5__. For example, the five rings represent the five continents that __6__ the 1912 Games. In addition, the five interlocked rings must be same in __7__, carrying the idea __8__ all continents are equal (平等的) at the Games.

__9__, we may think each color in the Olympic rings would stand for something specific, like a continent. But in reality, that's not the case at all. Coubertin __10__ six official Olympic colors—blue, yellow, black, green, red, and white (featured in the background). That's because when he introduced the symbol in 1913, every single flag of the nations taking part in the games could be reproduced (复制；再造) using the colors in the Olympic symbol. Or, in his own words: "The six colors thus combined reproduce those of all nations without exception (例外)."

1. A. different   B. similar
   C. proud   D. correct
2. A. refuse   B. remember
   C. forget   D. include
3. A. symbol   B. problem
   C. dream   D. advantage
4. A. for   B. before
   C. since   D. after
5. A. special   B. important
   C. light   D. common
6. A. took part in   B. ran out of
   C. got away from D. looked forward to
7. A. color   B. size
   C. space   D. material
8. A. which   B. what
   C. that   D. where
9. A. Clearly   B. Luckily
   C. Easily   D. Lastly
10. A. caught   B. chose
    C. closed   D. covered

词汇碎片

consider v. 视为，认为   remain v. 一直是，保持不变   specific adj. 特定的；具体的

重难句讲解

That's because when he introduced the symbol in 1913, every single flag of the nations taking part in the games could be reproduced using the colors in the Olympic symbol. 这是因为当他在 1913 年推出这一标志时，每个参加运动会的国家的国旗都可以用奥林匹克标志中的颜色来再现。

本句是复合句。when 引导时间状语从句，take part in 意为"参加，参与"。

043

Tuesday B 阅读理解

Shadow theater (皮影戏) is a special art form and a type of opera in China. The puppets (木偶) for the show are carved (雕刻) from the skins of cows, horses or sheep. Making puppets includes several steps, such as choosing materials, carving, painting, sewing (缝) and inking (上油墨). No matter how complex the puppets are, two tools—a carving knife and a wax (蜡) board, are necessary and enough to produce a play. Performers (表演者) use these puppets to tell various stories.

In the past, the shadow theater was performed in the fields, with all performers hidden behind the scenes. Some controlled the puppets and sang, while others managed the music. A team was made up of six or seven people and a box of puppets. When putting on a play at a market or square, performers would start the show after the installation (安装) of light boxes and curtains. A team could perform up to 30 or 40 times a day, even into the night at times, and when the curtain fell, the performers would pack up and move on.

Rooted in China's northwestern Shaanxi Province during the Western Han, the shadow theater is considered the oldest active film art in the world. Some people call shadow theater "the ancestor (祖先) of the modern art of making films".

And among all the country's branches (分支), Beijing shadow theater stands out for its techniques in carving and modeling the puppets, as well as its specific tunes (曲调). Beijing shadow theater was divided into two <u>schools</u>: east and west. The eastern school disappeared very early on, while the western school came into being during the Ming Dynasty. In 1842, Lu Decheng inherited (继承) this art and established the Beijing Xiangshun Shadow Theater. Since then, the art of Beijing western-school shadow theater has been passed down generations (代) of the Lu family.

1. Which of the following is NOT the step to create puppets?
   A. Sewing.   B. Painting.
   C. Inking.   D. Cutting.

2. According to the second paragraph, we can infer (推断) that _____.
   A. it was not easy to make puppets for the show
   B. the ticket for a shadow play was very expensive
   C. the shadow theater was closely linked to light and shadow
   D. the shadow theater was not very popular among the public

3. Which of the following is TRUE?
   A. The shadow theater is a form of modern art.
   B. The shadow theater has a very long history.
   C. The shadow theater is from China's southeast.
   D. The shadow theater has no branches at all.

4. What does the underlined word "schools" mean in this passage?
   A. 学校   B. 流派
   C. 机构   D. 区域

5. This passage is mainly about _____.
   A. the introduction to the shadow theater
   B. how to enjoy a shadow play
   C. the importance of the shadow theater
   D. all kinds of puppets for the shadow theater

词汇碎片

special *adj.* 特殊的   produce *v.* 制作；生产   divide *v.* 划分

重难句讲解

No matter how complex the puppets are, two tools—a carving knife and a wax board, are necessary and enough to produce a play. 无论木偶有多复杂，一把刻刀和一块蜡版这两种工具是必要的，也足以制作一出戏。

本句是复合句。No matter how 引导让步状语从句，意为"无论多么……"；complex 意为"复杂的"。

Wednesday C 阅读理解

China's various traditional minority (少数民族) dress codes (行为规范) have had a large influence on their clothing. Traditionally, their textiles (纺织品), techniques (技术), and accessories (配饰) are used to protect some of the histories of the minorities who never used a written language to document their stories. They are a work of art.

Located in China's western region, Xinjiang Uygur Autonomous Region (新疆维吾尔自治区) has green grasslands, pretty blue lakes, wide deserts and rapidly developing large cities. The most distinctive (独特的) Uygur feature in their dress code would have to be their daily hat, which tells age, job, and ethnic origin (族源). And "Atlas", a traditional hand-made pattern on silk, is colorful and produced in this area. It shows the Uygur people's wisdom and history, and establishes a connection to their lively past and hopes for a bright future.

As we turn our eyes to southern areas, we will know another dressing code. "Without silver (银) or flowers a girl won't be a girl," an old Miao minority saying goes. Silver is an important part of their culture. It is mostly seen in Guizhou Province, but also across Guangxi, Yunnan, Hunan, and Hainan.

Silver shows beauty and affluence (富裕), and has the role of driving away bad spirits. Bigger and more ornate (华丽的) silver jewelry is better. For example, one Miao woman's silver ensemble (全套服装) can weigh more than 20 kg. The patterns of flowers, butterflies and animals are always seen. From the time a Miao woman is a child, she has silver jewelry she inherits (继承) from her family. By the time she gets married, her collection grows as her family buys more accessories.

1. Textiles of minorities are used for _____.
   A. protecting their languages
   B. being different from others
   C. protecting their histories
   D. avoiding bad luck

2. Which of the following is NOT the information that we can get from Uygur people's hat?
   A. Age.   B. Job.
   C. Address.   D. Origin.

3. _____ play(s) a great role in Miao minority's culture.
   A. Silver   B. Gold
   C. Flowers   D. Animals

4. How did a Miao woman get silver jewelry when she was a child?
   A. She bought it.
   B. She received it from her family.
   C. Her family made it for her.
   D. Her friends sent it to her.

5. What is the main idea of this passage?
   A. China has lots of minorities.
   B. Xinjiang has a special kind of hat.
   C. Miao people prefer silver clothes.
   D. Clothing is influenced by the dress code.

词汇碎片

various *adj.* 各种各样的   influence *n.* 影响   protect *v.* 保护   connection *n.* 联系

重难句讲解

By the time she gets married, her collection grows as her family buys more accessories. 当她结婚时，由于她的家人购买了更多的首饰，她收集的银饰也就更多了。

本句是复合句。By the time引导时间状语从句，意为"到……的时候"；as引导原因状语从句。

Thursday D任务型阅读

阅读短文，从下列选项中选出能填入文中空白处的最佳选项，选项中有两项为多余选项。

When it comes to gifts, flowers are a classic choice. __1__ Of course, Valentine's Day roses aren't strictly for expressing romantic (浪漫的) love. Thanks to different rose color meanings, the classic flowers make great Valentine's Day gifts for friends and family members too.

Why is a rose given on Valentine's Day? __2__ And like the history of Cupid and Valentine's Day, it's rooted in Greek mythology (神话). "Some stories say that the first red rose was created when the Greek goddess (女神) Aphrodite was hurt by a white rose's thorn (刺), causing that rose to turn red," says Sara Cleto, a folklorist (民俗学家). "Others say that the first red rose grew on the ground where Adonis, Aphrodite's lover, died and the goddess's tears fell."

__3__ She is the wife of a British ambassador (大使) to Turkey during the 1700s. "Lady Montagu wrote letters home excitedly talking about the Turkish 'flower language,' or the process of giving certain symbolic (有象征意义的) meanings to certain flowers. __4__ It had more to do with rhyming (押韵的) words than the importance of the flowers themselves," Cleto says. "Still, the concept of 'flower languages' caught on, especially in 19th-century England, and over the course of that century, roses became ever more closely linked to romantic love."

In fact, a huge reason for giving roses for Valentine's Day is simple. __5__ Cleto says, "Flowers are usually shipped over long distances, and roses are both very beautiful and hardy (适应力强的), so that's a huge part of why this practice has continued."

A. But she seemed to have understood this local custom in the wrong way.
B. And among all the Valentine's Day gifts, none are as popular as the rose.
C. The tradition of giving roses for Valentine's Day has several different stories.
D. In addition, an early person connecting roses with romance is Lady Montagu.
E. Another advantage is that this particular rose has no thorns, which is perfect for gift-giving.
F. Roses are beautiful flowers with wonderful smells and happen to travel really well.
G. However, it's not the only choice.

词汇碎片
classic *adj.* 经典的　　express *v.* 表达　　tear *n.* 眼泪　　importance *n.* 重要性

重难句讲解
Some stories say that the first red rose was created when the Greek goddess Aphrodite was hurt by a white rose's thorn, causing that rose to turn red. 有些故事版本说，第一朵红玫瑰是因希腊女神阿佛洛狄忒被一朵白玫瑰的刺刺伤，导致那朵玫瑰变成红色而产生的。

本句是复合句。that 引导宾语从句，作 say 的宾语；宾语从句中包含一个 when 引导的时间状语从句，causing that rose to turn red 为现在分词短语作状语。

Friday E 任务型阅读

Porcelain-making (制瓷) in Liling dates back to the Han Dynasty. It developed fast at the end of the Qing Dynasty, when polychrome porcelain (釉下五彩瓷)—green, blue, black, brown and agate red (玛瑙红)—was introduced in 1908. A porcelain vase won gold at the Panama Pacific World's Fair (巴拿马太平洋万国博览会) in 1915, making it known worldwide. Unluckily, the wars of the first half of the 20th century cut short this success. It was after 1949 that the industry was active again. Porcelain-making continued to develop to an industrial level and other types of ceramics (陶瓷制品) appeared.

At present, there are more than 4,000 types of ceramic products in five kinds. Liling has about 700 specialized (专门的) companies, employing over 200,000 people. The number of companies with annual (年度的) income of 20 million yuan or more is 162, forming a large industrial groups.

The production of porcelain for domestic use (家用) is the third-largest in China. The products are exported (出口) to more than 150 countries. A porcelain valley (谷) was built in the city in 2014, which has even become a tourist attraction in this area.

More than 20 great masters of polychrome porcelain are active in Liling. Among them, Huang Xiaoling decides to pass on this skill, which is beautiful and elegant. She also teaches part-time at the Liling Porcelain Institute of Hunan University of Technology. "Though it doesn't make us millionaires, working in the porcelain industry allows us to have a comfortable life while passing on the skills and culture of our ancestors," Huang said.

阅读短文，回答下面 1~5 小题。

1. When did the porcelain-making in Liling start?

2. Why did the porcelain-making in Liling become famous?

3. What suddenly stopped the success of porcelain-making in Liling?

4. How many types of ceramic products are produced in Liling now?

5. What does Huang Xiaoling think of working in the porcelain industry?

词汇碎片

date back to 追溯到 worldwide *adv.* 在全世界；在世界各地 continue *v.* 继续 tourist attraction 观光胜地

重难句讲解

Among them, Huang Xiaoling decides to pass on this skill, which is beautiful and elegant. 黄小玲是其中一位，她决定将这一美丽而优雅的技术传承下去。

本句是复合句。which 引导非限制性定语从句，修饰前面的 this skill。elegant 意为"优雅的"。

We all know carrying a four-leaf clover (四叶草) will bring you good luck, but the history of this (1) _____ symbol may surprise you.

Why is the four-leaf clover considered lucky? One story has it that the lucky meaning comes (2) _____ Eve herself. As Adam and Eve were (3) _____ the Garden of Eden, Eve is said to have picked a single four-leaf clover as a souvenir (纪念品) of paradise (天堂), and this has led to them being considered lucky ever since. The Celts (凯尔特人) considered four-leaf clovers to have magical (神奇的) powers of protection, able to drive away bad luck. It was also believed (4) _____ carrying a clover allowed the bearer to see fairies (精灵). Celtic fairies were dangerous little creatures who might play terrible tricks (戏弄) (5) _____ steal your children, so carrying a clover meant that you could take (6) _____ to avoid danger if you saw one.

(7) _____ story says that when St. Patrick brought Christianity (基督教) to ancient Ireland, he used the three-leaf shamrock (三叶草) to explain the Holy Trinity (三位一体): one leaf represented the Father, the next the Son, and the (8) _____ the Holy Ghost (圣灵). (9) _____, the belief that four-leaf clovers are lucky may have already been among the Celtic peoples, probably because it is difficult to find one clover with four (10) _____. Many Celtic traditions were mixed with the new religion (宗教) over the years, and the importance of the clover was one of them. The four-leaf clover meaning became connected with Christianity so that the first three leaves came to represent faith (信仰), hope, and love, and the fourth leaf, luck.

Week Nine 科学技术

Monday — A 完形填空

体 裁	记叙文	题 材	科学技术	正 确 率	___/15	词 数	227
难 度	★★★★☆	建议用时	16 分钟	实际用时		答案页码	110

Engineers at Beijing-based China Electronics Technology Group have developed a cutting-edge air disinfector (消毒机). __1__ can neutralize (使无效) more than 10 kinds of pathogenic (致病的) bacteria (细菌) and viruses (病毒), __2__ novel coronavirus (新型冠状病毒) that caused the COVID-19 pandemic. The __3__ has been accepted by a group of medical experts and virologists (病毒学家).

Peng Ke, one of the chief designers, said __4__ Friday that more than 100,000 units of the __5__ product have been transported to Zhangjiakou in Hebei Province, one of the host regions of the Beijing 2022 Olympic Winter Games, and are being __6__ at public places. __7__, government buildings, hospitals, railway stations and other crowded places in densely (密集地) populated cities __8__ Beijing, Chongqing and Chengdu have also prepared the disinfectors.

__9__ by designers and disease control specialists (专家) __10__ that the disinfector is able to kill almost all novel coronavirus pathogens (病原体) within its effective working radius (半径) in just 15 minutes, Peng Ke said, stressing that it is absolutely __11__ for humans and animals. "__12__ with other disinfection methods such as chemical agents (剂) and ultraviolet (紫外线的) lamps, our product features zero health hazards (危害), faster disinfecting processes, __13__ effectiveness and longer operating times. It is __14__ to use, requires no further costs and is suitable for indoor places with many people," the engineer also said. Product managers said they have received 13 patents (专利权) on technologies and techniques created during the development __15__.

1. A. We   B. It
   C. He   D. They
2. A. except   B. above
   C. including D. around
3. A. product   B. game
   C. information D. phone
4. A. at   B. in
   C. on   D. of
5. A. new   B. simple
   C. old   D. beautiful
6. A. taken   B. sold
   C. used   D. held
7. A. In particular B. Even if
   C. By accident D. In addition
8. A. such as   B. for example
   C. because of D. according to
9. A. Choices   B. Tests
   C. Decisions D. Inventions
10. A. made   B. showed
    C. spoke   D. shared
11. A. dangerous B. bad
    C. active   D. safe
12. A. Forgotten B. Compared
    C. Stopped D. Covered
13. A. higher   B. lower
    C. worse   D. lighter
14. A. difficult B. impossible
    C. easy   D. popular
15. A. process B. result
    C. history D. goal

词汇碎片

develop *v.* 开发，研制　　cause *v.* 造成；引起；导致　　medical *adj.* 医学的，医疗的

重难句讲解

Tests by designers and disease control specialists showed that the disinfector is able to kill almost all novel coronavirus pathogens within its effective working radius in just 15 minutes, Peng Ke said, stressing that it is absolutely safe for humans and animals. 彭科说，设计师和疾病控制专家的测试表明，该设备能够在短短15分钟内杀死其有效工作半径内的几乎所有新型冠状病毒病原体，并强调它对人类和动物绝对安全。

本句是包含宾语从句的复合句。主句是 ...Peng Ke said，为主谓宾结构。宾语是 Peng ke said 前面的整个句子，即宾语从句。该宾语从句中又嵌套了一个 that 引导的宾语从句，作 showed 的宾语。stressing... 为现在分词短语作伴随状语。

Tuesday B 阅读理解

An unmanned (无人操纵的) vehicle carried the Olympic torch (火炬) this month for the first time in Games history, showing China's driverless (无人驾驶的) vehicle ambitions (雄心) and abilities. The driverless car, developed by Chinese information technology company Baidu, carried the torch for the 2022 Beijing Winter Olympic Games about 800 meters on Feb 2 at the capital's Shougang Industrial Park.

"We'd prefer to call it a robot because we will increasingly engage (使融入) with more moving robots in our daily lives," said Wei Dong, vice-president of Baidu's automatic (自动的) driving sector, adding that the vehicle represents the automobile industry's future. The vehicle, which does not have a steering wheel (方向盘), is a prototype (原型). The development team will continue to improve its functions.

While the robot involved in the torch relay (传递) represents the future of unmanned vehicles, many unmanned cars using mature (成熟的) technologies have been put into operation in other areas. In Yizhuang, a southern suburb of Beijing, residents have been able to hail (示意停下) robot taxis by a mobile phone app since Nov 25. It's the first commercialized (商业化的) autonomous driving project in China.

Passengers can press the "start" button on screens in front of the back seats, and they go. Though a safety officer is required to sit in the driver's seat, in accordance with current regulations in China, he or she does not need to lift a finger unless an emergency happens. The vehicles follow a preprogrammed (预编的) route and can operate automatically throughout the whole trip, including making turns, changing lanes (车道), using turn signals when changing lanes and stopping for pedestrians (行人) or at traffic lights.

1. Who developed the driverless car that carried the Olympic torch?
   A. Shougang Group.   B. Baidu.
   C. Yizhuang.   D. Alibaba.

2. Which of the following is TRUE according to Paragraph 1?
   A. China used driverless cars for some important games before.
   B. The driverless car carried a driver about 800 meters.
   C. Driverless car is very common in China.
   D. The driverless car was invented by a Chinese company.

3. Why does the unmanned vehicle represent the automobile industry's future according to Paragraph 2?
   A. Because there will be more moving robots in daily lives.
   B. Because people are getting lazy.
   C. Because technology is developing faster and faster.
   D. Because people will increasingly buy the driverless car.

4. What's the first commercialized autonomous driving project in China?
   A. Industrial robot.   B. Robot buses.
   C. Robot taxis.   D. Robot planes.

5. According to the passage, which of the following is NOT TRUE?
   A. A safety officer is required to sit in the driver's seat in a robot taxi.
   B. A robot taxi follows a preprogrammed route.
   C. A robot taxi can't operate automatically throughout the whole trip.
   D. A robot taxi can use turn signals when changing lanes.

词汇碎片

vehicle n. 交通工具，车辆   capital n. 首都   prefer v. 更喜欢   press v. 按；压；挤

重难句讲解

"We'd prefer to call it a robot because we will increasingly engage with more moving robots in our daily lives," said Wei Dong, vice-president of Baidu's automatic driving sector, adding that the vehicle represents the automobile industry's future. 百度智能驾驶事业群副总裁魏东说："我们更愿意称它为机器人，因为我们将在日常生活中越来越多地接触到移动机器人。"他补充说，这辆汽车代表着汽车行业的未来。

本句是包含宾语从句和原因状语从句的复合句。主句是...said Wei Dong，为主谓宾结构，主语是 Wei Dong，谓语是 said，宾语是前面的直接引语，即宾语从句。该宾语从句中还包含一个由 because 引导的原因状语从句。vice-president of Baidu's automatic driving sector 是 Wei Dong 的同位语，对 Wei Dong 进行补充说明。adding that... 是现在分词结构作伴随状语，that 引导的是宾语从句。

Traffic jams are a common problem in cities around the world. Some frustrated drivers wish they could fly over vehicles blocking their path. Such goals may be achieved sooner than many expect, with "flying cars", commonly known as electric vertical (垂直的) takeoff and landing vehicles, or eVTOLs, fast becoming a reality.

HT Aero, an affiliate (子公司) of Chinese electric vehicle maker Xpeng, showed a flying car late last month, saying it plans to introduce these vehicles in 2024.

The cars will feature a lightweight (轻量的) design and rotors (旋翼) that fold away, so that the vehicles can be driven on roads before and after flight. With a number of safety features, including parachutes (降落伞), each vehicle will cost less than 1 million yuan, the company said. Globally, some 250 companies are developing and producing flying vehicles, and the list is growing, according to a report by consultancy McKinsey. Robin Riedel, a McKinsey partner, said the flying cars sector has existed for more than a decade, and the "convergence (趋同性) of several trends" has led to increased interest in it.

"First, on-demand services have changed the way we think about mobility (移动能力). Second, there's a focus on sustainability (可持续性), which these vehicles support. Third, there's a lot of funding available from investors who want to be a part of the next big thing," Riedel said.

The emerging (新兴的) flying vehicles sector is now viewed as a serious solution to urban traffic jams and a new alternative (可供选择的事物) to personal mobility in cities. It is expected to grow into a market valued at $1 trillion (万亿) by 2040 and $9 trillion by 2050, according to global financial services company Morgan Stanley. Flying vehicles are typically about the size of ordinary ones, or slightly larger. Most of them will fly at speeds of 100 to 300 kilometers per hour and carry several passengers.

1. What can solve the problem of traffic jams according to Paragraph 1?
   A. Flying buses.   B. Flying cars.
   C. Planes.   D. Subways.
2. When will HT Aero introduce those flying cars?
   A. In 2024.   B. In 2025.
   C. In 2022.   D. In 2023.
3. How much will each flying car cost?
   A. 1 million yuan.
   B. Less than 2 million yuan.
   C. Less than 1 million yuan.
   D. More than 1 million yuan.
4. How many reasons did Riedel mention that have led to increased interest in flying cars?
   A. 3   B. 4
   C. 5   D. 1
5. Which of the following is TRUE about the difference between flying vehicles and ordinary vehicles?
   A. The speed of flying vehicles can reach 400 kilometers per hour.
   B. The speed of ordinary vehicles can reach 100 to 300 kilometers per hour.
   C. Flying vehicles are smaller in size than ordinary ones.
   D. Flying vehicles are usually about the same size as ordinary ones, or slightly larger.

traffic jam 交通拥堵   block v. 堵塞，阻塞   reality n. 现实   value v. 给……估价

The cars will feature a lightweight design and rotors that fold away, so that the vehicles can be driven on roads before and after flight. 这些汽车的特点是轻量化设计并配以可折叠的旋翼，因此在飞行前后都能在路上行驶。

本句是包含定语从句和结果状语从句的复合句。主句的主干是 The cars will feature a lightweight design and rotors，为主谓宾结构。that fold away 为定语从句，修饰 rotors。so that 引导的是结果状语从句，before and after flight 为时间状语。

Thursday D 阅读理解

Researchers at China Aerospace (航天) Science and Industry Corp (CASIC) have developed and made the world's first robot whale shark. The robotic shark has been on display in an aquarium (水族馆) at Shanghai Haichang Ocean Park in the city's Pudong New Area since January. The whale shark is a slow-moving carpet shark and the largest known living fish.

Designed and built by engineers at the Shenyang-based No. 111 Factory, a subsidiary (子公司) of the CASIC Third Academy, the underwater robot is 4.7 meters long, weighs 350 kilograms and can move 42 meters a minute. Powered (驱动) by a lithium (锂) battery, it can swim, turn, float and dive like a real shark by moving its mechanical fins. The mouth and gills (鳃) can also open and close like a shark's.

The robot is able to reach a depth of 10 meters and can operate for as long as 10 hours, said Fang Xuelin, a researcher at the factory's Underwater Propulsion (推进) Technology Laboratory who is in charge of the robot shark program. The shark can be remotely controlled and can also swim based on <u>preset</u> programs or its own sensors (传感器), he said.

Having observed the huge market potential (潜力) of underwater robots, the factory decided several years ago to take advantage of its expertise (专长) in space propulsion systems to develop robotic aquatic (水生的) animals. The factory now plans to develop more types of aquatic robots, including some extinct mammals (哺乳动物), for display in parks and schools. It will also promote the products to businesses engaged in fields such as underwater salvage (打捞) and mineral prospecting (矿产勘探).

1. According to this passage, in which city was the robotic shark displayed?
   A. Beijing.   B. Shenzhen.
   C. Shanghai.   D. Shenyang.
2. Which of the following is NOT TRUE about the robot whale shark?
   A. It was designed and built by engineers at the Shenyang-based No. 111 Factory.
   B. It is 4.2 meters long and weighs 350 kilograms.
   C. It can move 42 meters a minute.
   D. It can swim, turn, float and dive like a real shark.
3. What does the underlined word "preset" in Paragraph 3 mean in Chinese?
   A. 预设的   B. 重复的
   C. 调整的   D. 加工的
4. The Shenyang-based No. 111 Factory decided to use its expertise in _____ to develop robotic aquatic animals.
   A. market potential
   B. land propulsion systems
   C. space propulsion systems
   D. robotic aquatic systems
5. Which of the following companies will the factory most probably promote its products to?
   A. Weilong Information Technology Co., Ltd.
   B. Guangtian Culture Media Co., Ltd.
   C. Xingye Education Consulting Co., Ltd.
   D. Rungang Underwater Engineering Co., Ltd.

Friday E 短文填空

China's Chang'e 5 lunar (月球的) lander has discovered the first on-site (现场的) evidence (证据) of water molecules (分子) on the moon's surface, according to a study published in the journal *Science Advances* on Friday. This puts a long-running scientific debate about the moon's humidity (湿度) to rest.

Since the mid-20th century, scientists thought the moon was (1) _____ dry. But in 2020, NASA confirmed through remote observation (远程观测) that water molecules should be widely distributed (使分布) across the lunar surface, though it lacked actual on-site evidence to support its claims.

Lunar samples (样本) taken by the Chang'e 5 in December 2020 (2) _____ that the soil at its landing site contains (包含) less than 120 parts per million (百万分率) water, or 120 grams of water per metric ton (公吨). A rock from the region was found to carry 180 ppm of water, much (3) _____ than those found on Earth. Scientists believe most of the water in the lunar soil was implanted (植入) by the solar (太阳的) wind. Interestingly, (4) _____ the rock is somehow wetter than its surrounding (周围的) soil, this suggests that there may be extra sources of water on the moon, such as from its interior.

Lin Honglei, the first author of the study and an associate researcher at the Chinese Academy of Sciences' Institute of Geology and Geophysics (中国科学院地质与地球物理研究所), said detecting water signals, like water molecules and hydroxyl (羟基), is (5) _____ from finding actual liquid (液态的) water. Scientists would need to treat rock and soil with heat to extract (提取) water molecules and hydroxyl from them and turn it into liquid water, he said.

阅读短文，从方框中选择合适的单词并用其正确形式填空，使短文通顺、意思完整。每空限填一词，每词限用一次。（其中有两项为多余选项。）

because

dry

completely

show

but

clear

different

词汇碎片

discover v. 发现   surface n. 表面   support v. 支持

重难句讲解

But in 2020, NASA confirmed through remote observation that water molecules should be widely distributed across the lunar surface, though it lacked actual on-site evidence to support its claims. 但在2020年，美国国家航空航天局通过远程观测证实，水分子应该广泛分布在月球表面，尽管它缺乏实际的原位探测证据来支持其说法。

本句是包含宾语从句和让步状语从句的复合句。主句的主干是NASA confirmed that..., 为主谓宾结构。that引导宾语从句，though引导让步状语从句。

Saturday F 短文填空

体 裁	说明文	题 材	科学技术	正确率	___/10	词 数	234
难 度	★★★★☆	建议用时	11分钟	实际用时		答案页码	112

阅读短文，根据首字母提示，在短文空缺处填入适当的单词，使短文通顺、意思完整。

Metal 3D printing can produce the most complex rocket parts, using combustion-resistant (抗燃的) material. While 3D printing isn't new, how has the (1) t_____ developed to face the more extreme (极端的) conditions of space?

Since the first 3D printers appeared in the 1980s, their applications (应用) have continued to grow. At (2) f_____, the technology was relatively unknown, according to *Live Science*, but gained popularity in the 21st century. In the early years of 3D printing, it was (3) u_____ mainly for speedy prototyping (原型制作).

At room temperature, metal doesn't naturally lend itself to being printed as a fluid (液态). (4) H_____, this is exactly what today's machines allow. To make small shapes in metal, 3D printing is a far quicker (5) m_____ compared with metal cutting. Metal cutting is a subtractive (减去的) process, the (6) b_____ *Introduction to Plastics Engineering* (2018) explains, which can be extremely costly and time-consuming. Instead, 3D printing is (7) a_____ additive (添加的) process that uses carefully selected dimensions (尺寸) to build up a 3D piece layer by layer.

Some metal printing methods have more steps (8) t_____ others, based on the method of printing. Selective metal sintering (烧结) prints metal by combining it with plastic. This makes the printing process (9) s_____ to that of printing with plastic. The (10) d_____ is that when it is removed from the machine, it isn't a fully metal piece yet. Further steps strengthen the printed part and remove the unwanted plastic.

(1) _____
(2) _____
(3) _____
(4) _____
(5) _____
(6) _____
(7) _____
(8) _____
(9) _____
(10) _____

词汇碎片

produce v. 生产；制造　　condition n. 条件；状况　　appear v. 出现　　temperature n. 温度；气温

重难句讲解

The latter is a subtractive process, the book *Introduction to Plastics Engineering* (2018) explains, which can be extremely costly and time-consuming. 《塑料工程概论》（2018年）一书解释说，金属切割是一种"减法"工艺，成本极高且耗时。

本句是包含定语从句和宾语从句的复合句。主句是...the book explains，为主谓宾结构，宾语是前面的整个句子，即宾语从句。which 引导的是定语从句，修饰 a subtractive process。

Week Ten 人物传奇

Monday A 完形填空

体 裁	记叙文	题 材	人物传奇	正确率	/10	词 数	303
难 度	★★★☆☆	建议用时	10 分钟	实际用时		答案页码	114

Born in Zigong, Southwest China's Sichuan Province, Zhang Meili, 22, comes from a poor but loving family. Zhang was deeply __1__ by the film *Shaolin Temple* when she was a child. __2__ the age of 12, she was keen (热衷的) to learn martial arts (武术).

In 2017, Zhang __3__ to Chengdu Sport University with excellent grades to study *sanda* (散打). In 2020, after finishing her college study, she __4__ to be a bodyguard (保镖). After three months of basic training in Chengdu, Zhang arrived in Beijing to study and improve herself.

After several special training camps for bodyguards at Genghis Security Academy (学院) in Beijing, Zhang Meili __5__ training in hundreds of subjects. She gradually became a female (女性的) bodyguard up to __6__ and thus got a job in the academy to teach security and defense (防御) training programs.

Female bodyguards may be not as strong as male bodyguards. They have to spend more effort and have a more difficult time than the male bodyguards during training. However, in Zhang's view, compared with male bodyguards, women also have many __7__: they usually make people feel relaxed and can easily __8__ people's emotions; they are careful, and have a strong sense of defense; their movements are lighter and they have great skills.

"In each special training camp, female bodyguards have to experience __9__ examination, and at last only 20 percent of them can become bodyguards," Zhang says. "As long as female bodyguards train and fight hard, they could be the best. They are more popular __10__ male bodyguards when seeking jobs."

Good physical fitness and skills are not the most important standards for a good bodyguard. These are just the most basic conditions. They have to master more skills such as driving and sometimes they even have to learn foreign languages.

1. A. cared   B. divided
   C. impressed   D. held
2. A. At   B. In
   C. On   D. To
3. A. walked   B. went
   C. swam   D. prepared
4. A. offered   B. chose
   C. feared   D. hated
5. A. fought   B. gave
   C. paid   D. experienced
6. A. step   B. station
   C. standard   D. storm
7. A. advantages B. tasks
   C. tastes   D. exercises
8. A. hide   B. complete
   C. clear   D. sense
9. A. light   B. easy
   C. slow   D. strict
10. A. until   B. before
    C. than   D. as

词汇碎片

training *n.* 训练，培训　　compare with 与……相比较

重难句讲解

In 2020, after finishing her college study, she chose to be a bodyguard. 2020 年，大学毕业后，她选择当一名保镖。

本句是简单句。句子的主干为 she chose to be a bodyguard; after finishing her college study 为介词短语，作时间状语; In 2020 为时间状语。

When the Winter Games started in Beijing on February 4, fashion was one of a few focuses of the opening ceremony (开幕式). This time, China has created a strong fashion statement. The younger generation (一代人) of designers combines traditional culture with the Olympic spirit, creating something new through the Olympic stage. Here are two outstanding designers among them.

Chen Peng: a Chinese local designer	Wang Fengchen: a London-based Chinese designer
Design works for the 2022 Winter Olympics: looks for the five parts of opening ceremony	Design works for the 2022 Winter Olympics: down jackets worn by flagbearers in the opening ceremony
Features of the works: simple, classic and close to the taste of young people	Features of the works: modern, inclusive (包容的) and diversified (多样的)
Design ideas: offering the best wishes for the international viewers; using a lot of Chinese cultural background, like the elements of the Chinese ice lantern (冰灯) and Chinese ice sculpture (雕塑), or the Yuxian County paper cutting (蔚县剪纸), or the Chinese notes and Chinese paintings	Design ideas: including her own modern style; building a bridge between Chinese culture and western culture and thus to express the idea of international togetherness; using a mix pattern (图案) of snow-white mountains surrounded (包围) by white and blue line drawings of Beijing landmarks (地标)

Truly, for the 2022 Winter Olympics, local designers came into the spotlight with their creations for the Team China athletes and for the performers at the opening ceremony in Beijing. The Winter Olympics appears to have offered an opportunity, not just to young athletes, but also to young Chinese designers who aim to make it on the international stage.

1. Which of the following comments is for Wang Fengchen's works?
   A. They express the best wishes for people around the world.
   B. They are classic and are liked by young people.
   C. They have the element of Chinese ice sculpture.
   D. They have a modern and inclusive style.

2. What is the common feature of the works of these two designers?
   A. Simple.
   B. Young.
   C. International.
   D. Modern.

3. In which part of a magazine can we read the passage?
   A. Fashion.
   B. Travel.
   C. Environment.
   D. Economy.

spirit n. 精神   taste n. 品味

The younger generation of designers combines traditional culture with the Olympic spirit, creating something new through the Olympic stage. 年轻一代的设计师将传统文化与奥运精神相结合，通过奥运这个舞台创造了一些新的东西。
本句是简单句。句子的主干为 The younger generation... spirit。creating something... 为现在分词短语作状语。

Wednesday C 阅读理解

体裁	记叙文	题材	人物传奇	正确率	/3	词数	319
难度	★★★☆☆	建议用时	5分钟	实际用时		答案页码	114

For many Chinese people, Lantern Festival, which fell on Feb 15 this year, marks an end to two weeks of Lunar New Year. For folk artist Wang De, it is also the busiest, best time for him to show his craft (手艺)—creating molten (熔化的) iron fireworks (烟花).

Wang, who is a blacksmith (铁匠) of the 500-year-old art of *dashuhua*, which means "creating tree flowers", lives in Yuxian County in the city of Zhangjiakou, North China's Hebei Province.

To create molten iron fireworks, scrap iron (铁屑) is melted to 1,600℃ and thrown against a cold wall to blinding effect.

Wang, 58, and his assistants put on over a dozen *dashuhua* shows for local people and tourists as part of Spring Festival activities each year.

The folk artist hopes the tradition can bring more visitors to his hometown of Zhangjiakou, which drew international attention following its successful bid (投标) to host the 2022 Olympic Winter Games together with Beijing.

Dashuhua is a traditional form of fireworks show that takes place during certain festivals. In ancient times, this was a show that only those people with wealth and high social position could afford. There are only four people left in China who have mastered the ancient practice, and three of them are not young, according to local media reports.

Due to the risk of the show, it's easy for *dashuhua* artists to get injured when they are giving shows. But the high-risk tradition is still only kept for the brave.

During a show a few years ago, Wang got serious burns on his leg and he took two months to recover (康复).

Both Wang's father and grandfather were blacksmiths.

"I learned the craft from my father. When I was young, I thought it was exciting. But years later I also felt it was my duty to pass it on to the next generation," he says.

1. Who might afford the show of *dashuhua* in ancient times?
   A. A farmer who worked in the fields.
   B. A person who sold breakfast in the street.
   C. A son of a rich family.
   D. A waiter in a tea house.

2. Wang De and his assistants perform *dashuhua* during _____ every year.
   A. the Dragon Boat Festival
   B. Tomb Sweeping Day
   C. the Spring Festival
   D. the Double Ninth Festival

3. Which of the following word can best describe the show of *dashuhua*?
   A. Easy.
   B. Dangerous.
   C. Useful.
   D. Well-known.

词汇碎片

artist *n.* 艺术家　　create *v.* 创作，创造　　ancient *adj.* 古代的

重难句讲解

Wang, who is a blacksmith of the 500-year-old art of *dashuhua*, which means "creating tree flowers", lives in Yuxian County in the city of Zhangjiakou, North China's Hebei Province. 王德是一名表演"打树花"的铁匠，居住在中国北方河北省张家口市蔚县；"打树花"这门艺术已有500年的历史。

本句是复合句。主句的主干为 Wang lives in Yuxian County。who is... dashuhua 为非限制性定语从句，修饰 Wang。which means "creating tree flowers" 为非限制性定语从句，修饰 dashuhua。

Thursday D 阅读理解

Ancient coloring craft (手艺) is catching young people's eyes.

Ni Shenjian can still easily remember the time when he started to learn the craft of making blue calico (蓝印花布) about ten years ago. Ten years later, he has become a city-level inheritor (继承人) of the craft, following the steps of his father-in-law Wu Yuanxin and his wife Wu Lingshu.

The craft of dyeing (染色) and treating calico was started from the Song Dynasty. Blue calico was used by people across China.

In 2006, Nantong blue calico dyeing craft was listed as a national-level intangible cultural heritage (国家级非物质文化遗产), and Wu Yuanxin became a national-level inheritor of the craft.

"Inheriting and passing on crafts in a family is relatively stable. Other people often give up halfway since it's difficult to make much money in a short time," says Ni.

He received encouragement from the famous artist Han Meilin. "Your change of job is very important, and I hope you can pass it on to the next generation," Han said to Ni.

In 2012, Ni opened a course of blue calico craft at Nantong University and Nantong Open University. He also carried out activities in a number of universities, middle and primary schools.

Some of Ni's students, as fashion design majors, later used blue calico elements in their designs. Others who became teachers also used what they learned at Ni's lessons in their own classes.

To give blue calico something more modern, Ni and his family have been trying to make a change in the craft.

Over the years, Ni has found his life busy but meaningful. "Some jobs can give you wealth and make you become famous, and people are often keen on such jobs. But for some others, if you don't do them, maybe nobody else will do so in the future," Ni says.

Our family are trying to keep the craft alive, he adds.

1. Ni Shenjian inherited the craft of making blue calico from _____.
   A. his parents
   B. his teacher
   C. his grandparents
   D. his father-in-law and his wife

2. Which of the following is NOT the feature of the craft of making blue calico?
   A. It is traditional.
   B. It is valuable.
   C. It is easy to make much money.
   D. It has become more modern.

3. What did Ni Shenjian do to pass on the craft?
   A. He opened a course of blue calico craft.
   B. He carried out some activities in schools.
   C. He made some changes in the craft.
   D. All of the above.

4. You may see this article on _____.
   A. a book of cooking
   B. a magazine of art
   C. a website of math
   D. a comic book

---

step n. 步伐，脚步　　list v. 把……列入名单　　pass on 传递

Ten years later, he has become a city-level inheritor of the craft, following the steps of his father-in-law Wu Yuanxin and his wife Wu Lingshu. 十年后，他跟随岳父吴元新和妻子吴灵姝的脚步，成了这门手艺的市级传承人。

本句是简单句。句子的主干为 he has become a city-level inheritor。following... 为现在分词短语作状语，表示伴随；Ten years later 为时间状语。

Friday E 阅读理解

It was noon time on Sunday, two days after the opening ceremony (开幕式) of the Beijing 2022 Winter Olympics, which was directed by Zhang Yimou and held at the National Stadium, also known as the Bird's Nest.

The excitement of choreographer (编舞者) Wang Yuanyuan was still clear, even showing in her voice.

As one of the creative teams for the opening ceremony, Wang directed a 5-minute dance piece, titled *Forming a Snowflake*. She says she can finally sleep well.

"We were very nervous and worried. We were not sure whether people would love the dance piece and we were also worried about making mistakes during the show," says Wang, during a telephone interview. "After it was over, we won the hearts of many viewers, which finally made us feel relaxed."

Viewers shared their excitement and praised the dance on Chinese social media, saying it was "romantic" (浪漫的) and "beautiful".

Wang received the invitation (邀请) to join the creative team for the opening ceremony over a year ago from director Zhang. Then, along with her six team members, including visual (视觉的) artist Tan Shaoyuan, Wang began the choreography of the dance piece last summer.

"We tried many times, hoping to express the message of togetherness and unity," Wang says, adding that the dance piece echoes (呼应) the official motto for the Beijing 2022 Winter Games, "together for a shared future".

As an old friend of Zhang, Wang is widely known for choreographing the ballet piece, *Raise the Red Lantern*, directed by Zhang in 2001.

"He is full of energy and ideas. He always works day and night," says Wang of the film director.

"The grand opening ceremony is a result of the efforts of many people and he trusted us," she adds.

Born in Beijing, Wang started to learn Chinese dance at age 10. In 2008, she founded Beijing Dance Theater, one of the country's most important dance companies, which tours worldwide. Wang has adapted (改编) some of the most famous Chinese stories and works of literature into her choreography pieces.

1. Which of the following word can describe Wang Yuanyuan's feeling after the opening ceremony?
   A. Excited.   B. Worried.
   C. Nervous.   D. Scared.

2. What did Wang Yuanyuan and her team worry about before the opening ceremony according to the passage?
   A. Whether they could perform in the opening ceremony.
   B. Whether people would love the dance piece.
   C. Whether Zhang Yimou would trust them.
   D. All of the above.

3. Which of the following was NOT done by Wang Yuanyuan?
   A. Directing *Forming a Snowflake*.
   B. Directing *Raise the Red Lantern*.
   C. Founding Beijing Dance Theater.
   D. Adapting Chinese stories into choreography pieces.

4. What is Wang Yuanyuan's comment on Zhang Yimou?
   A. He is full of energy and ideas.
   B. He works very hard.
   C. He showed trust in her.
   D. All of the above.

词汇碎片

direct v. 导演   mistake n. 错误，过失   praise v. 赞美，表扬

重难句讲解

It was noon time on Sunday, two days after the opening ceremony of the Beijing 2022 Winter Olympics, which was directed by Zhang Yimou and held at the National Stadium, also known as the Bird's Nest. 时间是周日中午，也就是由张艺谋执导的在国家体育场（鸟巢）举行的 2022 年北京冬奥会开幕式的两天后。

本句是复合句。主句的主干为 It was noon time。two days... Winter Olympics 是 Sunday 的同位语。which... Bird's Nest 是 which 引导的非限制性定语从句，修饰 the opening ceremony。

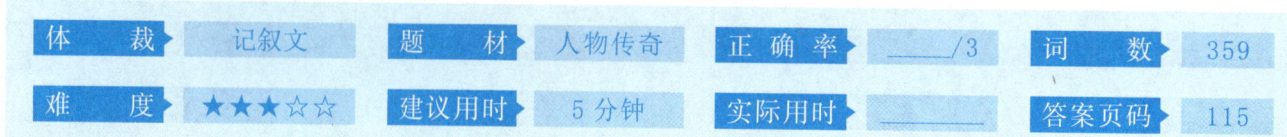

During this year's Spring Festival holiday, Huang Yangwei's mother and elder sister were dressed in new clothes with an ethnic brocade (织锦) he had woven (编，织) for them.

"It's just beautiful," says Huang's sister. "I love it."

Huang, 24, is a native of South China's Hainan Province. Born into a family of the Li ethnic group (黎族), he was deeply influenced by Li culture as a child, especially the ethnic brocade, which is famous for its bright colors. But he had no idea how to weave it.

"My parents are farmers, and no one in the family really knew much about weaving the brocade," he says.

Huang did not know much about craftsmanship (手工艺) until he was in high school, when local authorities organized an activity to introduce intangible cultural heritage (非物质文化遗产) to the school in 2016.

Since then, he fell in love with Li brocade and became the only boy in his home village who can weave it.

"I developed a deep love for the ethnic craft, but some villagers (村民) cannot understand why a man loves weaving so much," he says. "They think it's a girl's thing." However, Huang continued chasing after his weaving dream.

With great efforts, Huang made rapid progress and even won some awards in this field. In 2019, he went to a college in Haikou to study business administration (工商管理学). But he still wanted to weave.

He kept practicing during his college years and tried to make some changes to the traditional brocade patterns. Now, Huang is busy weaving a traditional dress for a customer from Harbin, the capital of Heilongjiang Province on the other end of the country. It is his first order that he has spent over half a year on.

Huang pays much attention to every piece of Li brocade he weaves by hand. In June, Huang will graduate from college. He has opened a clothing store with his elder sister in Wuzhishan.

"I hope I can bring Li ethnic culture to more parts of the world by weaving brocade," he says.

阅读短文，回答下面1~3小题。

1. How did Huang Yangwei know more about craftsmanship?

2. Why can't some villagers understand Huang's love for weaving?

3. What is Huang Yangwei's wish about weaving brocade?

词汇碎片

elder *adj.* 年龄较大的；资格老的   order *n.* 订单；订货

重难句讲解

Huang did not know much about craftsmanship until he was in high school, when local authorities organized an activity to introduce intangible cultural heritage to the school in 2016. 直到2016年黄杨伟上高中，当地政府在学校里组织了一场介绍非物质文化遗产的活动，他才对手工艺有了更多的了解。

本句是复合句。主句为 Huang did not know much about craftsmanship。until 和 when 分别引导时间状语从句。

Week Eleven 旅行交通

Monday A 完形填空

| 体 裁 | 记叙文 | 题 材 | 旅行交通 | 正确率 | ___/10 | 词 数 | 268 |
| 难 度 | ★★★★☆ | 建议用时 | 11分钟 | 实际用时 | | 答案页码 | 116 |

The 2022 Spring Festival travel rush (春运) officially starts today (January 17). It is __1__ that 1.18 billion trips will be made nationwide (遍及全国) during the Spring Festival travel rush this year, with 29.5 million trips per day, up 35.6 percent from 2021.

Also, New Year's Eve train tickets are officially __2__ sale from Monday. This year's 40-day travel rush is expected to __3__ on February 25. To better ensure the smooth management of the Spring Festival travel rush, relevant departments (有关部门) have also taken measures to __4__ the passenger experience.

First, precise (精准的) transport capacity will be organized to meet the travel needs of passengers in the context of epidemic (疫情的) prevention and __5__. During the Spring Festival travel rush, more than 10.5 million seats can be provided per day, up more than 10 percent from 2019. If the COVID-19 epidemic occurs in some areas, relevant departments will __6__ change the transportation capacity, stop or reduce the operation of passenger trains in affected (受影响的) areas, and control the movement of people.

Contactless (无接触的) services will __7__ be promoted to create a healthy travel environment for passengers. __8__, the number of self-service equipment at the stations will be increased, and fast channels for entering the station will be added. __9__ meal-order services will also be used.

To ensure the smooth progress of the 2022 Winter Olympics, relevant departments will also do their best to ensure the transport services for the Games. Forty pairs of Winter Olympics trains will be organized daily, and special trains will be added to handle the potential (潜在的) increase in passengers during the opening and __10__ ceremonies (仪式).

1. A. known B. expected C. agreed D. believed
2. A. on B. for C. in D. with
3. A. start B. continue C. end D. complete
4. A. share B. improve C. influence D. change
5. A. protection B. control C. report D. research
6. A. slowly B. quietly C. quickly D. completely
7. A. instead B. therefore C. however D. also
8. A. For example B. In addition C. At the same time D. By contrast
9. A. Online B. Offline C. Basic D. Standard
10. A. important B. public C. moving D. closing

词汇碎片
on sale 出售   smooth *adj.* 顺利的；平稳的   in the context of 在……的背景下   progress *n.* 进展；进步

重难句讲解
If the COVID-19 epidemic occurs in some areas, relevant departments will quickly change the transportation capacity, stop or reduce the operation of passenger trains in affected areas, and control the movement of people. 如果部分地区出现新冠肺炎疫情，有关部门将迅速调整运输能力，停止或减少受影响地区的旅客列车运行，控制人员流动。
本句是复合句。If引导的从句为条件状语从句，主句为and连接的三个并列句，并列句都是主谓宾结构。

Tuesday B 阅读理解

The China-Laos railway connecting the city of Kunming in Yunnan Province with the capital of Laos, Vientiane, is going to be officially open in December. Check out some of the can't-miss destinations (目的地) along the Chinese section (部分) of the railway.

Fuxian Lake in Yuxi	Fuxian Lake in Yuxi is China's largest deep-water lake sitting on a plateau (高原). Famous Chinese travel writer Xu Xiake once paid a visit and wrote about its clean water. What makes the lake more mysterious is the possibility that an ancient city lived under its quiet and calm surface. A diver (潜水员) once found the stone remains (遗迹) in the lake, which led to a series of underwater archaeological (考古的) research.
Sun River National Park in Pu'er	The word "Pu'er" may remind many of the famous tea from Yunnan Province, but it is also the name of a city. Back in ancient China, the region served as an important stop along the trade route Tea Horse Road (茶马古道). That's because it is close to three other countries—Vietnam, Laos and Myanmar. Apart from its tea, Pu'er holds rich natural resources (自然资源). The dense subtropical (亚热带的) rainforests in the Sun River National Park provide habitats (栖息地) for many different animals and plants.
Wild Elephant Valley in Xishuangbanna	A group of wandering (游荡的) Asian elephants in Yunnan made the headlines this year when they set off from Xishuangbanna, a major habitat for wild elephants in China. For those wishing to communicate with the giant creatures themselves, the Wild Elephant Valley is a must-visit. It will take three hours to get to Xishuangbanna from Kunming once the China-Laos railway is open.
Starlight Night Market in Xishuangbanna	It offers a dazzling (眼花缭乱的) nightlife experience. A large number of local delicacies (佳肴), ethnic (民族的) costumes and beautiful handicrafts (手工艺品) are displayed at shops along the Lancang River. The spot has become an internet hit for its unusual culture and the Instagram-friendly photos it produces.

1. Fuxian Lake becomes more mysterious because _____.
   A. a diver found a few special stones in the lake
   B. there is a quiet and rich city in the lake
   C. a diver has done some research about the lake
   D. there might be an ancient city in the lake

2. Which city is rich in both historical and natural resources?
   A. Kunming.
   B. Yuxi.
   C. Pu'er.
   D. Xishuangbanna.

3. If Li Ming is a fan of huge animals, you'd like to recommend _____ to him.
   A. Fuxian Lake
   B. Sun River National Park
   C. Wild Elephant Valley
   D. Starlight Night Market

---

pay a visit 参观，游览   mysterious adj. 神秘的   make the headlines 成为头条新闻

What makes the lake more mysterious is the possibility that an ancient city lived under its quiet and calm surface. 使这个湖更加神秘的是，在它平静的表面下可能存在着一座古城。

本句是复合句。What引导的从句作主语，is是系动词，the possibility是表语。that引导同位语从句，解释说明the possibility。

Wednesday C 阅读理解

China saw a strong recovery in its tourism sector (部门) during the seven-day Spring Festival holiday. New vacation choices, including ice and snow tourism, short-distance travel and cultural tourism, not only brought people more fun but also helped heat up (使升温) the tourism market.

Ice and Snow Tourism

The Beijing 2022 Olympic Winter Games, which opened during the Spring Festival holiday, have promoted the growth of the ice and snow industry.

According to online information, the order volume (订单量) for snow and ice tourism destinations during the Chinese New Year holiday jumped 68 percent from a year ago.

According to online news, cities with many ice and snow sports activities in the south, such as Shanghai and Guangzhou, have also joined the list of popular destinations for ice and snow travel.

Short-distance Travel

It is said that over 80 percent of tourists chose to travel locally. On the online platform, bookings for local tourist attractions and hotels respectively (分别) accounted for 82 percent and 60 percent of all orders.

Shanghai, Nanjing and Hangzhou were among the most popular tourist destinations and also major sources (来源) of tourists over the holiday.

Cultural Tourism

According to the China Tourism Academy, 91.4 percent of all tourists experienced cultural tourism during the holiday, and 81.8 percent took part in more than two cultural activities. Most tourists chose to visit museums and art galleries.

Shanghai held nearly 500 cultural and tourism activities themed around intangible cultural heritage (非物质文化遗产) during this year's Spring Festival holiday.

1. Which is NOT included in the new vacation choices?
   A. Ice and snow tourism.
   B. Short-distance travel.
   C. Long-distance travel.
   D. Cultural tourism.

2. _____ have been on the list of popular tourist attractions for ice and snow travel.
   A. Shanghai and Guangzhou
   B. Shanghai and Hangzhou
   C. Nanjing and Hangzhou
   D. Nanjing and Guangzhou

3. _____ of tourists attended more than two cultural activities.
   A. 68%
   B. 80%
   C. 91.4%
   D. 81.8%

4. What is the purpose of this passage?
   A. To introduce several new vacation choices.
   B. To make an ad for Olympic Winter Games.
   C. To offer some useful advice about travel.
   D. To predict the development of travel industry.

---

booking n. 预订   account for 占……比例；对……负责   take part in 参加   gallery n. 展览馆

词汇碎片

New vacation choices, including ice and snow tourism, short-distance travel and cultural tourism, not only brought people more fun but also helped heat up the tourism market. 冰雪旅游、短途旅游和文化旅游等新的度假选择，不仅给人们带来了更多的乐趣，也有助于旅游市场升温。

本句是 not only... but also... 连接的并列句。including... cultural tourism 为介词短语作后置定语，修饰 New vacation choices。

重难句讲解

Thursday D 阅读理解

体裁：记叙文　题材：旅行交通　正确率：___/4　词数：240
难度：★★★☆☆　建议用时：5分钟　实际用时：___　答案页码：117

Chiranjib Chakraborty from India is one of the city image recorders. Crazy about photography (摄影) and impressed by the beautiful landscapes (风景) Shenzhen has, Chakraborty tries to express the beauty of this metropolis (大城市) with his camera. In this passage, he will share with readers the beauty of Shenzhen Bay Park.

It all started in 2014 when I arrived in Shenzhen for the first time. From my 18th floor balcony in Baishizhou, I looked towards Hong Kong and saw this beautiful park that I later came to know as Shenzhen Bay Park.

The park occupies a 13-kilometer-long stretch (一段) of reclaimed land (填海地) along the southern coast of Shenzhen on the north shore of Shenzhen Bay, starting at the west near Shenzhen Bay Bridge and ending at the Hongshulin Nature Reserve (自然保护区).

For me, the park is unique for its sunrise and sunset views and as a habitat for a variety of bird species (物种). If you are a landscape photographer, the park has many opportunities for you. Recommended (推荐) places to shoot the sunrise are where Dasha River Park Road meets Shenzhen Bay Park and the park entry point near the Shenzhen Bay Park Metro Station (地铁站).

Shenzhen Bay Park is home to a variety of species of birds, especially during winter. Many bird photography enthusiasts (爱好者) gather at this time of the year to photograph birds.

Overall, Shenzhen Bay Park is one of the best places to visit in Shenzhen. Its nature and serenity (宁静) will attract its visitors.

1. Chakraborty went to Shenzhen in _____ for the first time.
   A. 2012
   B. 2014
   C. 2018
   D. 2022

2. The underlined word "occupies" in Paragraph 3 probably means _____.
   A. 得到
   B. 开发
   C. 占据
   D. 管理

3. How many places does the author recommend to shoot the sunrise?
   A. One.
   B. Two.
   C. Three.
   D. Four.

4. Many people gather in Shenzhen Bay Park during winter to take photos of _____.
   A. sunrise
   B. sunset
   C. birds
   D. insects

词汇碎片
impressed *adj.* 留下深刻印象的　especially *adv.* 尤其；特别　gather *v.* 聚集　overall *adv.* 总的来说，总体上

重难句讲解
From my 18th floor balcony in Baishizhou, I looked towards Hong Kong and saw this beautiful park that I later came to know as Shenzhen Bay Park. 在白石洲18楼的阳台上，我朝香港望去，看到了这座美丽的公园，后来我才知道它就是深圳湾公园。
本句是and连接的并列句。第一个并列分句是简单句；第二个并列分句是复合句，其中包含that引导的定语从句，修饰this beautiful park。句首From... Baishizhou介词短语是地点状语。

Friday E 任务型阅读

| 体 裁 | 记叙文 | 题 材 | 旅行交通 | 正确率 | ___/4 | 词 数 | 245 |
| 难 度 | ★★★☆☆ | 建议用时 | 5分钟 | 实际用时 | ___ | 答案页码 | 117 |

Universal Beijing Resort (度假胜地) is expected to get 100,000 visitors per day in 2022, more than the average of 80,000 for the Shanghai Disney Resort. Another 2.2 square kilometers of attractions and five hotels are planned for the phase (阶段) II of the Universal resort.

The theme park, which has just completed its phase I, covers 1.8 square kilometers and has more than a dozen programs and 40 rides (供骑乘的游乐设施). It has received positive comments from tourists, Cui Shuqiang, vice mayor (副市长) of Beijing, said.

According to Cui, construction is planned on another 2.2 square kilometers, part of phase II. The original plan of the Universal Beijing Resort was to build a cultural tourist area with seven hotels. But only two hotels have been built, so the number of rooms is limited. Visitors who want to spend several days in the park must stay in nearby areas, which has pushed the development of homestay tourism (民宿旅游).

The Universal Beijing Resort officially opened on September 20, 2021, after nearly 20 years of planning. Due to recent COVID-19 flare-ups (暴发), the theme park only got about 10,000 visitors a day, compared with a peak capacity (容纳能力) of about 110,000 visitors. The resort has taken strict epidemic control measures and adopted the reservation system (预约制).

"After the winter, more people will visit the Universal Beijing Resort, with about 100,000 visits expected per day, meaning tens of millions of tourists a year. It will promote the development of Tongzhou district, the sub-center (副中心) of Beijing," said Cui.

阅读短文，回答下面1~4小题。

1. How many square kilometers does the phase II cover?

2. Why is the number of rooms limited?

3. When did the Universal Beijing Resort officially open?

4. According to Paragraph 4, what should tourists do before they visit the Universal Beijing Resort?

词汇碎片

positive adj. 正面的；积极乐观的　　original adj. 原来的；起初的　　limited adj. 有限的

重难句讲解

The theme park, which has just completed its phase I, covers 1.8 square kilometers and has more than a dozen programs and 40 rides. 这个刚刚完成一期工程的主题公园占地1.8平方千米，拥有十几个项目和40处骑乘游乐设施。

本句是 and 连接的并列句。该句的主干是 The theme park covers... and has...。which 引导非限制性定语从句，修饰 The theme park。

Saturday F 短文填空

体裁	记叙文	题材	旅行交通	正确率	___/8	词数	266
难度	★★★★☆	建议用时	10分钟	实际用时	___	答案页码	118

阅读短文，在短文空缺处填入适当的单词，使短文通顺、意思完整。

With three weeks to go (1) _____ the opening of the 2022 Olympic and Paralympic Winter Games (冬季残奥会), the hosting Beijing city government gave details on traffic management measures during the Winter Games, supporting green and low-carbon travel, and asking for precedence (优先权) to be given to Olympic traffic.

Wu Shijiang, an official from Beijing's transportation authority, said that drawing on the experience of the (2) _____ Olympic Games, Beijing is ready to set up a transport service period for the Winter Games from January 21 to March 16, 2022, a total of 55 days.

Measures during the 55 days include setting (3) _____ an Olympic lane, preventing vehicles carrying dangerous chemical (化学的) materials, construction waste (4) _____ driving on the road. Besides, people in Beijing are encouraged to work from home and adopt flexible working plans to reduce commuting (通勤) and relieve (减轻) traffic (5) _____ on the nearby areas of Olympic venues (场馆).

Wu said that Olympics-related traffic is mainly concentrated in the north and west of the city, and traffic congestion (堵塞) is expected to occur at some times and on some specific road sectors (区域). (6) _____, the city will encourage green and low-carbon travel, prioritize (优先考虑) public transport, and (7) _____ rules governing Olympic lanes and give precedence to Olympic traffic. Wu said Beijing's subway and bus services will extend operating hours and may (8) _____ additional (额外的) routes depending on the situation to ensure people's travel during the Spring Festival holidays, which overlap (与……重叠) the Olympics.

Beijing's Olympic lane will officially open on January 21, covering 239.5 kilometers. During the Winter Paralympics, the length of Olympic lanes will be adjusted to 196.7 kilometers.

(1) _____
(2) _____
(3) _____
(4) _____
(5) _____
(6) _____
(7) _____
(8) _____

词汇碎片
set up 设立　　prevent sb. from doing... 阻止某人做……　　material n. 材料；原料　　concentrate v. 集中

重难句讲解
With three weeks to go before the opening of the 2022 Olympic and Paralympic Winter Games, the hosting Beijing city government gave details on traffic management measures during the Winter Games, supporting green and low-carbon travel, and asking for precedence to be given to Olympic traffic. 在2022年冬奥会和冬残奥会开幕三周前，主办方北京市政府详细介绍了冬奥会期间的交通管理措施，支持绿色低碳出行，并要求优先保障冬奥交通。

本句是简单句。句子的主干为 the hosting Beijing city government gave details，为主谓宾结构。句首的 With three weeks... 是时间状语，on traffic management measures during the Winter Games 是介词短语作后置定语修饰 details，supporting... and asking for... 是 and 连接的现在分词短语作伴随状语。

Week Twelve 异国风情

Monday A 完形填空

体 裁	记叙文	题 材	异国风情	正确率	___/15	词 数	372
难 度	★★★★☆	建议用时	16分钟	实际用时	___	答案页码	119

In India's northeast, the village of Kongthong is only accessible by a three-hour drive from the state capital, Shillong. The village is surrounded (环绕) by high mountains and deep valleys (峡谷). It's also home to a special __1__ called *jingrwai iawbei*, which has been popular here for centuries. According to this tradition, each newborn baby in Kongthong is given both a(n) __2__ name and a special melodious tune (悠扬的曲调) at __3__ by their mother. While their name is only used __4__ official purposes (目的), this tune becomes their identity (身份) throughout their lives. __5__ a person dies, their tune dies with them, never to be __6__ for anyone else ever.

"It is an expression of a mother's __7__ love and joy at the birth of her child. It's like a mother's heart song, full of kindness, almost like a lullaby (摇篮曲)," said Shidiap Khongsit, a woman __8__ the Khasi tribe (部落)—one of the three tribes of Meghalaya and the one that lives in Kongthong.

In the past, the melodies were used to keep track (跟踪) of one another in the __9__ while hunting, and also to drive away bad spirits. "We believe __10__ bad spirits that live in the forests cannot tell our tunes from each other or from animal calls. Therefore, no __11__ comes to you when you're called by your tunes in the forest," Khongsit said. She explained that there's a __12__ version (版本) of a long tune too. That is __13__ to a nickname (昵称). When heard from afar, the tunes sound like whistles (口哨), which is why Kongthong has been given the __14__ name "Whistling Village".

When asked about the __15__ of this practice, Khongsit replied, "Nobody can say for sure when it began, yet most agree that it has been around ever since Kongthong came into being. Kongthong itself has been here even before the kingdom of Sohra was established by our people and by those from other villages in the area." Considering that the kingdom of Sohra was founded in the early 16th century, it places the village's age or the practice's beginning at more than 500 years.

1. A. festival   B. dance
   C. song   D. tradition
2. A. important B. famous
   C. strict   D. regular
3. A. birth   B. work
   C. heart   D. present
4. A. with   B. for
   C. by   D. from
5. A. Although   B. Because
   C. Once   D. Until
6. A. refused   B. forced
   C. repeated   D. regretted
7. A. mad   B. strong
   C. hard   D. interesting
8. A. giving up   B. getting up
   C. belonging to D. arriving in
9. A. farm   B. river
   C. village   D. forest
10. A. that   B. what
    C. how   D. when
11. A. rule   B. hope
    C. manner   D. danger
12. A. longer   B. shorter
    C. heavier   D. older
13. A. different B. similar
    C. simple   D. strange
14. A. particular B. confident
    C. proud   D. boring
15. A. top   B. end
    C. beginning D. bottom

词汇碎片

village *n.* 村庄   popular *adj.* 流行的，受欢迎的   reply *v.* 回答，答复   considering that 考虑到

重难句讲解

Nobody can say for sure when it began, yet most agree that it has been around ever since Kongthong came into being. 没有人能够确定它是从什么时候开始的，但大多数人认为自孔通村形成以来，它就一直存在。

本句是 yet 连接的并列句。when 引导宾语从句，作 say 的宾语；yet 为转折连词，表示"但是"；that 引导宾语从句，作 agree 的宾语；since 引导时间状语从句；come into being 意为"形成，产生"。

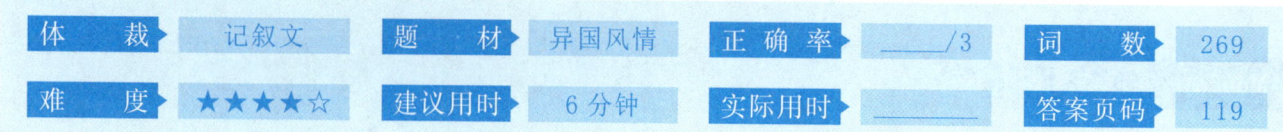

Gaelic (盖尔语) had been the main language in Scotland for centuries. It began to be canceled from the early 17th century, beginning with The Statutes of Iona (《爱奥那法令》) of 1609, under the rule of King James VI. He called it "barbaric (野蛮的)" and called upon local chiefs to send their heirs (继承人) to English-speaking schools. Many emigrations (移居) of Gaelic speakers in the 18th and 19th centuries, forced or voluntary (自愿的), didn't help, and the language was further weakened after the Battle of Culloden (卡洛登战役)—the Jacobites' (雅各布派) failed last stand.

But in rural areas, Gaelic speaking remained strong, though increasingly by the 20th century it was limited to the home. In the past, a lack (缺乏) of jobs led young people to leave the Isle of Skye and look for opportunities elsewhere. And the Gaelic language was considered old-fashioned and incompatible (不相容的) with this need to progress.

Since the 1970s, the town of Eilean Iarmain has been at the center of Scotland's Gaelic revival. Now, a new generation of locals is ready to share their culture with tourists. Noble believed that the Gaelic language could be used to stop population decline (下降) in Skye and actually become an economic driver in its own right.

Decades (十年) on, Noble's idea has slowly been proven. Sabhal Mòr Ostaig is now one of the biggest employers on the Isle of Skye and a third of islanders speak Gaelic as either their first or second language. The college has led to a new generation of Gaelic speakers skilled in TV, business and other industries that have enabled them to create more jobs on the island.

1. Gaelic had been the main language in Scotland for centuries until _____.
   A. the 17th century
   B. the 18th century
   C. the 19th century
   D. the 20th century

2. What does the underlined word "revival" in the third paragraph probably mean?
   A. 衰退   B. 替换
   C. 建立   D. 复兴

3. From the last two paragraphs, we can infer that _____.
   A. Gaelic speaking becomes popular in cities of Scotland
   B. Gaelic language improves the economic development in Skye
   C. a lot of young people begin to give up Gaelic language
   D. a new generation takes Gaelic as their official language

词汇碎片

cancel v. 废除；取消   call upon 要求；拜访   remain v. 保持不变；剩余   share v. 分享

重难句讲解

But in rural areas, Gaelic speaking remained strong, though increasingly by the 20th century it was limited to the home. 但在农村地区，盖尔语仍然很强势，尽管到了20世纪，盖尔语越来越局限于在家庭中使用。

本句是复合句。主句是 Gaelic speaking remained strong；though 引导让步状语从句。

If you've lived in Norway (挪威) for a while, some of the social norms (社交准则) will now be part of everyday life. However, if you are new to the country, they'll come as more of a culture shock.

Small talk with strangers	For many, a little chat with a stranger on a train or in the queue at the supermarket is one of life's small joys. However, this isn't the case in Norway, where casually greeting strangers is just not the done thing. This can feel unfriendly if you're not used to it, but that doesn't mean Norwegians are rude and cold. Instead, they prefer to focus their energy on more important and comfortable relationships.
Wearing shoes indoors	Wearing shoes indoors is considered impolite in many places like Japan and other parts of Asia. And this is especially true in Norway during the winter months. Your host won't be pleased if you wear shoes with snow into their house.
Splitting the bill (平均分摊账单)	It may not be a big surprise to find out that splitting the bill is pretty standard whatever the occasion (场合) is in Norway. This is regardless of (不管) whether you are eating in or out, or just with friends. You should expect the bill to be split in most cases. This can be especially strange if you are the one invited over for dinner by a friend.
The "Norwegian arm"	One thing that might surprise people new to Norway is the "Norwegian arm". The "Norwegian arm" is the practice of everyone reaching for their favourite dish when having a big meal with friends or family. This can often mean people reaching over you or stopping you while you are trying to enjoy your meal. Actually, they think that it is a lot more polite to grab (取) what they want, rather than often disturb your meal by asking for you to pass them things.

1. According to this passage, Norwegians seldom _____ with strangers.
   A. have a dinner
   B. have a small talk
   C. play sports
   D. queue up

2. In winter, if you go into a house wearing shoes, your Norwegian host may feel _____.
   A. unhappy   B. satisfied
   C. friendly   D. strange

3. Which of the following is TRUE about social norms in Norway?
   A. Having a small talk with strangers is common.
   B. Wearing shoes indoors is polite.
   C. Splitting the bill is not necessary if you are invited.
   D. Reaching over someone to grab favourite dish is polite.

4. What is the purpose of this passage?
   A. To tell us that Norway is really cold.
   B. To tell us that Norwegians are rude and cold.
   C. To tell us what we can't do and can do in Norway.
   D. To tell us the best season to have a trip to Norway.

词汇碎片

culture n. 文化   chat n. 聊天，闲聊   rude adj. 无礼的，粗鲁的   standard adj. 标准的

重难句讲解

It may not be a big surprise to find out that splitting the bill is pretty standard whatever the occasion is in Norway. 在挪威，无论是什么场合，分摊账单都是相当标准的做法，这也许并不令人惊讶。

本句是复合句。It 作形式主语，to find out... pretty standard 为真正的主语，其中 that 引导的宾语从句作动词短语 find out 的宾语；whatever 引导让步状语从句。

Thursday D 阅读理解

Teh tarik, or "pulled tea", is often drunk in Southeast Asia, but it's the unofficial (非官方的) national drink of Malaysia, where it was invented. It's a simple mixture of strong black tea, condensed (浓缩的) milk and enough sugar. If you take a walk in any Malaysian city at any time of day, you'll see locals of all backgrounds crowded around plastic tables outdoors, drinking the mocha-colored (深咖啡色的) drink while chatting about anything and everything.

Each family-run (家庭经营的) store has its own closely guarded recipe, and the quality of teh tarik is measured by its "pull". It is a skill that allows air into the liquid (液体), improves its deep flavour (风味) and helps it develop the perfect froth (泡沫) that sets it apart from any other tea. Whoever can master this skill becomes a local famous person with honest fans.

While its sweet and simple taste is the reason for teh tarik's popularity, its cultural importance runs much deeper, and the drink in nature shows the country's strong sense of tolerance (容忍) and diversity (多样性).

"In Malaysia, we have had many years to familiarise (熟悉) ourselves with living in a multicultural (多元文化的) society," said Salma Nasution Khoo, an author from Penang (槟城). "Despite our differences, everyone is aware of the importance of going back to a state of balance and mutual respect."

Just as Malaysia is a cultural melting pot (熔炉) of indigenous (本土的) Malay, Chinese, British and South Indian, teh tarik is a liquid mixture of different cultures and customs. Black tea was first introduced by the Chinese in the 1830s; the skill of pulling was developed by South Indian street cooks after 1850, and milk and sugar were introduced nearly 100 years later during the end of British colonialism (殖民主义). Because many of the country's cultures contributed to the creation of teh tarik, most Malaysians, regardless of ethnicity (种族渊源), deeply like it today.

"Teh tarik is something that can connect people from different races (种族), cultures and religions (宗教)," said Mohd Azmi, an author from George Town. "We can all still sit together in one place, have the same drink and forget our differences for the moment."

1. Teh tarik doesn't include _____.
   A. black tea   B. chocolate
   C. milk   D. sugar
2. The quality of teh tarik depends on _____.
   A. its recipe   B. mixing
   C. pulling   D. heating
3. Which of the following statements is TRUE?
   A. The Malaysian population is made of Malay, Chinese and Japanese.
   B. Black tea was first introduced by the Chinese in the 1930s.
   C. The skill of pulling was developed by South Indian street cooks.
   D. Milk and sugar were invented by local Malay.
4. What is the best title for this passage?
   A. Malaysia: a Multicultural Society
   B. Teh Tarik: Malaysia's National Drink
   C. The Cultural Meaning Behind Teh Tarik
   D. Sitting Together and Having a Drink

---

national *adj.* 全国的；国家的   honest *adj.* 真诚的；诚实的   in nature 本质上

Just as Malaysia is a cultural melting pot of indigenous Malay, Chinese, British and South Indian, teh tarik is a liquid mixture of different cultures and customs. 正如马来西亚是一个由本地马来人、中国人、英国人和南印度人组成的文化大熔炉，拉茶是一种混合不同文化和习俗的液体。

本句是复合句。Just as 引导方式状语从句，意为"正如"；cultural melting pot 意为"文化大熔炉"。

Friday E 任务型阅读

We know the Hawaiian lei (夏威夷花环) as a tradition for celebration in the islands. __1__, but they are part of a Hawaiian tradition dating back 250 years. A feather lei is filled with the memory of past generations (代).

With their roots in Hawaiian culture dating back to 1,500 years ago, feathered clothing and accessories (配饰) have long represented royalty (皇室) and respect. __2__. In fact, leis, capes (披风), helmets (头盔) and *kahili* (a long pole decorated with feathers on one end) could only be worn by the various classes of Hawaiian *ali'i* (the high chiefs, who were considered to be gods' children). The longer the cape, the higher the class.

__3__. The famous yellow cape of King Kamehameha, who ruled Hawaii until 1819, was made from the most prestigious (有声望的) feather color. It took around 450,000 of these rare (罕见的) yellow feathers (taken from a kind of now-extinct bird living on the Big Island) to make up the cape. Skilled catchers caught the birds, took away the needed feathers, treated the birds with medicine and then let them go.

__4__. A single feather lei takes about 40 hours for one person to complete. For every inch of featherwork, 30 to 40 feathers are needed, which are woven (编织) together one by one. This is also part of why such an accessory is the ultimate (终极的) form of gratitude (感恩), respect and love. While a feather lei can cost between $200 and $1,000 and is generally used for special occasions, the receivers are touched by the gift of time. __5__, but reminding to keep this piece of culture alive.

阅读短文，从下列选项中选出能填入文中空白处的最佳选项，选项中有一项为多余选项。

A. Feather leis are not as famous as flower leis

B. It is still not easy to make feather lei today

C. It will take a lot of time to find those valuable feathers

D. All kinds of patterns and colors also showed class

E. Feathers were regarded as the symbol of power and class in Hawaii

F. Wearing a feather lei with history is much more than a celebration

be filled with 充满　　represent v. 代表　　class n. 阶级；班级　　treat v. 治疗

The famous yellow cape of King Kamehameha, who ruled Hawaii until 1819, was made from the most prestigious feather color.
统治夏威夷直到1819年的卡美哈美哈国王的著名黄色披风是由最能彰显威望的颜色的羽毛制成的。
本句是复合句。who引导的定语从句修饰King Kamehameha；be made from 意为"由……制成"。

Saturday F 短文填空

| 体 裁 | 说明文 | 题 材 | 异国风情 | 正确率 | ___/10 | 词·数 | 339 |
| 难 度 | ★★★★☆ | 建议用时 | 11分钟 | 实际用时 | ___ | 答案页码 | 121 |

In every Italian city, the day's rhythm (节奏) begins at the cafe. Cafes are a (1) _____ (two) living room for many Italians. This is where social life often begins, as people from all generations gather (聚集) with friends to share the (2) _____ (late) news and pass the time.

But in Trieste (的里雅斯特), a city on Italy's northeast coast, walk into any cafe here and you'll hear people (3) _____ (order) "Capo in B": a mini cappuccino (卡布奇诺) served in a glass that's a favourite of Triestini (的里雅斯特人). It's one of the many (4) _____ (reason) why this city sandwiched between Slovenia and the Adriatic is (5) _____ (difference) from anywhere else in Italy.

Many people might be (6) _____ (surprise) to learn that this border (边境) city is often considered Italy's unofficial (非官方的) "Coffee Capital". Not only are the Triestini said to drink twice as much of the coffee per year as anywhere else in Italy—a surprising 10kg of coffee beans for one person each year, but it's also home to the Mediterranean's (地中海) main coffee port (港口) and one of Italy's biggest coffee brands (品牌): Illy.

The coffee business continues to develop. In addition to Illy, founded in 1933, dozens of other smaller (7) _____ (company) roast (烤) and mix the millions of bags of coffee beans that arrive from all (8) _____ the world to Trieste each year.

"Coffee is definitely a thing here," said Alessandra Ressa, an English teacher who (9) _____ (move) from San Francisco to Trieste 20 years ago. "Instead of just standing at the bar and drinking a quick coffee like in other Italian cities, here we sit (10) _____ and take our time, making appointments with each other for the cafe. And you never see anyone walking with a to-go cup."

Each October, there's the Trieste Coffee Festival. Roasteries (烘焙工坊) open for tastings, restaurants create dishes spiced with coffee and there's a "Capo in B" championship to choose the city's best barista (咖啡师).

阅读短文,在短文空缺处填入适当的单词,或用括号内所给单词的适当形式填空。

(1) _____
(2) _____
(3) _____
(4) _____
(5) _____
(6) _____
(7) _____
(8) _____
(9) _____
(10) _____

词汇碎片
serve v. 端上;服务   main adj. 主要的   business n. 商业;买卖   make an appointment 约定;预约

重难句讲解
Not only are the Triestini said to drink twice as much of the coffee per year as anywhere else in Italy—a surprising 10kg of coffee beans for one person each year, but it's also home to the Mediterranean's main coffee port and one of Italy's biggest coffee brands: Illy. 据说的里雅斯特人每年喝的咖啡是意大利其他地方的人喝的两倍——一个人每年消耗的咖啡豆达到惊人的10千克。不仅如此,这里还是地中海的主要咖啡港口和意大利最大的咖啡品牌之一——Illy 的所在地。

本句是 Not only... but also... 连接的并列句。破折号后面的内容为插入语,补充说明的里雅斯特人的咖啡消费量; be home to 意为"是……的所在地"。

Week Thirteen 自然生态

Monday A 完形填空

体　　裁	记叙文	题　　材	自然生态	正 确 率	___/10	词　　数	285
难　　度	★★★☆☆	建议用时	10分钟	实际用时	___	答案页码	122

Professor Zhang Peidong from the Ocean University of China (OUC) has devoted the past 15 years to one thing: planting "grass" in "undersea prairies (大草原)" to restore (恢复) lush (郁郁葱葱的) habitats to protect coasts, increase the __1__ of wild animals and store carbon.

The "prairies" are seagrasses, widely recognized to be one of __2__ typical marine (海洋的) coastal ecosystems (生态系统) in the world, along with mangroves (红树林) and coral reefs (珊瑚礁). Growing in coastal bays, seagrasses used to be abundant (丰富的), but the beds became barren (贫瘠的) __3__ coastal development and pollution from waste water and artificial (人工的) sea farming. "Seagrasses are the only flowering plants that grow in marine environments and provide habitats for marine creatures," Zhang said.

"Seagrasses are as meaningful to marine life as prairies are to __4__ and sheep," said the 46-year-old professor. Seagrasses also play an important __5__ in carbon sinks (碳汇). The decline (减少) of seagrasses is a __6__ problem around the world. In coastal bays around __7__ such as Qingdao, Yantai and Weihai in Shandong Province, eelgrasses (鳗草) are one of the major plants in seagrass beds, and more than 80 percent of them have disappeared, according to a research team led by Zhang.

Zhang launched the team at the Qingdao-based OUC in 2006 for a seagrass restoration project. The team developed technology to breed (培育) eelgrasses and __8__ ways to restore seagrass beds. Swan (天鹅) Lake in Rongcheng, a county-level city in Weihai, was the first place for the team's __9__. More seagrasses greatly improved water quality and increased the number of birds and shellfish (水生有壳动物) around the lake. China Central Television reported that nearly 10,000 swans __10__ the winter there every year, creating amazing scenes for tourists and photographers.

1. A. weight   B. number   C. quality
2. A. three   B. four   C. five
3. A. except for B. even if C. due to
4. A. cows   B. dogs   C. cats
5. A. name   B. life   C. role
6. A. simple   B. common   C. positive
7. A. cities   B. countries C. villages
8. A. shared   B. talked   C. found
9. A. research B. ability C. danger
10. A. come   B. leave   C. spend

devote v. 致力；献身　　protect v. 保护　　increase v. 增加　　meaningful adj. 有意义的

词汇碎片

China Central Television reported that nearly 10,000 swans spend the winter there every year, creating amazing scenes for tourists and photographers. 据中国中央电视台报道，每年有近1万只天鹅在那里过冬，为游客和摄影师创造了令人惊叹的场景。

本句是包含宾语从句的复合句。主句是 China Central Television reported that...，为主谓宾结构。that 引导的是宾语从句，creating... 为现在分词短语作状语。

重难句讲解

Tuesday B 阅读理解

| 体 裁 | 说明文 | 题 材 | 自然生态 | 正确率 | ___/5 | 词 数 | 276 |
| 难 度 | ★★★☆☆ | 建议用时 | 6分钟 | 实际用时 | | 答案页码 | 122 |

What do bats (蝙蝠) and humans have in common? Not much. We're separated by more than 65 million years of evolution. However, our two species share a common feature about learning how to speak: babbling (咿呀学语).

Just like when human babies babble from "ma-ma-ma" to "mom," wild bat pups (幼崽) of one species learn the mating (交配) and territorial (地盘性的) songs of adults by babbling out streams of syllables (音节). "These findings suggest that humans and baby bats have a lot in common in how they learn to control their vocal apparatus (发声器官)," said Tecumseh Fitch, a cognitive (认知的) biologist at the University of Vienna.

In humans and in greater sac-winged bats (大银线蝠), babbling is a way of practicing—learning to express the syllables that make up their species' vocabulary and training these vocalizations. A baby's "babbling" may sound like gibberish (胡言乱语), but it is an important step in learning how to talk. While many songbirds learn to babble their songs too, sac-winged bats are the only other mammals discovered to babble like humans. The nature of the bat pups' babbling changes over time as they perfect their songs. Analysts (分析者) recorded over 216 babbling bouts of 20 bat pups in Costa Rica and Panama. "It immediately reminds you of human babies," said Ahana A. Fernandez of the Museum of Natural History in Berlin, who analyzed the recordings.

Researchers think there are more babbling species. Scientists are looking to mole rats (鼹鼠), giant otters (巨獭), and dolphins (海豚) as potential research subjects for more exploration into babbling in mammals. Further study of babbling may help to reveal the basic modules (模块) of language in the brain.

1. What do bats and humans have in common according to this passage?
   A. They can babble "ma-ma-ma" when they're young.
   B. They can't make any sounds when they're born.
   C. They babble when they learn how to speak.

2. What does the underlined word "biologist" mean in Chinese in Paragraph 2?
   A. 生物学家
   B. 艺术家
   C. 总经理

3. Where did analysts record over 216 babbling bouts of 20 bat pups?
   A. In Costa Rica and Panama.
   B. In Costa Rica and Canada.
   C. In Las Vegas and Panama.

4. According to the passage, which of the following is NOT TRUE?
   A. Fernandez works in the Museum of Natural History in Berlin.
   B. Researchers think there are more babbling species.
   C. Scientists are looking to elephants as potential research subjects.

5. In which column of a newspaper can we find this passage?
   A. Natural History.
   B. Discovery of Nature.
   C. Environmental Protection.

have... in common 有……的共同点　　separate v. 使分开，分离　　wild adj. 野生的；自然生长的

"These findings suggest that humans and baby bats have a lot in common in how they learn to control their vocal apparatus," said Tecumseh Fitch, a cognitive biologist at the University of Vienna. 维也纳大学的认知生物学家特库姆塞·费奇说："这些发现表明，人类和幼年蝙蝠学习控制发声器官的方式有很大的相似之处。"

本句是包含宾语从句的复合句。主句是 ...said Tecumseh Fitch，为主谓宾结构，主语是 Tecumseh Fitch，谓语是 said，宾语是前面的直接引语，即宾语从句。该宾语从句中还包含一个由 that 引导的宾语从句。a cognitive biologist at the University of Vienna 是同位语，对 Tecumseh Fitch 进行补充说明。

Wednesday C 阅读理解

体裁	说明文	题材	自然生态	正确率	/5	词数	253
难度	★★★★☆	建议用时	7 分钟	实际用时		答案页码	123

Some insects, especially those honey bees that produce honey, are usually social creatures that live in large colonies (群落).

A single hive (蜂房) can contain (容纳) between 20,000 and 80,000 worker bees. Colonies are also highly organized, with a queen, drones (雄蜂) and workers caring for the hive. There are up to 60,000 female worker bees in each colony. Their life span is about 4 to 6 weeks in summer. Males in the hive are called drones. They live during the spring and summer months, and their only purpose is to mate with new queens.

Bees are usually docile (驯服的) creatures that don't attack humans. All bees have segmented (分段的) bodies, consisting of a head, thorax (胸部) and abdomen (腹部). The females' hind legs have pouches (袋), which they use to carry pollen (花粉) back to the hive. Bees feed on pollen and nectar (花蜜) from flowering plants. Honey bees take the nectar and pollen back to the colony where they produce honey—a source of food for those bees that never leave the hive.

Honey gives energy to the bees' flight muscles, allowing their wings to beat up to 12,000 times a minute. Honey bees can visit up to 5,000 flowers in a single day, and they would have to visit about 2 million to make a 453-gram jar of honey. If the queen dies, the worker bees create a new one by choosing a young larva (幼虫) and feeding it with royal jelly (蜂王浆), a special kind of food that allows it to develop into a fertile (能繁殖的) adult queen.

1. How many worker bees can there be in a single hive?
   A. 50,000
   B. 200,000
   C. 800,000
2. Which of the following is TRUE about honey bees?
   A. There are up to 60,000 female worker bees in each colony.
   B. There are only drones and worker bees in each colony.
   C. Their life span is about 4 to 6 months.
3. Why do female bees have pouches on their hind legs?
   A. Because they use pouches to store pollen and water.
   B. Because they use pouches to carry pollen to flowers.
   C. Because they use pouches to carry pollen back to the hive.
4. Do all bees leave their hives?
   A. Yes, they do.
   B. No.
   C. Not mentioned.
5. How many flowers do honey bees need to visit to make three 453-gram jars of honey?
   A. About 2 million.
   B. About 4 million.
   C. About 6 million.

词汇碎片

especially *adv.* 尤其，特别　　honey *n.* 蜂蜜　　creature *n.* 生物；动物　　purpose *n.* 目的；意图

重难句讲解

The females' hind legs have pouches, which they use to carry pollen back to the hive. 雌蜂的后腿上有囊袋，用来将花粉带回蜂房。

本句是包含定语从句的复合句。主句是 The females' hind legs have pouches，为主谓宾结构。which 引导的是非限制性定语从句，修饰 pouches。

Thursday D任务型阅读

Recently, the footprints of wild Siberian tigers (东北虎) were found in northeast China's Greater Khingan Range by a Chinese research team. __1__. The reappearance of these tigers was confirmed (证实) after discoveries of snow footprints and feces (粪便) of tigers and following DNA identification (鉴定) tests, said the National Forestry and Grassland Administration Sunday.

The team led by Zhou Shaochun, a zoologist (动物学家) of the wildlife research institute (机构) of Heilongjiang Province, found footprints in the snow in Beijicun national natural reserve (保护区) on Dec. 29, 2021. __2__. Four feces samples were collected during footprint tracking. __3__. "The discovery comes more than 50 years after the last time the trail of Siberian tigers was found on record in the Greater Khingan Range," Zhang Minghai, an expert on wildlife and habitat (栖息地) protection at the Northeast Forestry University, said.

Along with the Lesser Khingan, the Greater Khingan is one of the most important virgin (原始的) forest reserves in northeast China. __4__, it still reveals the improvement of wildlife habitats in the region and the restoration (恢复) of food chains.

Siberian tigers mainly inhabit eastern Russia, northeast China, and the northern part of the Korean Peninsula, and are on China's first-class protection list. The species were widely distributed (分布) in northeast China at the beginning of the 20th century, with the Greater Khingan Range as one of their main habitats. __5__.

A. However, a survey made from 1974 to 1976 showed the tigers had disappeared in the mountain area due to some reasons

B. It's the first appearance of the trail of the rare species in the mountain area in over 50 years

C. These footprints might be those of Siberian tigers

D. But Zhang said the tigers will be properly protected in China

E. Although the recent finding does not mean the long-term living of Siberian tigers

F. Later, these feces samples were proved to belong to Siberian tigers

Friday E 任务型阅读

Chinese researchers have discovered 31 new species of wild orchids (兰科植物) in China, according to the National Forestry and Grassland Administration (NFGA). In recent years, the number of wild orchids has decreased sharply. Some varieties (品种) have even become extinct (灭绝的) due to the exploitation (开发) and degradation (退化) of their native ecosystem. In order to strengthen the protection of orchids and establish a scientific management and monitoring system, the NFGA carried out a special investigation (调查) project aiming at the nation's wild orchid resources in 2018.

So far, the project has discovered 31 new orchid species and 12 orchid species first recorded in China. The species and distribution of wild orchids were investigated across 16 regions including Yunnan Province, Guangxi Zhuang Autonomous Region and Tibet Autonomous Region.

According to the NFGA, the project is expected to end in 2023. Nearly 1,260 orchid species have been recorded, of which about 800 native orchids are under ex-situ conservation (迁地保护) in botanical (植物的) gardens, and about 65% are distributed in national or provincial nature reserves. The orchid family has important economic value and unique viewing value. China is one of the countries with the richest orchid species in the world, with 1,745 species belonging to 181 genera (属) recorded so far.

阅读短文，根据短文内容，完成方框中所缺信息。

Wild Orchids

China is (1) _____ in orchid species. 31 new species of wild orchids have been found in China according to the NFGA. Here is further information about wild orchids in China.

Values	Economic value (2) _____ value
Present Situations	Problem: Some wild orchids (3) _____ out.
	(4) _____: exploitation and degradation of their native ecosystem.
	Action: The NFGA set up an investigation project to (5) _____ orchids.
	Result: Almost 1,260 orchid species have been recorded, and about 800 of them are protected by the way of ex-situ conservation in botanical gardens.

词汇碎片

establish v. 建立；确立   project n. 项目   aim at 针对；瞄准

重难句讲解

In order to strengthen the protection of orchids and establish a scientific management and monitoring system, the NFGA carried out a special investigation project aiming at the nation's wild orchid resources in 2018. 为加强对兰科植物的保护，建立科学的管理和监测体系，2018年，国家林业和草原局开展了一项针对全国野生兰科植物资源的专项调查项目。

本句是包含目的状语的简单句。句子的主干是 the NFGA carried out a special investigation project，为主谓宾结构。In order to... 为目的状语；aiming at... 为现在分词短语作后置定语，修饰 project。

Saturday F 短文填空

体裁 记叙文　题材 自然生态　正确率 ___/10　词数 217
难度 ★★★☆☆　建议用时 10分钟　实际用时 ___　答案页码 124

A total of 39 wild Asian elephants inhabiting (栖息于) different areas gathered together recently to eat in Jiangcheng County, southwest China's Yunnan Province, according to local authorities on Monday. Due to the shortage of (1)_____ sources in the forest during winter, when the corn planted in the villages is gradually harvested (收割), herds of elephants, along with their cubs (幼崽), have come here for food, said Diao Faxing, an Asian elephant observer. "They do nothing (2)_____ eat every day," said Diao.

According to the head of the county's wildlife protection station, the 39 elephants (3)_____ to two populations. They gathered in batches (批) near Kangping Township and Zhengdong Township, and mainly (4)_____ for food on the farmland during the day, which has caused damage (5)_____ villagers' agricultural facilities (农业设施) and crops. "We are trying to (6)_____ these elephants back to the mountains by (7)_____ them with food," he said.

Local authorities have taken measures such as strengthening monitoring (监测) and early warning, traffic control and setting up roadblocks (路障) to ensure the safety of (8)_____ and elephants.

Wild Asian elephants, a flagship (旗舰) species in the rainforest, are (9)_____ A-level state protection in China. Thanks to stronger environmental and wildlife protection efforts, the population in the country has (10)_____ to about 300, mostly scattered (分散) around Yunnan.

阅读短文，从方框中选择合适的单词并用其正确形式填空，使短文通顺、意思完整。每空限填一词，每词限用一次。（其中有两项为多余选项。）

people
look
buy
food
but
grow
lead
book
belong
provide
under
to

词汇碎片
authority n. 当局，官方　　shortage n. 不足，缺少　　along with 和……一起

重难句讲解
They gathered in batches near Kangping Township and Zhengdong Township, and mainly looked for food on the farmland during the day, which has caused damage to villagers' agricultural facilities and crops. 它们在康平镇和整董镇附近分批聚集，白天主要在农田上觅食，对村民的农业设施和农作物造成了破坏。

本句是包含定语从句的复合句。主句的主干是 They gathered in batches and mainly looked for food，包含由 and 连接的并列谓语结构。which 引导的是非限制性定语从句，修饰前面的整个句子。

Week Fourteen 环境保护

Monday A 完形填空

体 裁	记叙文	题 材	环境保护	正确率	___/10	词 数	241
难 度	★★★☆☆	建议用时	10 分钟	实际用时		答案页码	126

The concentration (浓度) of PM 2.5 in Beijing hit a record low during the Winter Olympics, officials said.

On Feb. 4, when the Games __1__, the air density (密度) of the unhealthy particles (微粒) in the capital stood __2__ 5 micrograms (微克) per cubic meter (立方米). As of Thursday, the average density of the pollutant during the Games was 24 mcg/cubic m, __3__ the Ministry of Ecology and Environment.

The air quality was the best __4__ has been recorded since monitoring (监测) of PM 2.5 began in 2013, Wang Jinnan, head of the ministry's Chinese Academy of Environmental Planning, said on Friday. "In the past five years, as __5__ of both Summer and Winter Olympics, Beijing has produced a miracle in improvements to air quality in big cities," said Wang, __6__ is also an academician (院士) of the Chinese Academy of Engineering. The average PM 2.5 density in the city in 2021 was 33 mcg/cubic m, down 40 percent from 2017, he noted.

Zhang Dawei, an official of the ministry, said that the air quality in Beijing, Tianjin and Hebei Province so __7__ during the Winter Olympics has been much __8__ than during the same period last year, with a year-on-year drop of 40 percent in average PM 2.5 density. The huge improvement is the __9__ of consistent (持续的) government efforts to control air pollution in the area, although meteorological (气象的) conditions favoring (有利于) the decrease of air pollutant concentration have also __10__, he said.

原创试题

1. A. opened   B. continued
   C. stopped   D. closed
2. A. in   B. on
   C. at   D. by
3. A. because of B. according to
   C. apart from D. on behalf of
4. A. that   B. who
   C. whose   D. which
5. A. member   B. guest
   C. volunteer D. host
6. A. that   B. who
   C. whose   D. which
7. A. far   B. that
   C. much   D. high
8. A. less   B. clearer
   C. worse   D. better
9. A. reason   B. result
   C. record   D. review
10. A. failed   B. changed
    C. helped   D. occurred

词汇碎片

hit a record low 创历史新低   so far 到目前为止   pollution n. 污染

重难句讲解

The air quality was the best that has been recorded since monitoring of PM 2.5 began in 2013, Wang Jinnan, head of the ministry's Chinese Academy of Environmental Planning, said on Friday. 中国生态环境部环境规划院院长王金南周五表示，这种空气质量是自 2013 年开始监测 PM 2.5 以来记录的最佳水平。

本句是复合句。主句的主干是 ...Wang Jinnan... said，前面的部分可以被看作省略 that 的宾语从句。其中 that 引导定语从句，修饰 the best，since 引导时间状语从句。

Dear friends,

I'm Cao Jianjun, a photography enthusiast (爱好者). I'm writing this letter to introduce my "friends" to you. Every winter, I wait for them at a national wetland park in Hunan Province.

In 2013, I caught the Chinese merganser (中华秋沙鸭), an endangered (濒危的) bird species for the first time in the province's Shuangpai County. Since then, my camera lens (镜头) has caught more and more of the beautiful birds.

I did not know the birds when I first caught them, but I realized they were different from other birds that I usually saw. So I was quite excited when experts told me they were one of the oldest species in the world. The Chinese merganser, also called "the giant panda in bird species", has high requirements (要求) for its habitat (栖息地) and water environment.

Over the past eight years, I have taken more than 60,000 pictures of the birds in the county, which has become a major habitat for the merganser and other migratory birds (候鸟). I often sit alone on the bank of the river for a whole day in order to take perfect pictures.

The county has made a lot of efforts to handle the ecological (生态的) problems in recent years. With the improving environment, the county is not only a habitat for migratory birds but a hot tourist destination featuring bird watching and leisure activities.

China is creating a better environment for migratory birds. Nets and other fishing gear (用具) were a huge threat to the birds along the Yangtze River, but the threat is <u>vanishing</u> as the country has put a complete 10-year fishing ban in the key waters of the Yangtze since the beginning of 2020.

Besides photography, I also volunteer to patrol (巡逻) the habitat for the purpose of protecting the birds. Many villagers and retired teachers volunteer to guard the birds too. I believe protecting their habitat is to protect our home and hope more people join us.

Sincerely,
Cao Jianjun

1. What is NOT TRUE about the Chinese merganser?
   A. Cao Jianjun first caught them in 2013.
   B. They are an endangered bird species.
   C. They are one of the oldest species.
   D. You can see them at a national wetland park in Hunan in autumn.

2. What does the underlined word "vanishing" in Paragraph 6 mean?
   A. Happening.
   B. Disappearing.
   C. Remaining.
   D. Working.

3. What's the main idea of the passage?
   A. Cao jianjun loves taking pictures of birds.
   B. The Chinese merganser is one of the rare species.
   C. Shuangpai County is a hot tourist attraction.
   D. Protecting the birds' habitat is to protect our home.

---

make efforts to do sth. 努力做某事   leisure n. 休闲   threat n. 威胁   purpose n. 目的

I did not know the birds when I first caught them, but I realized they were different from other birds that I usually saw. 当我第一次拍到这种鸟时，我并不认识它们，但我意识到它们不同于我通常看到的其他鸟类。

本句是 but 连接的并列句。第一个并列分句是复合句，包含 when 引导的时间状语从句；第二个并列分句也是复合句，包含省略 that 的宾语从句，作 realized 的宾语，宾语从句中又嵌套了 that 引导的定语从句，修饰 other birds。

Wednesday C 阅读理解

体 裁	记叙文	题 材	环境保护	正确率	___/5	词 数	307
难 度	★★★☆☆	建议用时	6分钟	实际用时		答案页码	127

  The fireworks that lit up the night sky above the National Stadium during the opening ceremony for the 2022 Beijing Winter Olympic Games on February 4 not only presented beautiful images, but also showed state-of-the-art (最先进的) technologies and environmental awareness, industry insiders (知情者) said.

  The fireworks display for the opening ceremony paid great attention to environmental protection, said Liu Yongzhang, deputy general manager of Dancing Fireworks Group, one of the leading companies involved. "The chemicals (化学品) used to make fireworks have no heavy metals and low sulfur (硫)," he said. Li Chuang, president of Shenggu Fireworks Manufacturing (制造) Company in Hebei Province, said that compared with normal fireworks, the ones used for the opening ceremony reduced pollutants by about 70 percent.

  "No residue (残留物) was left when the fireworks burned out in the night sky," he said. "The Winter Olympic Games required that the event be 'green', and we were so glad that we could contribute to an environmentally friendly Games." "The reason why no residue was produced was that we adopted the technology of 'slight-smoke fireworks', which produce less smoke and waste while burning. A new type of slight sulfur chemical was also chosen as one of the raw materials to produce the special shining part of the fireworks." Li said the number of fireworks burned was just 10 percent of those used for the 2008 Beijing Summer Olympic Games.

  "High technologies have been used to produce the eco-friendly fireworks," Liu said. "We tried countless times to finally decide the layout (布局) and the angles to show the patterns perfectly." The research team used 3D technology to design drafts (草稿) on a computer, and then improved the drafts through many experiments so that the height and inclination (倾斜度) of the fireworks presented the best show without pollution.

1. What didn't the fireworks above the National Stadium show?
   A. Beautiful images.
   B. High technologies.
   C. Environmental awareness.
   D. Industry secrets.

2. How much did the fireworks used for the opening ceremony cut pollutants by?
   A. About 50%.   B. About 60%.
   C. About 70%.   D. About 10%.

3. Which of the blanks can NOT be filled with the underlined word "green"?
   A. We need to develop _____ cleaning products.
   B. Wait for the light to turn _____.
   C. Her eyes were _____ from crying.
   D. After the rains, the land was _____ with new growth.

4. Why was no residue left?
   A. Because the fireworks were totally burned.
   B. Because the technology of "slight-smoke fireworks" was used.
   C. Because no sulfur chemical was chosen.
   D. Because the fireworks had no metals.

5. What can NOT the research team do through 3D technology?
   A. Deciding the layout.   B. Designing drafts.
   C. Adjusting the height.   D. Changing the shape.

词汇碎片

light up 照亮　　awareness *n.* 意识　　contribute *v.* 做贡献　　environmentally friendly 环保的

重难句讲解

The fireworks that lit up the night sky above the National Stadium during the opening ceremony for the 2022 Beijing Winter Olympic Games on February 4 not only presented beautiful images, but also showed state-of-the-art technologies and environmental awareness, industry insiders said. 业内人士表示，在2月4日举行的2022年北京冬奥会开幕式上，点亮国家体育场上方夜空的烟花不仅呈现出美丽的画面，还体现了最先进的技术和环保意识。

本句是复合句。主句的主干是 ...industry insiders said，前面可以被看作省略 that 的宾语从句。宾语从句是 not only... but also... 连接的并列句，并列句的主语是 The fireworks，后面的 that 引导定语从句，修饰 The fireworks，定语从句一直到 not only 前结束。

Thursday D任务型阅读

体裁	记叙文	题材	环境保护	正确率	___/10	词数	250
难度	★★★★☆	建议用时	11分钟	实际用时	___	答案页码	127

China passed a new law on wetlands (湿地) protection, establishing the country's first specialized (专门的) law on the problem. The law will take effect (生效) on June 1, 2022.

Governments at all levels should raise public awareness of protecting wetlands through various activities, such as setting up "wetland protection day" or "wetland protection week," according to the law. Education authorities and schools are also asked to increase the awareness of students on the protection of wetlands.

According to the law, the country will manage wetlands at different levels, and important wetland areas should be brought under the ecological conservation (生态保护) red lines. A national list of important wetlands will be released (公布) by forestry (林业) and grassland authorities and other related departments of the State Council (国务院) for the better management of wetlands. Protection signs should also be set up, according to the law.

The law prohibits any organization or individual from destroying the habitat of birds and aquatic (水生的) life in wetlands.

Stipulations (规定) on the protection of peat swamps (泥炭沼泽) and mangrove (红树林) wetlands are emphasized in the newly adopted law. It is forbidden to exploit (开采) peat from peat swamp wetlands or to exploit their groundwater without authorization (批准), according to the law. It is also forbidden to occupy (占用) or dig ponds in mangrove wetlands, as well as to fell (采伐), excavate (挖掘) or transplant mangroves, or to over-exploit mangrove seeds, among other activities.

The law includes rules on setting up a system of compensation (补偿) for ecological conservation, requiring more government funding in protecting important wetlands.

阅读短文，根据短文内容，完成表格中所缺信息。

	China adopts a new law on wetlands protection
Some facts about the law	◆ The law is about wetlands (1) _____. ◆ The law is China's (2) _____ specialized law on this problem. ◆ The law will come into force on (3) _____ 1, 2022.
Some rules in the law	◆ Different activities should be held to raise (4) _____ awareness. ◆ Education departments and schools should increase the awareness of (5) _____. ◆ The country should manage wetlands at (6) _____ levels. ◆ Related departments should make a national (7) _____ of important wetlands public. ◆ Organizations and (8) _____ are not allowed to destroy the habitat in wetlands. ◆ It's not allowed to (9) _____ groundwater without permission. ◆ A system of compensation for ecological conservation should be (10) _____.

词汇碎片: establish v. 确立；确定　raise awareness of 提高对……的意识　forbidden adj. 禁止的　require v. 要求；需要

重难句讲解: According to the law, the country will manage wetlands at different levels, and important wetland areas should be brought under the ecological conservation red lines. 根据该法律的要求，国家将对湿地实行分级管理，重要湿地应划入生态保护红线。

本句是 and 连接的并列句，第一个并列分句是主谓宾结构；第二个并列分句是被动句。

Week Fourteen 环境保护

Friday E 短文填空

| 体 裁 | 记叙文 | 题 材 | 环境保护 | 正 确 率 | /5 | 词 数 | 266 |
| 难 度 | ★★★☆☆ | 建议用时 | 6 分钟 | 实际用时 | | 答案页码 | 128 |

Shanghai is making itself a better and lovelier place to live in with less air pollution and cleaner water.

From January to September, the city's average PM 2.5 concentration (浓度) was 26 micrograms per cubic meter, down 16 percent from last year, and the percentage of days with "excellent" or "good" air quality index (指数) (AQI) (1) _____ 91.6 percent, an increase of 5.1 percent from last year, the city's bureau (局) of ecology (生态) and environment announced.

In the bureau's new Five-Year Plan (2021-2025), the goal is to achieve an annual average concentration of PM 2.5 in Shanghai (2) _____ 35 micrograms per cubic meter and a stable (稳定的) AQI of about 85 percent (equivalent to over 300 days with good air quality in a year) by 2025.

In addition, the city is (3) _____ making its water cleaner. From January to August of 2021, the rate of surface water ranked "good" was 77.3 percent, an increase of 5.1 percent over the same period of last year.

From 2015 to 2020, Shanghai managed to prevent and control water (4) _____, resulting in consistent (持续的) improvement of the overall water quality. The water quality of four centralized (集中的) drinking water sources at the upper reaches of the Huangpu River have kept Class Ⅲ since 2018. The city has eliminated (清除) heavily (5) _____ bodies of water since the end of 2018. By the end of 2020, the city had basically eliminated bodies of water inferior (较差的) to Class-V. More than 60 percent of the main river's water quality will reach or exceed (超过) Class Ⅲ by 2025.

阅读短文，从方框中选择合适的单词或短语填空，使短文通顺、意思完整。

polluted

reached

focused on

below

pollution

词汇碎片

announce v. 宣布　　　result in 造成，导致　　　overall adj. 总体的

重难句讲解

From January to September, the city's average PM 2.5 concentration was 26 micrograms per cubic meter, down 16 percent from last year, and the percentage of days with "excellent" or "good" air quality index (AQI) reached 91.6 percent, an increase of 5.1 percent from last year, the city's bureau of ecology and environment announced. 上海市生态环境局宣布，从1月到9月，上海PM 2.5的平均浓度为每立方米26微克，比去年下降了16%，空气质量指数为"优"或"良"的天数比例达到91.6%，比去年上升了5.1%。

本句是复合句。主句的主干是 ...the city's bureau of ecology and environment announced，前面的部分可以被看作省略 that 的宾语从句。宾语从句是 and 连接的并列句，第一个并列分句的主干是 the city's average PM 2.5 concentration was 26 micrograms per cubic meter，为主系表结构；第二个并列分句的主干是 the percentage of days with "excellent" or "good" air quality index (AQI) reached 91.6 percent，是主谓宾结构。

Saturday F 短文填空

| 体裁 | 记叙文 | 题材 | 环境保护 | 正确率 | ___/10 | 词数 | 247 |
| 难度 | ★★★★★ | 建议用时 | 12分钟 | 实际用时 | ___ | 答案页码 | 129 |

阅读短文，根据首字母提示，在短文空缺处填入适当的单词，使短文通顺、意思完整。

World's top scientists called for global cooperation and joint efforts in green energy development and climate change at the 4th World Laureates Forum (世界顶尖科学家论坛) in Shanghai.

At a sub-forum themed on dual carbon governance (双碳治理), science and environmental experts explored ways to deal with problems (1) i_____ renewable (可再生的) energy storage, carbon sink (碳汇) and the balance (2) b_____ managing climate change and economic growth.

Steven Chu, the 1997 Nobel Prize laureate in physics, said rising temperature is the main environmental (3) r_____. The best solution is (4) c_____ greenhouse gas emissions (排放) through the development of renewable energy.

Noting that China is a leader in clean energy transmission (传输) and distribution (分配), Chu said China and other (5) c_____ can "work together in trying to share best practices and how we can organize electrical distribution and (6) t_____ systems."

Zhou Chenghu, a (7) m_____ of the Chinese Academy of Sciences, said China has been building a carbon sink ecosystem and has (8) p_____ a lot of efforts into strengthening the management of carbon emissions from animal husbandry (畜牧业). China has also been expanding afforestation (植树造林) and urban greening and adopting biological (生物的) technology to capture carbon dioxide.

Professor Yang Peidong, who has been named a MacArthur "genius" Fellow, has developed new solar cells (电池) and artificial photosynthesis (人工光合作用) devices. He (9) b_____ technology can significantly raise the possibility of clean energy application (应用) in the future. "If humans can simulate (模拟) photosynthesis and use carbon dioxide catalysts (催化剂) and nanomaterial (纳米材料) technology to separate water, it can (10) p_____ infinite (无限的) clean energy," said Yang.

(1) _____
(2) _____
(3) _____
(4) _____
(5) _____
(6) _____
(7) _____
(8) _____
(9) _____
(10) _____

词汇碎片

call for 呼吁　　themed adj. 以……为主题的　　practice n. 做法　　strengthen v. 加强

重难句讲解

Noting that China is a leader in clean energy transmission and distribution, Chu said China and other countries can "work together in trying to share best practices and how we can organize electrical distribution and transmission systems." 朱棣文指出，中国是清洁能源输送和分配的领导者。他说，中国和其他国家可以"共同努力，分享最佳做法，以及（讨论）我们如何协调配电和输电系统"。

本句是复合句。主句的主干是 Chu said，后面是省略 that 的宾语从句，作 said 的宾语。宾语从句中又嵌套一个 how 引导的宾语从句，作 share 的宾语，和 best practices 并列。

答案解析

Week One

Monday【A 完形填空】

● 答案解析

1. C。考查名词辨析和上下文语义。A 项意为"树"，B 项意为"动物"，C 项意为"螃蟹"，D 项意为"花"。空格所在句意为：该博物馆占地 1 000 多平方米，藏有超过 323 种_____。结合上一句中的 The World Crab Museum（世界螃蟹博物馆）可知，该博物馆收藏的应该是螃蟹，故选 C。

2. B。考查上下文语义。A 项意为"除了……"，B 项意为"例如"，C 项意为"更别说"，D 项意为"超过"。空格所在句意为：这里 90% 以上的藏品都是罕见的螃蟹，展出的藏品中有十几种是濒临灭绝的物种，_____六足巨蟹。根据语境可知，"六足巨蟹"是作为例子来说明前面所说的"濒临灭绝的物种"，"例如"代入后符合语义，故选 B。

3. A。考查形容词辨析。A 项意为"有联系的"，B 项意为"相似的"，C 项意为"有害的"，D 项意为"有用的"。空格所在句意为：柳政鸿出生于一个海岛县，他从小就觉得自己与海洋是_____。根据语境可知，只有"有联系的"代入后符合语境，其他三项代入后均不符合逻辑，故选 A。

4. D。考查介词辨析。A 项意为"在……里面"，B 项意为"在……上面"，C 项意为"……的"，D 项意为"从……"。空格所在句意为：我_____小就对水上运动和海洋活动感兴趣。根据语境可知，空格所在处表示"从很小的时候就……"，from 符合语义，其他三项代入后均不符合逻辑，故选 D。

5. B。考查名词短语辨析。A 项意为"对……的恐惧"，B 项意为"对……的喜爱"，C 项意为"对……的仇恨"，D 项意为"对……的担忧"。空格所在句意为：他对螃蟹和海洋生物的_____深受家人的影响。根据上一句中的 interested in water sports and ocean activities（对水上运动和海洋活动感兴趣）可知，柳政鸿应该是喜欢螃蟹和海洋生物的，故选 B。

6. D。考查动词辨析。A 项意为"拒绝"，B 项意为"忘记"，C 项意为"停止"，D 项意为"开始"。空格所在句意为：我的父亲跟随他并_____制作螃蟹标本。根据语境可知，既然父亲跟随祖父，那么父亲应该是在祖父工作的基础上更进一步，"开始制作螃蟹标本"符合语境，其他三项代入后均不符合语境，故选 D。

7. C。考查动词辨析。A 项意为"保持"，B 项意为"邀请"，C 项意为"返回"，D 项意为"比较"。空格所在句意为：2017 年大学毕业后，20 多岁的柳政鸿决定_____家乡——澎湖，在当地的旅游行业工作。根据语境可知，"回到家乡"符合语境，故选 C。

8. B。考查动词辨析。A 项意为"加入"，B 项意为"开设"，C 项意为"发现"，D 项意为"进入"。空格所在句意为：2019 年，他在福建厦门_____了一家临时螃蟹博物馆，首次亮相并试水市场，该博物馆于当年 12 月关闭。根据该句中的"试水市场"和"关闭"可知，柳政鸿应该是开设了一家临时螃蟹博物馆，B 项符合语义，故选 B。

9. C。考查连词辨析。A 项意为"在……之前"，B 项意为"如果"，C 项意为"随着"，D 项意为"除非"。空格所在句意为：_____家人收集螃蟹数量的增加，柳政鸿了解了自然界和海洋生物的多样性。将四个选项分别代入后发现，只有 As 符合语义，故选 C。

10. A。考查副词辨析。A 项意为"逐渐"，B 项意为"最近"，C 项意为"几乎不"，D 项意为"突然"。空格所在句意为：于是，他的爱好_____成了他的事业。结合上一句"随着家人收集螃蟹数量的增加，柳政鸿了解了自然界和海洋生物的多样性"和柳政鸿开设螃蟹博物馆可知，柳政鸿的爱好成了他的事业，而这一变化是逐渐发生的，A 项符合语境，故选 A。

Tuesday【B 阅读理解】

● 答案解析

1. D。细节理解题。第一段指出 Wang Zhipu, a student at Yongtai No. 1 High School, taught himself astrophotography by reading books and by searching online（永泰一中的学生王至璞通过看书和在线搜索自学了天文摄影）。由此可知，王至璞是自学了天文摄影，故选 D。

2. A。细节理解题。第三段最后一句指出 Wang's photo took

first prize in the Young Competition category, an award for photographers aged 15 and under（王至璞的照片在青年竞赛组中获得一等奖，该奖项是为年龄在15岁及以下的摄影师设立的）。由此可知，参加青年竞赛组的条件是年龄在15岁及以下，故选A。

3. C。细节理解题。第六段第二句指出Busy with his studies, Wang made use of every spare moment, getting up at dawn, sleeping early to wake up at midnight, and even taking time off from evening classes when necessary［虽然忙于学习，但王至璞利用所有空闲时间（进行拍摄），黎明就起床，为了半夜起床而早睡，甚至在必要的时候还会请假不上晚自习］。由此可知，王至璞在拍摄方面非常努力，C项符合文意，其他三项文中均未提及，故选C。

Wednesday【C 阅读理解】
● 答案解析

1. C。细节理解题。第二段中指出When Lingshiqi had too many bags to carry... He built a robot（当凌十七有太多背包要背时……他制造了一个机器人）。由此可知，凌十七制造的机器人"恶魔"可以帮他背包，C项符合题意，其他三项文中均未提及，故选C。

2. A。细节理解题。第三段第二句指出A 16-minute video clip features the 28-year-old Huawei engineer designing and creating a robotic arm（一段16分钟的视频片段展示了这位28岁的华为工程师设计和制造机械臂的故事）。由此可知，稚晖君制造了一条机械手臂，A项符合文意，故选A。

3. D。细节理解题。第四段最后一句指出The 22-year-old graduate from the Beijing University of Posts and Telecommunications posted a 7-minute video in October, which has been viewed more than 17 million times（这位来自北京邮电大学的22岁毕业生在10月份发布了一段7分钟的视频，该视频的播放量已超过1 700万次）。由此可知，何同学的视频在互联网上很受欢迎，D项符合文意。何同学没有制造火箭，他的视频时长为7分钟，且文中并未提及视频是由何同学的父母拍摄并发布的，因此A项、B项和C项均与原文不符，故选D。

4. B。词义猜测题。第五段第一句指出As if these feats were not surprising enough, the self-built model rocket launch of another young man, Liu Shang, may actually push the boundaries to a new horizon（就像这些_____还不够惊人一样，另一位年轻人刘上的自制模型火箭的发射，实际上可能会将边界推向一个新的层面）。根据语境可知，these feats指代上文提到的三位青年的成就，四个选项中，只有B项"成就"代入后最符合语境，故选B。

Thursday【D 阅读理解】
● 答案解析

1. C。细节理解题。第一段中指出he hopes to become a PE teacher and train China's future soccer players. Two years ago, though, his dream was even bigger. Ai hoped to join the men's national soccer team（他希望成为一名体育老师，培养中国未来的足球运动员。然而，两年前，他的梦想更大。岩坎香曾希望加入男足国家队）。由此可知，岩坎香最初的梦想是成为一名足球运动员，C项符合文意，故选C。

2. A。词义猜测题。第二段第一句中指出Ai drew public attention last year after videos of him playing soccer in a river went viral（去年他在河里踢足球的视频在网上_____后引起了公众的关注）。由"引起了公众的关注"可知，应该是视频在网上走红，A项代入后符合语境，故选A。

3. B。细节理解题。第三段中指出But when Ai finally played with the team, he was humbled. He was barely able to keep up. His skills were not as strong as he had imagined, and he had little awareness of teamwork（但当岩坎香最终和球队一起踢球时，他却被轻松打败了。他几乎无法跟上。他的技能并没有他想象中的那么强，他也没有什么团队意识）。由此可知，A项、C项和D项均为岩坎香改变梦想的原因，只有B项不是，故选B。

4. B。细节理解题。第四段第三、四句指出He needed more experience. So he set a new and more practical goal—to apply to university and become a PE teacher（他需要更多的经验。于是，他定下了一个更实际的新目标——申请大学，将来成为一名体育老师）。由此可知，他申请大学的原因是为成为体育老师积累更多经验，B项符合文意，故选B。

5. D。主旨大意题。第一段指出岩坎香曾希望成为体育运动员，后来改变梦想，希望成为体育老师；第二段讲述岩坎香成为名人的原因；第三段讲述岩坎香改变梦想的原因；第四段讲述岩坎香改变梦想后做出的行动及结果；第五段讲述岩坎香的感受。全文围绕岩坎香成为体育老师的梦想展开，D项可以概括文章主旨，其他三项均不符合文意，故选D。

Friday【E 任务型阅读】

● 答案解析

1. makes me strong and warm. 第一段第二句指出"I've had a lot of fun on the ice. It wasn't cold, and exercising makes me strong and warm," the 10-year-old said（"我在冰上玩得很开心。天气不冷，锻炼让我变得强壮和温暖。"这位10岁的孩子说）。题干中的前半部分是对I've had a lot of fun on the ice. It wasn't cold 的同义改写，skating对应原文中的exercising，因此后面应填makes me strong and warm。

2. The Beijing 2022 Olympic and Paralympic Winter Games allow. 第二段中指出Thanks to the Beijing 2022 Olympic and Paralympic Winter Games, many Beijing residents like Xu and her family have been able to enjoy winter sports-related activities（得益于北京2022年冬奥会和冬季残奥会，许多像徐德佩和她的家人这样的北京市民能够享受到与冬季运动相关的活动）。由此可知，是北京2022年冬奥会和冬季残奥会让北京市民能够享受到与冬季运动相关的活动，因此空格处应填The Beijing 2022 Olympic and Paralympic Winter Games allow。

3. Beijing has done a lot to promote winter sports. 一般主旨句位于段首或段尾，第三段首句指出Beijing has done a lot to promote winter sports（北京在推广冬季运动方面做了大量的工作）。后面两句讲述了北京的具体行动，是对首句的展开说明，因此首句就是该段的主旨句。

4. The following day. 第四段最后一句中提到adding that he planned to go skating the following day（他还补充说他计划第二天去滑冰）。该句中的"他"指张超，由此可知，张超打算第二天去滑冰。

5. 这位70岁的老人在中国东北部的黑龙江省——中国最寒冷的省份——出生并长大，他从小就喜欢冬季运动。Born and raised... Province 为过去分词短语作伴随状语，翻译时可以补充主语，即后面的the 70-year-old，放在句首。两个破折号中间的内容为插入语，对Heilongjiang Province进行补充说明，翻译时可以保留破折号。since引导的时间状语从句在翻译时可以放在谓语动词的前面。

Saturday【F 短文填空】

● 答案解析

（1）to。根据语境可知，此处为turn sb. from... to... 的结构，意为"使某人从……变成……"，故填to。

（2）me。空格处所填词充当动词taught的宾语，所给单词为主格，应变成相应的宾格，故填me。

（3）living。空格所在句意为：在我新泽西的家里，我在厨房、_____和家庭办公室里都放了几盆这种漂亮的室内植物。根据句子结构可知，_____room应为与厨房和家庭办公室并列的名词短语，room前面应填一个形容词，所给动词的形容词形式为living，代入后表示"客厅"，符合语境，故填living。

（4）came。空格所在句意为：当我们来到北京生活时，我发现兰花非常便宜。根据空格后的found out可知，此处应使用一般过去时，所给词为动词原形，其过去式为came，故填came。

（5）a。空格所在句意为：而在一家新泽西的店里，类似的东西至少要花30美元。空格后的名词store为可数名词，前面应使用冠词，因为不是特指，且Jersey不是以元音音素开头，所以应该使用不定冠词a，故填a。

（6）Sadly。空格位于句首，括号中所给词为形容词，放在句首即修饰整个句子，应使用副词，故填Sadly。

（7）and。空格所在句意为：在视频网站YouTube上，我学会了修剪花茎，用香蕉叶做肥料，_____多加一点水来延长它们的寿命。根据句子结构可知，prune stems、use banana leaves as fertilizer 和 just use a little more water to prolong their lives 三者并列，中间缺少连词，故填and。

（8）different。空格后为名词短语，所以此处应使用一个形容词来对其进行修饰，括号中所给词为名词，其形容词形式为different，故填different。

（9）would。考查固定搭配。根据空格后的love to have... 可知，此处为would love to do sth. 的结构，故填would。

（10）like。空格所在句意为：他说公寓开始看起来_____殡仪馆了！根据句子结构可知，空格前面为系动词look（看起来），空格后为名词短语，结合句意可知，此处可填like构成短语look like（看起来像），符合语境，故填like。

Week Two

Monday【A 完形填空】

答案解析

1. C。考查固定搭配。not... but... 是固定搭配，意为"不是……而是……"，代入后符合上下文语境，故选C。

2. D。考查上下文语义。A项意为"南部"，B项意为"北部"，C项意为"西部"，D项意为"东部"。根据第三段提到的 two software engineers from the east 可知D项符合上下文语义，故选D。

3. A。考查形容词辨析。A项意为"长的"，B项意为"（体积、程度、数量等）大的"，C项意为"深的；厚的"，D项意为"远的"。根据空格前的 mini rocket 和 1.37 meters 可知空格部分形容火箭的大小，A项代入原文后符合语境，故选A。

4. A。考查动词辨析。A项意为"飞行；航行"，B项意为"居住"，C项意为"呼唤；给……打电话"，D项意为"移动"。根据下文提到的 rocket 和 to see whether Mercury... breathe flames 可知这位男孩未来想乘坐火箭飞行，A项符合语境，故选A。

5. B。考查动词短语辨析。A项意为"关心"，B项意为"思考"，C项意为"担心"，D项意为"讨论"。上文提到了男孩的愿望，下文提到了火箭起飞，由此可推断男孩在看到火箭起飞时对未来产生了思考，B项代入原文后符合语境，故选B。

6. B。考查连词辨析。A项意为"尽管，虽然"；B项意为"当……时"；C项意为"自从"，通常用于完成时态中；D项意为"直到……为止"。根据语境可知，空格处描写的是孩子们观看神舟十三号载人飞船发射直播时的心情，A、D两项代入原文后不符合语境，故排除。C项不符合时态要求，故排除。故选B。

7. D。考查形容词辨析。A项意为"放松的"，B项意为"害怕的"，C项意为"无聊的"，D项意为"激动的"。根据文章可知孩子们对太空充满兴趣，故排除B、C两项。在神舟飞船发射这种举国瞩目的时刻，孩子们的心情应该是"激动的"，而不是"放松的"，D项代入原文后最符合语境，故选D。

8. C。考查动词辨析。A项意为"讨论"，B项意为"期待"，C项意为"自愿做"，D项意为"后悔"。下文提到，这两位软件工程师在课堂上耐心回答孩子们的问题，还帮助孩子们制造微型火箭。C项代入原文后意为"自愿为这些学生在线授课"，符合语境，故选C。

9. B。考查动词辨析。A项意为"同意"，B项意为"提及；提起"，C项意为"意识到"，D项意为"表达"。根据下文可知孩子们提出了许多关于太空的问题，raise questions 意为"提出问题"，符合语境，故选B。

10. A。考查动词辨析。A项意为"回答"，B项意为"强迫"，C项意为"检查"，D项意为"承诺"。空格后的 them 指代上文提到的 many questions，由此可知此处讲的是两位软件工程师解答孩子们提出的问题，A项符合语境，故选A。

11. C。考查名词辨析。A项意为"一份；股份"，B项意为"微笑"，C项意为"尝试；努力"，D项意为"转动；（依次轮到的）机会"。下文提到 Then an amateur rocket team was born（于是，一个业余火箭研发团队诞生了），由此可知空格处指两位软件工程师愿意尝试制造微型火箭。give it a try 为固定搭配，意为"试一试"，故选C。

12. C。考查形容词辨析。A项意为"危险的"，B项意为"有趣的"，C项意为"具有挑战性的"，D项意为"令人满意的"。下文提到，两位软件工程师在三个月的时间里一直在研究火箭的制造，需要的零件有100多个，由此可知制造火箭并不容易，C项符合语境，故选C。

13. A。考查副词辨析。A项意为"成功地"，B项意为"严肃地；严重地"，C项意为"容易地"，D项意为"秘密地"。文章第一句便提到软件工程师和孩子们发射了自己制造的火箭，由此可知引擎测试非常成功，A项符合语境，故选A。

14. B。考查形容词辨析。A项意为"突然的"，B项意为"准备好的"，C项意为"特殊的"，D项意为"确信的"。be ready for sth. 是固定搭配，意为"为某事做好了准备"，代入原文后意为"发射工作准备就绪"，符合语境，也与文章开头呼应，故选B。

15. D。考查名词辨析。A项意为"步骤；脚步"，B项意为"故事"，C项意为"预言；预测"，D项意为"梦想"。根据下文提到的 I want to be an astronaut when I grow up（我长大后想成为一名航天员）可知，D项最符合语境，故选D。

Tuesday【B 阅读理解】

答案解析

1. B。细节理解题。第二段提到 Our reporter today takes

us to southwest China's Sichuan Province, to a middle school…，结合下文可知此处的a middle school指的是"喜德中学"，故选B。

2. B。细节理解题。根据题干关键词Wenggu Wushamo定位到对应的表格，由My sister is a college student（我姐姐是大学生）可知B项符合原文，故选B。

3. C。细节理解题。根据题干关键词Lei Yousheng定位到对应的表格，由Teacher, Xide Middle School（喜德中学老师）可知C项符合原文，故选C。

4. A。细节理解题。根据题干中的some students 和 sent to other middle schools定位到对应的表格，表格中提到，We've piloted a program of sending some of our students to middle schools in more developed areas, where they have better chances of going to colleges（我们进行了一个项目的试点，把我校的部分学生送往更发达的地区上初中。在那里，他们考上大学的机会更大）。考上大学的机会更大意味着接受更好的教育，由此可知A项符合原文，故选A。

5. D。推理判断题。根据第二段中的reporter（记者）可知本篇文章最有可能是一篇新闻报道，故选D。

Wednesday【C 阅读理解】
● 答案解析

1. D。细节理解题。第一段提到a new plan designed to make sure such children have equal access to education（这项新规划旨在确保这些儿童拥有平等的受教育机会），其中such children指代上文提到的disabled children。由此可知，这项新规划旨在保护残疾儿童受教育的权利，D项符合原文，故选D。

2. A。细节理解题。根据原文第二段中的The average government expenditure on disabled children… will be raised（政府对……残疾儿童的平均支出将增加）和The plan also called for more efforts to develop… higher education… for disabled people（该规划还呼吁加大力度，发展面向残疾人士的……高等教育……）可知B、D两项符合原文。根据第三段中的 Special education is one of the most urgent needs for children with disabilities（特殊教育是残疾儿童最迫切的需求之一），以及下文提到的政府促进特殊教育的发展可知C项符合原文。文章并未提及政府为残疾儿童提供工作，A项属于无中生有，故选A。

3. B。语篇理解题。第四段中的integrating children with special needs in regular schools（将拥有特殊需求的孩子融入常规学校）是对integrated education（融合教育）的解释说明，即让有身体或心理缺陷的学生与普通学生一起学习。B项符合原文，故选B。

4. A。细节理解题。根据倒数第二段中的hiring a teacher for his daughter（为女儿聘请老师）可知A项符合原文。根据倒数第二段中的he was not willing to send his daughter to a special education school（他不愿意把女儿送到特殊教育学校）可排除B项。最后一段虽然提到齐永刚想送他的女儿去中等职业学校学习，但并不能推断出这件事已经发生，故排除C项。D项原文未提及。故选A。

5. C。主旨大意题。本文主要讲述了政府为残疾儿童的教育制订的新规划，C项"一个面向残疾儿童的规划"最能概括文章主旨，故选C。

Thursday【D 任务型阅读】
● 答案解析

1. B。空格前提到园岭小学允许学生在期末考试中携带"小抄"，B项是对这一举措的进一步说明，其中This move指"允许学生在期末考试中携带'小抄'"一事。故选B。

2. D。空格前提到burden-reducing policies（减负政策），空格后提到这些政策的目的，空格后的they指代policies。由此可知空格处的内容与"减负政策"有关。D项 These policies were introduced by Chinese authorities（这些政策是中国官方推行的）符合语境，起到承上启下的作用，故选D。

3. A。空格后提到了不同年级学生进行期末考试的形式，A项 The final exams in the school were taken in different forms（园岭小学采用不同的形式进行期末考试）是对本段内容的总结，故选A。

4. E。空格后提到了学生拥有概括知识能力的重要性，E项中的students' learning abilities（学生的学习能力）与下文对应，E项代入原文后符合语境，故选E。

5. C。根据空格后的冒号可知subject awareness, subject competence, class performance, after-school performance, and final assessment（学科意识、学科能力、课堂表现、课后表现和期末评估）是对空格处的补充说明。C项中的five aspects（五个方面）与下文对应，C项代入原文后符合语境，故选C。

Friday【E 短文填空】

答案解析

（1）caught。根据句子结构可知，空格所在句缺谓语动词。catch sb.'s eye(s) 为固定搭配，意为"引起某人注意"。根据第一段中的 went 和空格后的 said 可知时态为一般过去时。故填 caught。

（2）times。根据句子结构可知，about four _____ a week 作状语。time 可表示"次；回"，为可数名词，由空格前的 four 可用复数形式，代入原文后意为"一周四次"，符合语境。故填 times。

（3）least。空格所在句主干完整，故空格处和 at 搭配构成状语。at least 是固定搭配，意为"至少"，代入原文后符合语境。故填 least。

（4）in。become interested in 是固定搭配，意为"对……产生兴趣"，代入原文后符合语境。故填 in。

（5）practicing。opportunity for doing sth.是固定搭配，意为"做某事的机会"，故空格处需填入动词的动名词形式。将所给选项中的动词代入原文，再结合空格前提到的"地板曲棍球被列入课程"可知，此处指在课堂上练习地板曲棍球，practice（练习）符合语境。故填 practicing。

（6）courses。根据句子结构可知，空格处作宾语，且前有形容词 optional 修饰，故空格处需填入名词。结合下文提到的 skating and skiing（滑冰和滑雪）可知，course（课程）符合语境，且课程不止一种，故用此名词的复数形式。故填 courses。

（7）since。空格后是时间点 2017，空格前谓语动词的时态为现在完成时，since（自……以来）符合语境和语法要求。故填 since。

（8）number。根据句子结构可知，The _____ of the annual event's participants 作主语，结合下文提到的 500 和 1,700 可知空格所在部分与数字有关，number（数量）符合语境。故填 number。

（9）than。more than 是固定搭配，意为"多于；超出"，代入原文后符合语境。故填 than。

（10）helps。根据句子结构可知，空格所在句缺谓语动词，主语是动名词短语 Promoting ice and snow sports at school，故谓语动词为第三人称单数。选项中所剩动词 help（帮助）代入原文后符合语境。本句无明显的时间状语，故时态为一般现在时。故填 helps。

Saturday【F 短文填空】

答案解析

（1）by。根据句子结构可知，given _____ Longhua District No. 3 Experimental School 作后置定语，修饰 course。动词 give 和其逻辑主语 art course 为被动关系，动作的发出者为 Longhua District No. 3 Experimental School，介词 by 后面跟动作发出者。故填 by。

（2）an。spend time doing sth. 意为"花时间做某事"，_____ hour 作 spent 的宾语，hour 为可数名词单数，以元音音素开头，需用冠词 an。故填 an。

（3）designer。空格所在句意为：在每一个小组中，两名学生分别扮演客户和时装 _____。文章主题是学校开设时装设计课程，且下文提到了 young designers。由此可推断另一位学生扮演的是设计师。故填 designer。

（4）After。空格所在部分提到了反复修改，下文提到设计师们成功设计出了服装。由此可知，在反复修改后才成功设计出服装，after 表示"在……之后"，空格处位于句首，首字母需大写，故填 After。

（5）and。根据句子结构可知，fellow students 和 the tutor 并列，and 表示并列，代入原文后意为"同学和老师的评价"，符合语境。故填 and。

（6）in。根据句子结构可知，_____ 2019 作时间状语。月份、季节和年份前一般用介词 in，代入原文后意为"开设时装设计课程的想法出现于 2019 年"，符合语境。故填 in。

（7）to。decide to do sth. 是固定搭配，意为"决定做某事"。故填 to。

（8）students。根据句子结构可知，空格所在句缺宾语，主语是 the teachers，谓语是 guided。根据空格后提到的 to learn the basics of fashion design（学习时装设计的基本要点）可知，此处指老师引导学生学习，且学生不止一个，需填复数形式。故填 students。

（9）are。根据句子结构可知，空格所在句为 There be 句型，表示"有"。根据空格后的 two student manuals 可知 be 动词用第三人称复数。根据空格前的 aims 可知时态为一般现在时。故填 are。

（10）where。根据句子结构和语境可知，空格所在句是定语从句，修饰前面的 museums and galleries，表示学生可以在博物馆和美术馆内看到过去的客家服装，听著名设计师的讲座。空格所在句主干完整，故空格处需填入关系副词，museums and galleries 表示地点。故填 where。

Week Three

Monday【A 完形填空】

答案解析

1. C。考查名词辨析。A项意为"机会；机遇"，B项意为"理由；原因"，C项意为"瞬间；片刻"，D项意为"过程；步骤"。将四个选项代入原文，只有C项符合文意与逻辑，意为"从她第二个儿子出生的那一刻起就知道她有一个最喜爱的孩子"。其余选项代入后均不符合逻辑。故选C。

2. B。考查动词辨析。A项意为"给予"，B项意为"爱；喜欢"，C项意为"做；制造"，D项意为"提供"。空格后提到，在某种程度上，相比于她的长子，她最小的孩子就是更能得到她的"欢心"。由but可知，空格处讲的是两个孩子她都爱，只不过她更偏爱她的第二个儿子。故选B。

3. D。考查动词短语辨析。A项意为"把……拒之门外；解雇"，B项意为"扔掉，丢弃"，C项意为"抛弃；把……收起来放好"，D项意为"带走；拿走"。空格后提到，她有24小时不能见到刚出生的大儿子，可知她第一个儿子在出生后由于健康问题被立即抱走治疗了。故选D。

4. A。考查形容词辨析。A项意为"宝贵的；很重要的"，B项意为"滑稽的"，C项意为"艰难的；硬的"，D项意为"困难的"。由空格后的bonding period（建立亲子关系的时期）可知，孩子出生后与父母建立亲子关系的这段时期是重要且宝贵的。故选A。

5. B。考查上下文语义。第二段提到，乔安娜的第二个儿子更能得到她的"欢心"。由空格前的long-lasting preference（长期偏爱）可知，此处讲的是她对第二个儿子的长期偏爱。故选B。

6. A。考查动词辨析。A项意为"接受"，B项意为"发现"，C项意为"带来"，D项意为"保护"。将四个选项代入原文，只有A项符合文意与逻辑，意为"虽然乔安娜进行了多年的思想斗争，但她说现在她已经接受了这个事实"。其余选项代入后均不符合逻辑。故选A。

7. C。考查动词辨析。A项意为"负担得起"，B项意为"鼓励"，C项意为"注意到"，D项意为"离开"。由上文可知，乔安娜了解到自己内心对她两个孩子的感受不同，也没有避而不谈。又由空格前的Unlike Joanna（与乔安娜不同）及空格后的goes undiscussed（不会被讨论）可知，大多数父母和乔安娜不一样，他们很难注意到自己内心对孩子的偏爱，所以也不会讨论这一点。故选C。

8. B。考查上下文语义。空格前提到，拥有一个最喜爱的孩子可能是为人父母最大的禁忌；空格后提到，大多数父母确实会有一个最喜爱的孩子。空格前后构成转折。故选B。

9. D。考查动词短语辨析。A项意为"谈论，讨论"，B项意为"就（某事）撒谎"，C项意为"考虑"，D项意为"担心"。空格前提到"大量证据表明，成为最不受喜爱的孩子可能会从根本上塑造孩子的性格，并导致激烈的手足之争"，因此父母可能会担心自己的偏爱被（孩子们）注意到。故选D。

10. C。考查名词辨析。A项意为"决定"，B项意为"意外；事故"，C项意为"问题"，D项意为"梦；梦想"。将四个选项代入原文，只有C项符合文意与逻辑，意为"真正的问题在于，父母如何应对他们的孩子对偏爱的感知"。其余选项代入后均不符合逻辑。故选C。

Tuesday【B 阅读理解】

答案解析

1. C。细节理解题。由第一段第二句中的 from 15:00 to 18:00（15:00至18:00）可知，该派对将持续3个小时。故选C。

2. D。细节理解题。由第二段中的 basic materials such as construction paper, paper plates, and straws（基本材料，如彩色美术纸、纸盘和吸管）可知，candies（糖果）在丘比特箭投掷游戏中是用不到的。故选D。

3. D。细节理解题。由第五段第一句 Relay races are exciting ways for kids to work together as a team（接力赛是让孩子们齐心协力的激动人心的方式）可知，心形糖果拆包装接力赛是一个团队游戏。其他三个游戏中均未提及团队。故选D。

4. A。细节理解题。由第一段可知，该派对是在2月14日举办，又由最后一段 Please call me a day before the party if you can't come（如果你不能到场，请在派对前一天给我打电话）可知，如果不能参加派对需要提前一天，即最晚在2月13日给主办者打电话。故选A。

5. B。推理判断题。阅读全文可知，这是一份情人节亲子活动邀请函，又由最后的落款 Your neighbor from Building 101（101栋邻居）可知，这份邀请函是由邻居发出的，因此最有可能在社区内收到。故选B。

Wednesday【C 阅读理解】

答案解析

1. B。细节理解题。由题干中的 cause relationship problems for kids 定位到第一段最后一句。该句提到，The latter can leave lasting scars that can cause relationship problems for kids for years to come（而后者则会给孩子心里留下持久的创伤，可能会导致孩子未来出现情感问题）。上文提到了两种父母的做法，一种是从来不在孩子面前争论，另一种是争吵分歧过多。其中 The latter 指的就是后者，即 fights and disagreements。故选 B。

2. C。词义猜测题。画线单词上文提到，争吵通常涉及伤害性的语言、辱骂、提高嗓门，等等；下文提到，这些类型的争吵会对婚姻造成伤害，也会对孩子造成不良影响。由此可知，此处是在讲争吵的坏处，而非争吵的重要性、合理性或效率。C 项代入原文后与上下文联系最紧密。故选 C。

3. D。细节理解题。由第二段最后一句可知，争论的过程中可能会出现 a heated yet controlled discussion, difference of opinion, and an underlying desire to find a place of agreement（激烈但可控的讨论、意见分歧，以及达成共识的潜在愿望）。A、B、C 三项均是争吵的时候可能出现的情况，而非争论。故选 D。

4. C。细节理解题。由第三段最后一句 Kids will grow up and face conflicts with family members, teachers, bosses, and in relationships of their own（孩子们长大后会面临与家庭成员、老师、上司的冲突，并且在他们自己的恋爱关系中也会面临冲突）可知，冲突无处不在，在每种关系中都可能发生。故选 C。

5. D。主旨大意题。文章第一段描述了父母的两种常见的做法，即避免争论或过度争吵；第二段讲述了争吵和争论的区别；后面三段提出了作者的建议，即父母应该选择争论而非争吵，并给出理由。由此可知，文章的主旨是父母应该适度争论。故选 D。

Thursday【D 任务型阅读】

答案解析

1. C。由下文的回答"Yes, it is."可知，C、D 两项可能是正确答案，而对于 D 项 That's wonderful（太棒了）这种表示赞美的话一般的回答是表达感谢，代入原文后不符合语境。故选 C。

2. A。下文黛西的回答是对"包括你"组织的进一步介绍，因此 A 项 Tell us more about it（给我们具体介绍一下吧）符合此处语境。故选 A。

3. E。由上文 What specifically does your mother help you with（你妈妈具体帮你做什么呢）可知，空格处黛西的回答与妈妈给予她的帮助有关，E 项 She has been supporting me in any way that she can（她一直在竭尽所能地帮助我）符合此处语境。故选 E。

4. F。由空格后的 They 可知，空格处提到的人不止一个，F 项 I think it comes a lot from my parents（我想这在很大程度上是因为我的父母）符合此处语境，They 指代 my parents。故选 F。

5. B。空格前提到，看到别人受苦、被不友善地对待，黛西很难受；空格后提到，黛西想做一些力所能及的事帮助别人。剩余的三个选项中，只有 B 项 I want to do something about that（我想为此做点什么）代入后符合此处语境。故选 B。

Friday【E 短文填空】

答案解析

（1）friends。空格所在句意为：由于疫情，许多孩子与＿＿＿＿＿出去玩的时间减少了，而且学习方式变成了在线学习。friend 意为"朋友"，代入后符合文意与逻辑。空格前无冠词，所以这里应填其复数形式。故填 friends。

（2）children。空格所在句意为：远程学习对父母和＿＿＿＿＿来说都有一系列的挑战。由上文可知，本篇文章主要讲述在家学习期间家长可以给孩子提供的帮助。又由空格前的 parents 可知，空格所填词应该表示"孩子"，child 代入后符合文意。空格处与 parents 并列，所以这里应填其复数形式。故填 children。

（3）subjects。空格所在句意为：他们平时在学校学习有固定的安排，包括一天中的特定时间段学习什么特定＿＿＿＿＿。这里讲的是学校有日常的课程安排，subject 意为"科目"，代入后符合文意。由空格后的 times 可知，这里表达的是多个时间段对应学习多个科目，所以应填其复数形式。故填 subjects。

（4）helpful。空格所在句意为：在家里建立一个新的常规将是非常＿＿＿＿＿，因为这样你的孩子会确切地知道将要做什么。由本段小标题可知，本段讲的是父母应该为孩子的在家学习设定常规，由此可知空格处应该表达的是"有益的，有帮助的"，help 的形容词形式 helpful 代入后符合文意。故填 helpful。

（5）Learning。空格所在句意为：学校课程结束后，_____不一定要停止。空格所填词表示学校课程的继续，因此这里讲的是上完网课之后也可以进行"学习"。learn 代入后符合文意与逻辑。空格所在句缺主语，所以这里应填其动名词形式，单词位于句首，所以首字母大写。故填 Learning。

（6）activities。空格所在句意为：要让你的孩子知道，学习可以转变为你们一起做的超级有趣的_____。根据下文 Take a break from textbooks to do some crafts and creative projects with your kids（从课本中抽身出来，和你的孩子一起做一些手工和创意项目）可知，这里讲的是孩子上完学校网课之后父母可以和孩子一起做一些有趣的活动，activity 代入后符合文意。空格前无冠词，又由上下文可知，这里应填其复数形式。故填 activities。

（7）creating。空格所在句意为：像_____教育海报或透视画这类活动可以帮助你的孩子了解历史。由上文的 crafts and creative projects（手工和创意项目）可知，这里主要讲述父母可以和孩子一起动手做一些手工活动。create 意为"制作"，代入后符合文意。like 为介词，所以这里应填其动名词形式。故填 creating。

（8）skills。空格所在句意为：在树林这种自然环境里走一走，对孩子们来说是了解周围环境、学习一些基本生活_____的好方法。skill 意为"技能"，代入后符合文意且与 basic life 搭配合理。由 some 可知，这里应填其复数形式。故填 skills。

（9）lying。空格所在句意为：就像你_____在床上无法把工作做到最好一样，孩子们需要为上课和学习创造一个特殊的空间。由 in your bed 可知，这里指的是"躺"或"睡"在床上无法把工作做到最好，lie 意为"躺"，代入后符合文意。分析句子结构可知，该句结构完整，因此_____ in your bed 作状语，所以这里应填其分词形式，lie 与其逻辑主语 you 之间是主动关系，所以应填其现在分词形式。故填 lying。

（10）are full of。空格所在句意为：卧室里_____太多分散注意力的玩具和电子产品。be full of 意为"充满；装

满"，代入后符合文意。空格前的 Bedrooms 为名词复数，时态为一般现在时，所以这里的 be 动词应改为 are。故填 are full of。

Saturday【F 短文填空】

● 答案解析

（1）find。空格所在句意为：你可能不会在哈佛商学院的教科书中_____T and Sons 物业管理有限责任公司成功的秘诀。该句缺谓语，宾语是 the secret sauce（秘诀），因此空格处所填谓语动词应该表示"找到，发现"，find 符合文意。又由空格前的 won't 可知，此处应填动词原形。故填 find。

（2）neighbor。空格所在句意为：大约五年前，年轻的小托尔·亨德里克森看见他的一位_____在打扫院子，胳膊上打着石膏，于是他开始帮助她。空格处应该是小托尔·亨德里克森帮助的对象，由下文的 other neighbors（其他邻居）可知，托尔刚开始帮助的是一位邻居。又由空格前的 a 可知，此处应填名词单数。故填 neighbor。

（3）turned。turn into 为固定搭配，意为"发展为，演变为"，代入后意为"后来除了帮她打扫院子，他还帮她修剪草坪、搬家具和铲雪"，符合文意。又由整段的时态可知，此处应使用一般过去时。故填 turned。

（4）Lending。lend a hand 为固定搭配，意为"伸出援手，提供帮助"。将 lend 代入原文后意为"托尔还向其他邻居伸出援手，这很快就为他带来了有偿的景观美化和除雪工作"，符合文意。分析句子结构可知，该句主语为_____ a hand to other neighbors，所以此处应该填其动名词形式。故填 Lending。

（5）like/love。空格所在句意为：我_____走出去，帮助人们打理他们的院子之类的。由上文 I'm not a sit inside kind of person（我不是那种喜欢在家里坐着的人）可知，托尔应该是喜欢走出去的，like 或 love 都符合文意。又由上下文的时态可知，此处应使用一般现在时。故填 like/love。

（6）pay。空格所在句意为：如果他们不想_____，也没关系。由上文可知，托尔刚开始帮助邻居是不收费的，后来随着帮助的人越来越多，于是成立了一家物业管理公司。又由 I'm not a sit inside kind of person. I like/love to go out and help people with their yards and stuff

（我不是那种喜欢在家里坐着的人。我喜欢走出去，帮助人们打理他们的院子之类的）可知，托尔是一个闲不住的人，所以即便是免费提供帮助，也是没关系的。pay表示"付钱"，符合文意。故填pay。

（7）buy。空格所在句意为：在过去的一年里，托尔说服他的父亲给他的小货车_____一个雪犁，这样他们就可以一起帮助更多的人。由persuaded（说服）可知，获得雪犁需要花费一定的金钱或付出一定的努力。因此，空格处所填词应该表示"购买"或"安装"等，buy符合文意。故填buy。

（8）growing。空格所在句意为：他们全新的父子景观美化和除雪业务不断_____。由上文的Word spread（消息传开了）可知，他们父子的这项业务被越来越多的人知道了，所以他们的业务应该是不断增长，grow符合文意。keep doing为固定用法，意为"持续做，一直做"。故填growing。

（9）never。空格所在句意为：亨德里克森先生还提到，他的儿子在成长过程中被贴上了学习障碍的标签，但这_____阻止他。分析句子结构可知，空格处应填一个副词，修饰动词stopped。由but可知，空格所在分句的意思与上文发生了转折，所以此处应该填一个表示否定意义的副词。never表示"从未"，符合文意。故填never。

（10）teaching。空格所在句意为：这看起来确实是儿子在_____父亲如何将广施善行作为成功的助推剂。由倒数第二段第一句中的I wouldn't be doing what I'm doing with my son if it wasn't for his inspiration（如果不是受我儿子鼓舞，我不会和他一起做现在的事情）可知，儿子所做的事情对父亲产生了影响。分析句子结构可知，空格处应填一个可接双宾语的谓语动词，且其中一个宾语为从句how the currency of kindness can fuel success（如何将广施善行作为成功的助推剂）。由此可知，teach符合文意。又由is可知，此处使用的是现在进行时。故填teaching。

Week Four

Monday【A 完形填空】

● **答案解析**

1. C。考查形容词辨析。A 项意为"无聊的"，B 项意为"幸运的"，C 项意为"可能的"，D 项意为"不同的"。作者在上文针对喝汽水的话题连续提出三个问题，空格所在句是对这三个问题的回答，即如果是这样，那么你_____对汽水上瘾了。将选项代入句中可知"可能的"符合句意，故选 C。

2. D。考查名词辨析。A 项意为"羞耻"，B 项意为"骄傲"，C 项意为"满意"，D 项意为"需要"。空格所在句意为：汽水成瘾是指一个人每天_____喝大量的汽水。将选项代入句中可知"需要"符合句意，故选 D。

3. B。考查状语从句。空格所在部分意为"汽水成瘾在医学领域严格来说并不是一种健康状况"，下文又提到人们可能会对汽水中的咖啡因或糖分上瘾，前后语义发生转折。although 可引导让步状语从句，表示"虽然"，故选 B。

4. C。考查动词辨析。A 项意为"浪费"，B 项意为"偷，窃取"，C 项意为"形成；发展"，D 项意为"拒绝"。develop 后可跟 habit、interest、addiction 等名词，表示形成某种习惯、爱好，对……上瘾等，故选 C。

5. D。考查形容词辨析。A 项意为"友好的"，常与介词 to 搭配使用；B 项意为"害怕的"，常与介词 of 搭配使用；C 项意为"受欢迎的"，常与介词 with 搭配使用；D 项意为"相似的"，常与介词 to 搭配使用。将选项代入句中，"相似的"符合句意，故选 D。

6. A。考查动词短语辨析。A 项意为"从……中退出；摆脱"，B 项意为"照顾，关照"，C 项意为"从……朝外看"，D 项意为"用光，耗尽"。being hungry for soda, _____ control, headache, 即渴望汽水、_____控制、头痛，都是上瘾的症状，且 get out of control 为固定搭配，意为"失控"，符合句意，故选 A。

7. A。考查名词辨析。A 项意为"习惯"，B 项意为"方法"，C 项意为"爱好"，D 项意为"选择"。空格后面括号内的内容是对空格所在短语的解释，括号内的内容意为"吃饭时喝汽水"，再结合空格前面的修饰性短语 unhealthy eating 可知这是一种不健康的饮食习惯。故选 A。

8. B。考查名词辨析。A 项意为"任务"，B 项意为"原因"，C 项意为"结果"，D 项意为"课程"。空格所在句意为：令人上瘾的成分（如咖啡因和糖）、不健康的饮食习惯（吃饭时喝汽水）和个人偏好都可能是汽水成瘾的_____。将选项代入句中可知"原因"符合句意，故选 B。

9. B。考查形容词辨析。A 项意为"良好的"，B 项意为"有害的"，C 项意为"成功的"，D 项意为"特殊的"。根据下文提到的心脏病、高血压和蛀牙可知此处在讨论汽水成瘾的危害，故选 B。

10. D。考查固定搭配。be linked to 为固定搭配，意为"与……相关"，故选 D。

11. C。考查名词辨析。A 项意为"图片"，B 项意为"行为"，C 项意为"问题"，D 项意为"技能"。空格后列出了心脏病、高血压等健康问题，故选 C。

12. A。考查连词辨析。A 项表示选择，B 项表示并列，C 项表示转折，D 项表示因果。空格前意为：你认为自己喝了太多汽水。空格后意为：你可能已经对汽水上瘾。这两句在介绍同一种现象，由此可知这里用表示选择的连词 or，表示同一种现象的两种说法，故选 A。

13. D。考查副词辨析。A 项意为"悲伤地"，B 项意为"紧密地"，C 项意为"令人惊讶地"，D 项意为"逐渐地"。空格所在部分提到了减少饮用汽水的量。下文提到，You can set goals such as two sodas per day this week; one soda per day next week; half a soda per day the week after, and so on（你可以设定目标，例如本周每天喝两瓶汽水；下周每天喝一瓶汽水；再下一周每天喝半瓶汽水，以此类推）。由此可知这是一种循序渐进的方式，"逐渐地"符合句意，故选 D。

14. C。考查上下文语义。A 项意为"年"，B 项意为"月"，C 项意为"天"，D 项意为"小时"。由下文 two sodas per day this week; one soda per day next week（本周每天喝两瓶汽水；下周每天喝一瓶汽水）可知"天"符合句意，故选 C。

15. A。考查短语辨析。A 项意为"至少"，B 项意为"最多"，C 项意为"目前"，D 项意为"根本；究竟"。由下文 you should drink at least one cup of water along with it（那么你同时也应该至少喝一杯水）可知"至少"符合语境，故选 A。

Tuesday【B 阅读理解】

● **答案解析**

1. B。细节理解题。这家餐馆的营业时间是周二至周日的上午11点半到晚上8点半，B项"周二下午1点"在餐馆的营业时间内，故选B。

2. B。细节理解题。这家餐馆的地址是维克多路334号，所以B项符合原文，故选B。

3. D。细节理解题。根据题干中的关键词warm salad和soup定位到文中的菜单信息，可知一份沙拉是18美元，每日例汤是13美元，所以共需支付31美元，故选D。

4. B。细节理解题。由plant-based ingredients（植物性食材）可知A项表述错误；由Low temperature baking is important to keep nutrition in the food（低温烘烤有助于保留食物中的营养）可知B项表述正确；由It focuses on not only the nutrition of each meal, but also environmental protection（该餐厅不仅注重每一餐的营养，还注重环保）可知C项表述错误；由Seven kinds of sauces are prepared using the remaining ingredients like tomatoes, strawberries and apples（西红柿、草莓和苹果等剩余的食材被用来制成七种酱汁）可知D项表述错误，故选B。

5. D。推理判断题。本文介绍了一家餐馆的营业时间、地址、菜单、烹饪方式等，属于广告，故选D。

Wednesday【C 阅读理解】

● 答案解析

1. A。细节理解题。根据题干中的关键词The first step定位到第二段，该段指出，对谈话表现出兴趣是为那些可能正与心理健康问题做斗争的人创造一个安全空间的第一步，且该段的小标题是Start a conversation（开启谈话），因此A项符合要求，故选A。

2. C。细节理解题。根据题干中的关键词listening定位到第三段，由第二句中的When you are listening rather than lecturing, people with mental health problems are more likely to feel understood（当你在倾听而不是说教时，有心理健康问题的人更有可能感到自己被理解）可知C项符合要求，故选C。

3. B。细节理解题。根据题干中的关键词Support定位到第四段，由第二句中的asking "what can I do to help" isn't enough（问"我能做些什么来帮助你"是不够的）可知A项表述错误；由第一句You can offer support by focusing on concrete and specific tasks（你可以通过专注于具体、特定的任务来提供支持）可知B项表述正确；由第三句中的it's better just to provide support without waiting for an invitation（最好是主动提供支持而不是等待邀请）可知C项表述错误；由最后一句中的inviting the person to the movies can all be good starting points to give needed support（邀请对方去看电影都是给予他们所需支持的好的开端）可知看电影是有用的，所以D项表述错误，故选B。

4. C。语篇理解题。根据题干中的关键词labeling定位到第五段，文中提到不要给别人贴上"你很抑郁"或"你很焦虑"的标签，而这类描述都是来自他人的主观判断。由此可知，在所给选项中，C项little Mark being told "You are a loser" when losing a game（小马克输掉比赛时别人对他说"你是一个失败者"）符合文中"贴标签"的定义，loser就是他人给小马克贴的标签，其他三个选项都是在陈述事实，不涉及他人的主观判断，故选C。

5. C。主旨大意题。该题问本文的写作目的。本文主要介绍了一些帮助有心理健康问题的人的技巧，所以C项描述准确，故选C。

Thursday【D 阅读理解】

● 答案解析

1. D。细节理解题。根据题干中的19%定位到第一段，由该段中的more than 40 million US adults—a little more than 19%—feel anxious [超过4 000万（略超过19%）的美国成年人感到焦虑]可知超过19%的美国成年人感到焦虑，nervous与anxious是同义词，故选D。

2. B。词义猜测题。画线单词所在句子的意思为：虽然没有哪种食物或饮料是治疗焦虑或抑郁的_____，但你的饮食会影响你的平静程度。将所给选项代入句中，可知"良方"符合句意，故选B。

3. D。细节理解题。根据题干中的Top raw fruits and vegetables找到对应的表格栏，表格中指出Top raw foods linked to better mood are bananas, apples, carrots and lettuce（利于改善情绪的绝佳生食是香蕉、苹果、胡萝卜和生菜），由此可知D项不是利于改善情绪的绝佳生食，故选D。

4. C。细节理解题。根据Foods high in vitamin C一栏可知西红柿富含维生素C，所以A项表述正确；根据Whole grains一栏可知全谷物可以提升大脑内血清素的含量，所以B项表述正确；根据Whole grains一栏可知糙米属于全谷物，并没有提到其维生素D含量高，所以C项表述错误；根据Different types of milk一栏中的vitamin

D may be helpful in improving mood and sleep（维生素 D 有利于提升情绪和助眠）和 Milk can be a good source of vitamin D（奶液是摄取维生素 D 的一个好来源）可知牛奶有助于睡眠，所以 D 项表述正确。根据题意，故选 C。

5. B。主旨大意题。本文主要介绍了四类有助于缓解焦虑情绪的食物和饮料，所以 B 项最适合作为本文标题，故选 B。

Friday【E 任务型阅读】

● 答案解析

1. F。空格前面是一个问句，意为：但是这些松脆的零食对你的健康真的有好处吗？由此可知空格处是对前面问句的回答，结合选项可知 F 项 In fact, whether rice cakes are healthy or not depends on the type of rice cakes you buy（事实上，米饼是否健康取决于你买的米饼的类型）符合要求，故选 F。

2. B。空格处位于段首，一般为过渡句或段落的主旨句。下文列出了食用米饼的好处，B 项 Here are some benefits of rice cakes（以下是米饼的一些好处）能引出下文，符合语境，故选 B。

3. D。空格处位于段尾，通常是对该段落或前面内容的总结。空格前面提到全谷物可以控制人体的血糖水平及其原因，在所给选项中，D 项 Therefore, they don't cause an increase in blood sugar（因此，它们不会导致血糖升高）中有总结性的标志词语 Therefore，且有该段的关键词 blood sugar，故选 D。

4. G。该段主要是讲米饼有助于保持健康的体重。空格前面讲述如何吃米饼有助于保持健康的体重。在所给选项中，G 项 Making that three times a week could result in nearly six pounds of weight loss over a year（每周吃三次可以在一年内减少近 6 磅的体重）承接上文，继续讲述如何吃米饼有助于减重，其中 that 指代上文"吃一个原味百吉饼和两个糙米饼"的做法，故选 G。

5. A。空格处位于文章最后一段的段首，通常是对整篇文章或段落的总结。在所给选项中，A 项 In general, rice cakes are a healthy snack（总体来说，米饼是一种健康的零食）符合要求，In general 通常用于总结性的话语中，故选 A。

Saturday【F 短文填空】

● 答案解析

（1）experience。空格前面有不定冠词 a 和形容词 terrible，由此可知空格处需填入可数名词单数，在所给选项中只有 experience 符合语法要求，且代入句中符合句意，意为"一次糟糕的经历"，故填 experience。

（2）influence。空格前面有情态动词 can，由此可知空格处需填入动词原形，在所给选项中 influence、kill、prevent 符合语法要求。空格所在部分意为：CDC 的数据表明，根据目的地和季节的不同，它可能_____30%~70% 的旅行者。将符合语法要求的单词代入句中，只有 influence 符合句意。kill 意为"杀死"，旅行者腹泻致命的概率没有那么大，不符合常识，故填 influence。

（3）but。空格前后都是完整的句子，由此可知空格处需填入连词，且空格前后两句的句意发生转折，在所给选项中 but 符合要求，故填 but。

（4）possible。as... as possible 是固定搭配，意为"尽可能……"，符合句意，故填 possible。

（5）of。空格前面有单词 because，空格后面是名词短语，由此可知这里需填入一个介词，与 because 一起构成介词短语作原因状语，because of 为固定搭配，故填 of。

（6）difficult。空格前面有 be 动词，It 为形式主语，后面的不定式短语 to avoid travelers' diarrhea 为真正的主语，由此可知空格处需填入一个形容词，在所给选项中只有 difficult 符合要求，故填 difficult。

（7）prevent。the way to do sth. 意为"做某事的方式"，由此可知空格处需填入一个动词原形。在剩余的选项中，只有 prevent 和 kill 符合要求。空格所在句意为：_____旅行者腹泻的最佳办法是注意饮食。prevent 意为"预防"，符合句意，故填 prevent。

（8）where。空格前面是地点副词 anywhere，空格后面是一个完整的句子，由此可知空格处需填入一个定语从句的引导词，在所给选项中，只有 where 符合要求，引导定语从句修饰 anywhere，故填 where。

（9）attention。pay attention to 是固定搭配，意为"注意；重视"，符合句意，故填 attention。

（10）kill。空格前面是情态动词 can，由此可知空格处需填入动词原形，所剩的最后一个选项 kill 符合要求，代入句中意为"杀菌"，故填 kill。

Week Five
Monday【A 完形填空】
答案解析

1. B。考查名词辨析和上下文语义。A项意为"父亲",B项意为"邻居",C项意为"朋友"。空格所在句的意思是"在那些过着现代城市生活的人当中,许多人甚至不知道他们的_____是谁"。根据句意和常识可知,B项代入后最符合文意,故选B。

2. A。考查介词辨析。在表达时间时,in表示"在某世纪、年、季度、月、周";on表示"在具体某一天";at表示"在某一时刻"。空格后是Nov. 8,表示"11月8日",具体日期前要用介词on,故选A。

3. C。考查名词辨析和上下文语义。A项意为"医生",B项意为"老师",C项意为"导演"。空格所在句的意思是"_____在那些常常被忽视的角落里寻找那些不易被人察觉的动人时刻,这些时刻展现了人与人之间简单而真挚的关系"。上一句指出这档真人秀节目于11月8日在腾讯首播,该句应与上文呼应,C项代入后符合文意,故选C。

4. A。考查动词辨析。A项意为"帮助",B项意为"带走",C项意为"询问"。空格所在句的意思是"在这七期节目中,每一期都有两位受欢迎的明星花上几天时间与当地人一起工作,无论这些人是一群穿梭在城市里_____人们完成日常任务的跑腿员,还是哈萨克族的牧民家庭"。根据句意可知,跑腿员是帮助人们完成日常任务的人,故选A。

5. B。考查固定搭配。A项意为"即使",B项意为"不仅",C项意为"尽管"。空格所在句的意思是"这些明星走出他们的舒适区,他们的自我探索_____会丰富自身对生活的理解,也会丰富观众对生活的理解"。空格后出现了but also,由此可知空格处应填入not only, not only... but also...为固定短语,表示"不仅……而且……",符合句意,故选B。

6. C。考查形容词辨析和上下文语义。A项意为"简单的",B项意为"古老的",C项意为"现代的"。空格所在部分的意思是"你可以感受到_____中国人的总体风貌"。结合全文可知,《奇遇·人间角落》这档节目记录的是现代普通人的生活,C项符合文意,故选C。

7. B。考查固定搭配。be willing to do sth.是固定短语,表示"愿意做某事",故选B。

8. A。考查名词辨析。A项意为"条件",B项意为"目的",C项意为"承诺"。空格所在部分的意思是"(节目中的)一些人可能会在艰苦的_____下工作,他们可能会抱怨"。由此可知,只有A项代入后符合文意,故选A。

Tuesday【B 阅读理解】
答案解析

1. B。细节理解题。根据题干关键词the forum held定位到第一段最后一句。根据该句中的a forum that was held at Fosun Foundation in Shanghai(上海复星艺术中心举办的讨论会)可知,该讨论会在上海举办,故选B。

2. A。细节理解题。根据题干关键词Her Power Fashion Dialogue和women's power and responsibilities定位到第二段第一句。该句指出,Titled Her Power Fashion Dialogue and held by the Shanghai Fashion Week Organizing Committee, the forum used speeches and roundtable discussions to explore women's power and responsibilities through fashion...(该讨论会名为"她力量时尚对话",由上海时装周组委会举办,通过演讲和圆桌对话的方式……探讨了女性在时尚行业中的力量和责任)。由此可知,该讨论会通过演讲和圆桌对话的方式探讨了女性在时尚行业中的力量和责任,故选A。

3. B。词义猜测题。根据题干关键词定位到第二段最后一句。该句的意思是:作为主讲人,甄砚分享了自2021年4月起由联合会和上海时装周共同_____的"天才妈妈×东乡绣娘"等公益时尚活动。将三个选项代入文中,只有B项符合文意,故选B。

4. A。细节理解题。根据题干关键词women embroiderers定位到第三段第一句。根据该句中的these fashion events helped women embroiderers from underdeveloped areas display and sell their intangible cultural heritage handicrafts to cities, helping to improve their living conditions(这些时尚活动帮助不发达地区的绣娘展示并向城市出售她们的非物质文化遗产手工艺品,帮助改善她们的生活条件)可知A项正确。C项"帮助她们变得富有"言过其实。故选A。

5. C。细节理解题。根据题干关键词cross-disciplinary cooperation定位到第三段最后一句。该句指出,Cross-disciplinary cooperation, as well as today's dialogue, are

beneficial attempts at public welfare to join hands with fashion industry resources（跨领域合作，以及今天的对话，都是公益事业与时尚产业资源携手合作的有益尝试）。由此可知，跨领域合作对公益事业是有利的，故选 C。

Wednesday【C 短文填空】

● 答案解析

（1）including。根据句子结构可知，空格前的主句 The 66-year-old remembers almost every detail 主干完整，后面是 which 引导的非限制性定语从句，修饰 journey。根据语境可知，空格后的 the Chinese phrases she learned, the...she ate and the places she toured（她学过的中文短语、吃过的……和参观过的地方）是前面 every detail 的内容，故应填入一个表示"包括"的介词，故填 including。

（2）food。根据句子结构可知, the _____ she ate 与前面的 the Chinese phrases she learned 和后面的 the places she toured 并列，故空格处需要填入一个名词，且被 she ate 修饰，根据常识可知吃的东西就是食物，故填 food。

（3）order。空格所在句的意思是"2016 年，_____ 让人们更容易接触这项运动，霍夫罗斯特带领她的团队开设了一家全职乒乓球俱乐部"。由此可知，让人们更容易接触这项运动是霍夫罗斯特开设俱乐部的目的，且空格位于 in _____ to 结构中，in order to 为固定搭配，表示"为了"，符合句意，故填 order。

（4）play。空格处位于 and 后，visit China 与 _____ with top ping-pong players there 为并列关系，由此可知空格处需填入一个动词，且为动词原形。根据句意"她希望俱乐部的球员有更多的机会访问中国，与那里的顶尖乒乓球运动员一起_____"可知，空格处需填入表示"打球"的词，play 符合要求，故填 play。

（5）important。空格所在句的意思是"这很重要，但更_____的是，我们需要把'火炬'传递给下一代"。由 even more 可知，这里表达的意思是"……是重要的，但更重要的是……"，故填 important。

Thursday【D 任务型阅读】

● 答案解析

1. C。根据句子结构可知，空格所在句主干完整，空格前是人名 Chen Hezhen，有逗号隔开，可知空格处应填入同位语来解释说明 Chen Hezhen，选项中只有 C 项 a 71-year-old grandmother from Ningbo, Zhejiang（来自浙江省宁波市的 71 岁老奶奶）符合要求，故选 C。

2. D。空格前的 Since June 表示"自 6 月以来"，空格后的句子表示"并将其归还给了革命烈士的家属"。上一句指出"修复老兵和烈士的遗物是宁波财经学院社会实践项目的一部分"。第一段最后一句也提到陈荷珍很感激这群来自宁波财经学院的大学生，因为他们让自己珍贵的记忆得以重现。由此可知，空格处句子的主语应该是宁波财经学院的学生，只有 D 项 these young people have helped restore letters and other documents（这些年轻人帮助修复了信件和其他文件）符合要求，空格后的 them 指代的就是"信件和其他文件"，故选 D。

3. A。空格后的 But... 指出"但我们发现这些文书信件有着不同程度的破损，所以就想做些什么来帮忙"。将剩余选项代入文中，只有 A 项 Their family members have saved their letters in memory of them（家属保存了烈士的信件来纪念他们）符合上下文语义，空格后的 those objects 指代的就是"烈士的信件"，故选 A。

4. B。空格位于 However 后面，由此可知空格处的内容与上文构成转折关系。上文提到了"修复书信"，B 项 it isn't easy to restore these relics（要修复这些遗物并不容易）符合逻辑，故选 B。

5. F。空格前面内容的意思是"我需要特别小心和耐心"，空格前的 because 表明空格处的内容是说明需要特别小心和耐心的原因，F 项 the process can take a few weeks just to repair a single page（仅修复一页文件就可能需要几周的时间）符合上下文语义，故选 F。

Friday【E 任务型阅读】

● 答案解析

1. 15。根据题干关键词 female 和 spacewalk 定位到第一段第一句，该句指出 On Nov. 8, Wang Yaping... became China's first and the world's 16th female spacewalker（11 月 8 日……王亚平成为中国首位、世界第 16 位实现太空行走的女航天员）。由此可知，在王亚平之前世界上已有 15 位实现太空行走的女航天员，故答案为 15。

2. They are superior in communication and language expression. 根据题干关键词 Paragraph 2 和 female astronauts 定位到第二段第二句，该句指出, Women are superior in commu-

nication and language expression, and this helps female astronauts perform extravehicular activities(女性在沟通和语言表达方面更胜一筹,这有助于女航天员进行舱外活动)。由此可得出答案。

3. 庞之浩在接受《中国日报》采访时表示,女性通常身材小巧,这是一个优势,因为女性能够更好地控制她们的体重,从而完成更多任务。本句是一个复合句,as 引导的是原因状语从句。generally 表示"通常",control their weight 译为"控制她们的体重"。Pang told China Daily 在翻译时可放在句首,直译为"庞之浩告诉《中国日报》"不太地道,所以可译为"庞之浩在接受《中国日报》采访时表示"。

4. No, he can't. 根据题干关键词 the cabin of spacecraft 定位到第三段最后一句,该句指出,A taikonaut must weigh between 55 kilograms and 70 kilograms to fit in the cabin of spacecraft and consume less fuel, according to CGTN [据中国国际电视台(CGTN)报道,航天员须将体重控制在 55 至 70 千克之间,才能进入宇宙飞船舱,并且消耗更少的燃料]。由此可知,重达 80 千克的汤姆超过了文中所说的体重范围,故汤姆不能进入宇宙飞船舱。

5. I have learned that female astronauts play an important role in carrying out space missions. 本题为开放题,言之有理即可。

Saturday【F 短文填空】

● 答案解析

(1) next。空格所在句的意思是"在上海地铁运营一天后,一些人开始了他们的夜间工作,以确保_____早上的列车对乘客来说是干净和安全的"。根据常识可知,工作人员在夜间工作是为了保证第二天早上的列车是干净和安全的,"第二天早上"可用 the next morning 来表示,故填 next。

(2) manager。空格前有不定冠词 a,由此可知空格处需填入一个可数名词单数来描述杨文青的工作岗位,选项中只有 passenger 和 manager 符合要求。根据第二段第二句中的 A total of 82 workers on her team 和第四句中的 Yang and two of her fellow managers 可知,杨文青是一名经理,其团队有 82 人,故填 manager。

(3) around。根据句子结构可知,空格所在句主干完整,故 the city 前应填入一个介词,构成介词短语,在句中作状语。around the city 表示"在全市",符合文意,故填 around。

(4) go。根据句子结构可知,空格所在句包含两个并列谓语,由 and 连接,and 后的谓语 work 为一般现在时,故空格处的谓语也应用一般现在时。选项中只有 go 符合此处语境,go to work 表示"去工作",符合上下文语义,故填 go。

(5) quality。空格所在句的意思是"杨文青和她的两位经理同事也在夜间进行协调工作并检查他们的工作_____"。空格处应填入一个名词,选项中只剩下 quality、passenger、work、help 符合要求,将其一一代入文中,只有 quality 符合文意,表示"检查他们的工作质量",故填 quality。

(6) because。根据句子结构可知,空格前后是两个句子,空格前的句子意思是"列车清洁是一项要求很高的工作",空格后的句子意思是"所有工作都必须在特定的时间内完成",由此可知,空格前后是因果关系,且后一句为原因,故应填入表示原因的连词,选项中只有 because 符合要求,故填 because。

(7) between。空格后为 40 and 55(40 到 55 岁),表示年龄范围,由此可知空格处应填入 between,between...and...为固定用法,表示"在……和……之间",故填 between。

(8) worked。空格所在句是由 and 连接的并列句,and 前的句子意思是"杨文青从 1999 年开始在上海地铁做保洁工作",and 后的句子意思是"在 1 号线、2 号线和 3 号线的车站_____"。空格处需填入一个动词,选项中只有 work 符合此处语义,表示杨文青从 1999 年开始,一直到现在,都在地铁站工作,且在三条地铁线工作过,所以应用现在完成时,结合空格前的 has 可知空格处应填入 work 的过去分词形式,故填 worked。

(9) but。根据句子结构可知,空格前后是两个句子,空格前的句子意思是"我们的工作看似微不足道",空格后的句子意思是"我们将确保……的安全乘坐体验作为我们的责任",由此可知前后为转折关系,故填 but。

(10) passengers。空格所在部分的意思是"我们将确保_____的安全乘坐体验作为我们的责任"。空格处位于 for 后,故空格处应填入一个名词,passenger 符合上下文语义,而此处指的是所有乘客,要用复数,故填 passengers。

# Week Six

Monday【A 完形填空】

答案解析

1. **B**。考查动词辨析。A 项意为"切断"，B 项意为"开启"，C 项意为"连接"。空格后所接宾语是一个艺术节，B 项代入后意为"开启了一个艺术节"，即拉开艺术节的序幕，符合逻辑，将 A、C 两项代入原文都不符合逻辑，故选 B。

2. **C**。考查介词辨析。空格后的 October 为表示月份的名词，表示"在……月"用介词 in，故选 C。

3. **B**。考查动词辨析。A 项意为"唱"，B 项意为"写"，C 项意为"画"。空格前的 lyrics 意为"歌词"，由常识可知，应该是"写"歌词，因此只有 B 项符合逻辑，故选 B。

4. **A**。考查形容词辨析。A 项意为"欢迎的"，B 项意为"有趣的"，C 项意为"丢失的"。由文意可知，这首歌是为欢迎各国参与北京冬奥会和冬季残奥会的人们所作，因此只有 A 项符合文意，故选 A。

5. **C**。考查固定搭配。将 A、B、C 三项代入原文，只有 C 项能与 is 和 for 构成固定搭配 be known for，意为"因……而出名"，符合文意，其他两项皆无法构成合理搭配，故选 C。

6. **B**。考查动词辨析。A 项意为"找到"，B 项意为"表演"，C 项意为"开发；发展"。空格所在句为定语从句，修饰 the theme song。将 A、B、C 三项代入原文中只有 B 项符合文意，意为"由……在开幕式上演唱"，故选 B。

7. **A**。考查动词辨析。A 项意为"带领"，B 项意为"带走；拿走"，C 项意为"结束"。由上文可知，王平久是这首歌的词作者，将 A、B、C 三项代入原文，只有 A 项符合文意，意为"王平久……带领团队创作了《北京欢迎你》这首歌"，故选 A。

8. **C**。考查从属连词辨析。空格后为完整的句子，不缺成分，因此空格处所填词在从句中不作成分，只起到与主句连接的作用，只有 C 项 that 符合条件，该 that 从句补充说明 glad 的原因，故选 C。

9. **B**。考查动词辨析。A 项意为"借给"，B 项意为"带来"，C 项意为"支付"。将 A、B、C 三项代入原文，只有 B 项符合文意，意为"给人们带来像《北京欢迎你》所传递的那种温暖和快乐"，故选 B。

10. **A**。考查动词辨析。A 项意为"记得"，B 项意为"忘记"，C 项意为"期待"。将 A、B、C 三项代入原文，只有 A 项符合文意，意为"他记得他花了很长时间才给这首新歌起了个名字"，故选 A。

Tuesday【B 阅读理解】

答案解析

1. **A**。细节理解题。根据题干中的关键信息 tiger-themed exhibition 定位到表格第一栏，可知本展览开始向公众开放的时间为 2022 年 1 月 19 日，故选 A。

2. **B**。细节理解题。根据题干中的关键信息 at the art museum of China National Academy of Painting 定位到表格第二栏，可知在中国国家画院美术馆举行的展览是以"和谐"为主题的展览，故选 B。

3. **D**。细节理解题。根据题干中的关键信息 The style of *Sui Zhao Tu* paintings 定位到表格第三栏，可知《岁朝图》所采用的风格是为了庆祝春节而诞生。该栏第三段还提到此风格原本是为了迎合贵族和知识分子的品味，并不是普通民众，因此 A 项不符合原文内容。原文未提及宋朝皇帝以及齐白石的老师，因此排除 B 项和 C 项。故选 D。

Wednesday【C 阅读理解】

答案解析

1. **B**。细节理解题。根据题干中的关键信息 positive、future development 和 among young Chinese 定位到第一段最后 more than 60 percent have a positive view on its future development among young Chinese。由此可知，超过 60% 的受访者对冬季运动未来在中国年轻人中的发展持积极态度。题干中的 Over 和 opinion 分别为原文中 more than 和 view 的同义表达，故选 B。

2. **D**。细节理解题。根据题干中的关键信息 survey report 和 made 定位到第二段。根据本段中的 according to the survey report, which was made by Tsinghua University's Center for Development of Sports Industry and Youth.cn 可知，该调查报告由清华大学体育产业发展研究中心和中国青年网联合发布，故选 D。

3. **A**。细节理解题。根据题干中的关键信息 Young people follow winter sports mainly 定位到第七段。根据本段中的 Social media has become the main way for young people to follow winter sports 可知，社交媒体已经成为年轻人关注

冬季运动的主要渠道。题干中的 mainly by 为原文中 the main way 的同义表达，故选 A。

4. C。推理判断题。该文章围绕一项针对中国年轻人冬季运动参与情况的调查展开，由此可知文章主题是运动，因此该文章应该是被发表在与运动相关的报纸、杂志或者书籍上。C 项为"一份体育报"，故选 C。

5. B。观点态度题。文章列举了多项调查数据。从第一段中的 more than 60 percent have a positive view on its future development among young Chinese（超过 60% 的受访者对冬季运动未来在中国年轻人中的发展持积极态度）可知，超过一半人对冬季运动在年轻人中的发展持积极态度。此外，从第三段提供的调查数据可知，近一半的受访者对冬季运动有了更多的关注和了解，并且有相当一部分人愿意做冬奥会志愿者。因此，纵览文章可知，调查对象对冬奥会持支持的态度，故选 B。

Thursday【D 任务型阅读】

● 答案解析

1. D。空格处为欧盟驻华大使在开幕式上的致辞，那么可以推测此处应当是描述文学节主题类的总起性话语。五个选项中，D 项 We stress the diversity and creativity of women writers across the EU and China in this year's literary festival（今年的文学节我们着重探讨欧盟国家和中国的女性作家所具有的多样性和创造性）最符合文意，故选 D。

2. A。空格后有转折连词 but，因此可知空格处的内容与 but 后的内容意思相反。剩下的选项中，只有 A 项 The true value of women's writing was out of people's sight for a long time（女性写作的真正价值长期受到忽视）符合语境，其中 out of people's sight 和 has gradually been seen 意思相反。其他选项与空格后的内容在意思或者语法上无法连贯，故选 A。

3. C。该空位于段首，其作用可能是承接上文或者开启下文。下文中的 At this moment of social change 明显具有指向性，因此可推测空格处内容描述的就是与"社会变革"有关的内容。剩下的选项中，B 项和 E 项代入原文后意思与上下文不连贯；C 项代入后符合文意，与下文可以承接，故选 C。

4. E。该空为 Lidia 所说的话，剩下的选项中 E 项指出，在过去，女性无法写作。空格后指出，如今的情况变了。

两句为转折关系，且符合如今女性写作越来越重要的主题，故选 E。

5. B。空格处的内容仍然是 Lidia 所说的话，而空格后提到了另一个作家，因此可推测空格处的内容承接空格前的内容。空格前提到，葡萄牙开展了多次运动，使得女性可以捍卫自己的写作权；B 项指出，女性仍然有很多地方还没有涉足和探索过，因此该项从内容上可承接空格前的句子，故选 B。

Friday【E 任务型阅读】

● 答案解析

1. He is an actor and singer. 根据题干中的关键信息 Georgios Sochos 定位到第一段中的 Ten years after his last show as actor and singer with the Greek National Opera, Georgios Sochos stands...（距乔治奥斯·索科斯作为希腊国家歌剧院的演员兼歌手进行最后一次表演的十年之后，他站在……），由此可知，索科斯是一名演员兼歌手。

2. A similar project run by the English National Opera in London. 根据题干中的关键信息 a free-of-charge online program 定位到第五段中的 Inspired by a similar project run by the English National Opera in London, the National Theater of Greece started in May a free-of-charge online program（受伦敦英国国家歌剧院一个类似项目的启发，希腊国家剧院于 5 月推出了一个免费在线项目），由此可知，该项目的灵感来源于英国国家歌剧院的一个类似项目。

3. To help people who have difficulty in breathing and those who get great stress. 根据题干中的关键信息 purpose 和 free-of-charge online program 定位到第五段中的 a free-of-charge online program developed by a team of professionals to help people who have difficulty in breathing and those who get great stress（一个由专家团队开发的免费在线项目，以援助遭受呼吸困难和压力巨大的人），由此可知，该项目的目的是援助遭受呼吸困难和压力巨大的人。

4. By using voice and the mechanism of breathing. 根据题干中的关键信息 Aggeliki Toubanaki 和 to deal with their wounds 定位到倒数第二段中的 Toubanaki helps her students to use voice and the mechanism of breathing to deal with their wounds, both physical and psychological（图巴纳基帮助自己的学生使用声音和呼吸法来应对他

们的身体和心理创伤），由此可知，图巴纳基通过声音和呼吸法帮助学生治疗伤痛。

5. **They need to communicate their experiences, all those strong feelings that they have from their time in hospital.** 根据题干中的关键信息 patients 定位到最后一段中的 All patients need to communicate their experiences, all those strong feelings that they have from their time in hospital（所有的病人都需要交流他们的经历，以及他们在住院期间的所有强烈的感受），由此可知，病人需要交流各自的经历和感受。此题用文中原句回答亦可。

Saturday【F 短文填空】
● 答案解析

（1）display。try to do sth. 是 try 的固定用法，表示"试图（或设法）做某事"，因此空格处填 display 的原形，构成动词不定式，故填 display。

（2）means。空格所在句为解释"国风"一词的内容，陈述事实，用一般现在时即可，且 It 为第三人称单数，因此空格处应填 mean 的第三人称单数形式，故填 means。

（3）introduced。根据句意可知，此处的新风格是"被融入"，因此空格处应填 introduce 的过去分词形式，与空格前的 be 动词 were 构成被动语态，表示被动意义，故填 introduced。

（4）producing。根据句子结构可知，空格所在句的主语为 he，该句已经有了一个谓语动词 wanted，因此空格处只能填 produce 的非谓语动词形式；又因 he 与 produce 为逻辑上的主谓关系，所以此处应填 produce 的现在分词形式，表示主动意义，故填 producing。

（5）growing。根据句子结构可知，空格所在句已经有了系动词，因此空格处只能填 grow 的非谓语动词形式；又因 Young people 与 grow 为逻辑上的主谓关系，所以此处应填 grow 的现在分词形式，表示主动意义，故填 growing。

（6）experienced。空格后为名词，由此可知空格处应填 experience 的形容词形式 experienced，且 experienced 意为"经验丰富的"，符合句意，故填 experienced。

（7）tried。空格前为 has，空格后为 to，可知空格处应填 try 的过去分词形式 tried，与 has 构成现在完成时，并与 to 构成搭配，意为"试图"，故填 tried。

（8）hearing。根据句子结构可知，空格所在句已经有了谓语动词（will）get，故空格处只能填 hear 的非谓语动词形式；又因 they 与 hear 为逻辑上的主谓关系，所以此处应填 hear 的现在分词形式，表示主动意义，故填 hearing。

（9）moved。get moved 为固定用法，意为"被打动"，符合句意，其中 moved 为形容词，表示"受感动的"，故填 moved。

（10）to。encourage sb. to do sth. 为动词 encourage 的固定用法，表示"鼓励某人做某事"，故填 to。

Week Seven
Monday【A 完形填空】
● 答案解析

1. B。考查名词辨析。A项意为"书籍"，B项意为"机会"，C项意为"金钱"，D项意为"危险；风险"。空格所在句意为：我们几乎没有_____亲眼看到它们，更不用说触摸或阅读它们了。根据语境可知，"机会"代入后最符合语义，故选B。

2. C。考查动词辨析。A项意为"丢弃，扔"，B项意为"带来"，C项意为"保存"，D项意为"购买"。空格所在句意为：它们必须被_____在国家图书馆或私人机构中。根据语境可知，"保存"代入后最符合语义，故选C。

3. B。考查动词辨析。A项意为"毁坏"，B项意为"修复"，C项意为"选择"，D项意为"创造"。空格所在句意为：开发技术来保护这些书籍并_____那些……遭到部分损坏的书籍是非常重要的。根据语境可知，"修复"代入后最符合语义，故选B。

4. B。考查名词辨析。A项意为"次，回"，B项意为"原因"，C项意为"工作"，D项意为"梦想"。空格所在句意为：开发技术来保护这些书籍并修复那些因各种_____而遭到部分损坏的书籍是非常重要的。根据语境可知，"原因"代入后最符合此处语义，故选B。

5. D。考查连词辨析。A项意为"一……就"，B项意为"除非"，C项意为"尽管"，D项意为"以便；所以"。空格所在句意为：然而，把这些古籍以相同的外观和触感复制出来，_____将它们原本的风格、优美的字迹……呈现……，一直是许多学者的梦想。根据语境可知，"将它们原本的风格等呈现出来"是"把古籍以相同的外观和触感复制出来"的目的，so that（以便）代入后符合语义，故选D。

6. A。考查固定搭配。between the lines 为固定搭配，意为"在字里行间"，故选A。

7. D。考查名词辨析。A项意为"作者"，B项意为"工人"，C项意为"管理员"，D项意为"读者"。空格所在部分意为：以便将……以及古代文人写在字里行间的思想和感情呈现给_____。根据语境可知，书本中的内容应该是呈现给读者的，readers 最符合语义，故选D。

8. B。考查固定搭配。A项意为"寻找"，B项意为"做；使得"，C项意为"错过；想念"，D项意为"说"。空格所在句意为：一些出版社已经_____努力。根据空格后一句"但复制的古籍并没有按系列出版，其质量也可能有所差异"可知，空格处应表达积极含义，且 make the effort 表示"做出努力"，符合语义，故选B。

9. C。考查固定搭配。A项意为"在……之前"，B项意为"因为"，C项意为"直到……为止"，D项意为"自从；因为"。空格所在句意为：_____2018年华宝斋工作室出版了《中华善本百部经典再造》，复制的书籍的质量才变得比原版好。根据上文所说的"质量也可能有所差异"和该句中的"质量变得比原版好"可知，前后形成对比。结合空格前的 not 可知，此处为 It was not until...that... 的固定句型，且 until 代入后符合语义，故选C。

10. C。考查上下文语义。A项意为"最小的"，B项意为"最差的"，C项意为"最好的"，D项意为"最大的"。空格所在句意为：直到2018年华宝斋工作室出版了《中华善本百部经典再造》，复制的书籍的质量才变得比原版好，一些知名古籍的很多_____版本才可以被（人们）按照原版阅读。此处指复制书籍质量的改善，best 代入后最符合语义，故选C。

11. D。考查副词辨析。A项意为"立即"，B项意为"曾经"，C项意为"很少"，D项意为"经常，通常"。空格所在句意为：同一本古籍_____有好几个版本，不同学者的注解使得其质量……。根据空格后的"不同学者的注解"可知，同一本古籍应该是有多个版本，因此 usually 最符合此处语义，故选D。

12. A。考查名词辨析。A项意为"差异，不同"，B项意为"洞"，C项意为"猜想"，D项意为"希望"。空格所在句意为：同一本古籍往往有好几个版本，不同学者的注解使得其质量也有所_____。根据语境可知，只有"差异，不同"代入后符合此处语义，故选A。

13. D。考查形容词辨析。A项意为"令人愉快的"，B项意为"无聊的"，C项意为"容易的"，D项意为"重要的"。空格所在句意为：所以对那种系列图书来说，选择每本书的最佳版本_____，因为它会反映这套图书的整体质量。根据空格后的"因为它会反映这套图书的整体质量"可知，"选择每本书的最佳版本"是很重要的，D项符合语义，故选D。

14. D。考查介词辨析。A项意为"从……中出去"，B项意为"在……后面"，C项意为"……的"，D项意为"从；从……起"。空格所在句意为：（专家们）组织了一个团队，_____数千家图书馆保存的成千上万本古籍中选择最佳版本。根据语境可知，空格部分应表示"从……中选择"，from 符合语义，故选 D。

15. B。考查名词辨析。A 项意为"计划"，B 项意为"变化"，C 项意为"错误"，D 项意为"陈述"。空格所在句意为：甚至在整套书出版之后，特定书籍的版本也一直在发生_____。"计划""错误"和"陈述"三个选项代入后均不符合逻辑，只有"变化"符合语义，故选 B。

Tuesday【B 阅读理解】
● 答案解析

1. C。细节理解题。第二段第一句指出 My first visit, to Beijing, in 1987 was short, and I only paid attention to large and important architectural masterpieces dating back to the Ming Dynasty（1987 年我第一次来北京时，待的时间很短，我只关注了可追溯到明朝的大型、重要的建筑杰作）。由此可知，A、B、D 三项正确，C 项错误，故选 C。

2. B。细节理解题。第二段第三句指出 Walking daily, I started to understand a certain order about the direction of alleys, the location of buildings such as traditional *siheyuan* and how they were arranged（在每天散步的过程中，我开始了解有关小巷的走向、传统四合院等建筑物的位置以及布局的某种章法）。由此可知，作者是通过每天散步时观察得知北京小巷的走向章法的，故选 B。

3. A。细节理解题。第三段第二句指出 Gradually I started to concentrate on how the historic Beijing was built around a big plan that envisaged a central axis line at its heart（渐渐地，我的思绪开始集中在具有历史意义的北京是如何围绕着一个设想以中轴线为核心的宏伟计划建造的）。由此可知，在计划修建具有历史意义的北京时设想的核心是 a central axis line，故选 A。

4. B。细节理解题。第四段第二句指出 Forbidden City, built during 1406-1420, sits exactly on the axis, representing its position then at the center of China（于 1406 年至 1420 年修建的故宫正好位于轴线上，代表它当时处于中国的中心位置）。由此可知，将故宫修建在轴线上是为了展示它的重要性，故选 B。

Wednesday【C 任务型阅读】
● 答案解析

1. An interesting picture of ancient cultural exchange routes across the Qinghai-Tibet Plateau. 第一段指出 An interesting picture of ancient cultural exchange routes across the Qinghai-Tibet Plateau is appearing from below ground（一幅横跨青藏高原的古代文化交流路线的有趣画面正从地底浮现），由此可知本题答案。

2. Tashi Tsering. 第三段第二句指出 For Tashi Tsering, who introduced the findings during an online conference on Jan. 13, the site offers exciting prospects（扎西次仁在 1 月 13 日的在线会议上介绍了发现成果，对他来说，该遗址提供了令人振奋的前景）。由此可知，在在线会议上介绍发现成果的是扎西次仁，故答案为 Tashi Tsering。

3. By visiting the Damshung site. 第五段指出 As a result, communication between the two sides was certain to happen, and can be seen clearly by visiting the Damshung site（因此，双方之间的交流是必然会发生的，通过参观当雄墓地就可以清楚地看出这一点）。由此可知，可以通过参观当雄墓地看出吐蕃王国和唐朝之间的交流，故答案为 By visiting the Damshung site。

4. In Central China. 倒数第二段指出 Go, of course, originated in Central China and was very popular during the Tang Dynasty（围棋当然起源于中原，在唐代非常流行），由此可知答案为 In Central China。

5. Because it proves cultural exchanges between the Tang Dynasty and Tubo, explaining how different ethnic groups came together. 最后一段中指出 These discoveries provide important information to prove cultural exchanges between the Tang Dynasty and Tubo, explaining how different ethnic groups came together（这些发现为证明唐朝和吐蕃之间的文化交流提供了重要信息，解释了不同民族是如何融合在一起的），由此可知本题答案。

Thursday【D 任务型阅读】
● 答案解析

1. of; by。(A) 空格前为 the name，空格后为 their village，根据语境可知，此处要表达的是"他们村的名字"，表示所属关系应使用介词 of，故 (A) 空填 of；(C) 空格前为谓语部分 was built，空格后为表示对象的 Emperor Zhangzong of the Jin Dynasty，被动语态中表示"由……，被……"应使用介词 by，故 (C) 空格填 by。

2. research；found。(B) 处的 study 表示"研究"，其同义词可以填 research；(E) 处的 discovered 表示"发现"，其同义词可以填 found。

3. Emperor Zhangzong/the emperor visited the site twice。该句翻译起来比较简单，很多单词在文中都可以找到，"两次"的表达为 twice。

4. less；than。画线句子的意思为"其重要性仅次于金朝首都"，题干中将名词 importance 改成了形容词 important。此处要表达"没有金朝首都那么重要"，应使用形容词的比较级，所以前面应填 less，后面应填 than。

5. period；month。文中表示时间的名词有 period（时期，期间）、dynasty（朝代）和 month（月份）等，任意选择两个即可。注意不要填写表示具体年份或年代的词（如 1970s、1202 等）。

Friday【E 短文填空】
● 答案解析

（1）proved。空格所在处意为"陕西省省会城市西安一座具有 2 000 多年历史的大型墓地被证明属于西汉一位著名的皇帝"，根据句子结构可知，空格处为被动语态，应填动词的过去分词形式，故填 proved。

（2）third。空格所在处意为"刘恒，又被称为汉文帝，是西汉的第三位皇帝"。由句意和空格前的定冠词 the 可知，空格处应填序数词，括号中所给的单词 three 是基数词，其序数词为 third，故填 third。

（3）possible。空格所在处意为"古文献显示了文帝陵的可能位置，但其具体位置一直不清楚"。根据句子结构可知，空格处所填词修饰名词 location，所以应该填入一个形容词，括号中所给的单词为副词，其形容词为 possible，故填 possible。

（4）areas。根据空格前的限定词 some 和空格后的谓语 were raided 可知，主语应为复数名词，因此应该填入括号中所给名词的复数形式，故填 areas。

（5）were。根据句子结构可知，空格处为被动语态，因为主语是 the structure and objects，为复数，且"挖"的

动作发生在过去，所以此处的 be 动词应该使用过去式，故填 were。

（6）More。根据空格后的 than 可知，空格处应出现比较级，括号中所给词为 many，其比较级为 more，more than 表示"超过"，符合语义，故填 More。

（7）to rule。根据空格前的 wanted 和括号中所给的动词 rule（统治）可知，此处构成 want to do sth. 的结构，故填 to rule。

Saturday【F 短文填空】
● 答案解析

（1）ancient history。空格前一句指出广东省对当代中国的重要性，空格所在句指出"然而，在谈到其_____时，往往会出现一种刻板的观点"。根据空格所在句中的 However 可知，该句与上一句之间为转折关系，两句形成对比，即该句应该是在谈论广东省在古代的情况，ancient history 符合语境，故填 ancient history。

（2）rich documents。根据空格所在句中的 Compared with 可知，逗号前后形成对比，空格后指出"有关该时期的广东的信息和故事不够多"，空格所在部分指出"与现有的向我们讲述中原地区 2 000 多年前的生活的_____相比"，由前后的对比关系可知，rich documents 与 there isn't enough information and stories 相对应，符合逻辑，故填 rich documents。

（3）than people thought。根据空格前的比较级 greater 可知，than people thought 填入后构成完整的比较级，符合此处语境，故填 than people thought。

（4）an area of。根据空格后的 80,000 square meters 可知，空格处所填词需要能够修饰数词，an area of 代入后符合语境，故填 an area of。

（5）the lower-level。空格前一句指出 In high-level tombs, there are many jade artifacts and many other kinds of objects（在高级墓葬中，有很多玉器和许多其他种类的物品）。空格所在句指出 But in _____ ones, only some stones and pottery were found [但在_____墓葬中，（考古人员）只发现了一些石头和陶器]。根据语境可知，此处前后两句形成对比，讲述高级葬墓和低级葬墓中物品的区别，空格后面的 ones 指代 tombs，the lower-level 代入后符合语境，故填 the lower-level。

Week Eight
Monday【A 完形填空】

答案解析

1. **B**。考查形容词辨析。A项意为"不同的",B项意为"相似的",C项意为"自豪的",D项意为"正确的"。空格上文提到the meaning of wedding rings(婚戒的含义),这里是用婚戒的含义引出对奥运五环含义的解释,但是下文又提到much more than that(远不止于此),结合选项可知,奥运五环的含义与婚戒的含义相似,但比婚戒的含义更广,故选B。

2. **D**。考查动词辨析。A项意为"拒绝",B项意为"记得",C项意为"忘记",D项意为"将……算入;包括"。空格所在部分意为:1912年的奥林匹克运动会第一次_____来自五大洲的运动员。将选项中的单词代入句中可知,"将……算入;包括"符合句意,故选D。

3. **A**。考查名词辨析。A项意为"标志",B项意为"问题",C项意为"梦想",D项意为"优势"。空格所在句意为:顾拜旦设计了后来成为全球奥林匹克运动会_____的东西——奥运五环。根据常识可知,奥运五环是奥林匹克运动会的标志,故选A。

4. **C**。考查介词辨析。A项意为"达,计",后跟时间段;B项意为"在……之前";C项意为"自……以来",后跟具体的时间点,如年、月、日等;D项意为"在……之后"。空格后面是1920,为具体的年份,且本句时态为现在完成时,故选C。

5. **A**。考查形容词辨析。A项意为"特殊的",B项意为"重要的",C项意为"轻的",D项意为"常见的"。空格上文提到Humans have long used rings or circles as symbols(长期以来,人类一直使用圆环或圆圈作为象征),空格所在句中的but表示句意发生转折,说明奥运五环这个标志有别于其他圆环或圆圈,所以"特殊的"符合句意,故选A。

6. **A**。考查动词短语辨析。A项意为"参加(比赛、竞赛)",B项意为"用完",C项意为"逃离",D项意为"盼望"。空格后面为the 1912 Games(1912年奥运会),且空格所在定语从句修饰the five continents(五大洲),五大洲的运动员应该是"参加"奥运会,故选A。

7. **B**。考查名词辨析。A项意为"颜色",B项意为"尺寸",C项意为"空间",D项意为"材料"。根据下文all continents are equal at the Games(所有大洲在奥运会上都是平等的)可知,五环的大小(尺寸)应该相同,故选B。

8. **C**。考查同位语从句。空格后面的句子结构完整,解释说明空格前idea的具体内容,所以这里是一个同位语从句,引导词应用that,故选C。

9. **D**。考查副词辨析。A项意为"清楚地",B项意为"幸运地",C项意为"容易地",D项意为"最后地"。根据下文可知,空格所在段落讲的是奥运五环的最后一种象征含义,故选D。

10. **B**。考查动词辨析。A项意为"抓住",B项意为"选择",C项意为"关闭",D项意为"覆盖"。空格所在句意为:顾拜旦_____了六种官方的奥运颜色——蓝、黄、黑、绿、红和白(底色)。将选项中的单词代入句中可知,"选择"符合句意,故选B。

Tuesday【B 阅读理解】

答案解析

1. **D**。细节理解题。根据题干中的关键词the step to create puppets可以定位到第一段第三句,可知木偶的制作包括几个步骤,如选择材料、雕刻、绘画、缝制和上油墨,只有D项不是制作木偶的步骤,故选D。

2. **C**。推理判断题。文章第二段提到all performers hidden behind the scenes(所有表演者都隐藏在幕后),以及performers would start the show after the installation of light boxes and curtains(演出人员在安装好灯箱和幕布后就可以开始表演了),由此可以推断,皮影戏与光影紧密相关,故选C。

3. **B**。细节理解题。由第三段第一句可知皮影戏历史悠久,所以A项错误,B项正确;由第三段第一句可知皮影戏起源于中国西北,而不是东南,所以C项错误;由第四段第一句可知皮影戏有众多分支,所以D项错误。故选B。

4. **B**。词义猜测题。本题问schools在本文中的含义。画线单词所在句意为:北京皮影戏分为东、西两_____。下文介绍了皮影戏的西派代表路德成,由此可知schools在本文中指的是"流派",故选B。

5. **A**。主旨大意题。本文第一段介绍了皮影戏木偶的制作步骤,第二段介绍了皮影戏在过去的演出形式,第三段介绍了皮影戏的起源及其意义,第四段介绍了皮影戏的流派,所以本文的主要内容是介绍皮影戏,故选A。

Wednesday【C 阅读理解】

答案解析

1. C。细节理解题。根据题干中的关键词 Textiles 定位到第一段，由第一段第二句可知，少数民族的纺织品的作用是保护他们的历史，故选 C。

2. C。细节理解题。由第二段第二句中的 which tells age, job, and ethnic origin 可知，维吾尔族人民戴的帽子可以反映出他们的年龄、职业和族源，C 项 Address（地址）本文未提及，故选 C。

3. A。细节理解题。根据题干中的关键词 Miao minority 可以定位到第三段，由 Silver is an important part of their culture 可知，银（饰）在苗族文化中非常重要，故选 A。

4. B。细节理解题。根据题干中的关键词 silver jewelry 和 child 可以定位到最后一段，由 From the time a Miao woman is a child, she has silver jewelry she inherits from her family 可知，苗族妇女从家人那里继承银饰，故选 B。

5. D。主旨大意题。本文主要介绍了维吾尔族和苗族的服饰文化，且本文的第一句便是本文的主旨句，第一句意为：中国各种少数民族传统着装规范对他们的服装产生了很大的影响。在所有选项中，只有 D 项概括了文章大意，故选 D。

Thursday【D 任务型阅读】

答案解析

1. B。空格后提到"当然，情人节的玫瑰并不是只能用于表达浪漫的爱情"，由此可知，空格处应该讲的是人们通常会在情人节送玫瑰。在所给选项中，只有 B 项意思相近，符合此处语境，故选 B。

2. C。空格前面是一个问句：为什么在情人节送玫瑰？空格后面讲的是希腊神话中的关于红玫瑰的故事。由此可知空格处为空格后面内容的总结句。在所有选项中，只有 C 项符合要求，且 C 项中的 several different stories 与空格下文的 Some stories say... Others say... 对应，故选 C。

3. D。空格位于段首，一般为过渡句或段落的主旨句。下文主要提到了 Lady Montagu（蒙塔古夫人）与花语，在所有选项中，D 项提到了 Lady Montagu，符合此处语境，故选 D。

4. A。空格上文提到蒙塔古夫人在家书中谈到了土耳其的花语，空格下文提到这其实与押韵的词语有更大的关系，由此可知空格处句意发生转折。在所给选项中，只有 A 项符合要求，But 表示转折的含义，故选 A。

5. F。空格上文提到，其实在情人节送玫瑰的原因很简单，空格下文提到了鲜花的运输与玫瑰的特质。在所给选项中，F 项中的 Roses are beautiful flowers 对应下文的 roses are both very beautiful，happen to travel really well 对应 hardy。故选 F。

Friday【E 任务型阅读】

答案解析

1. From the Han Dynasty. 根据题干中的关键词 the porcelain-making in Liling 可以定位到第一段第一句 Porcelain-making in Liling dates back to the Han Dynasty，由此可知醴陵制瓷业起源于汉朝。

2. Because a porcelain vase won gold at the Panama Pacific World's Fair in 1915. 题干问的是醴陵制瓷业为什么会变得有名，文中的 making it known 与题干中的 become famous 为同义表达；根据 A porcelain vase won gold at the Panama Pacific World's Fair in 1915 可知，醴陵制瓷业变得有名是因为醴陵产的一个瓷器花瓶在 1915 年的巴拿马太平洋万国博览会上赢得了金奖。

3. The wars of the first half of the 20th century. 根据题干中的关键词 the success 定位到第一段第四句，由此可知是 20 世纪上半叶的战争打断了醴陵制瓷业的发展。

4. There are more than 4,000 types of ceramic products (in five kinds). 根据题干中的关键词 ceramic products 定位到第二段第一句，由此可知醴陵有（五大类）多达 4 000 多种陶瓷制品。

5. Huang Xiaoling thinks that working in the porcelain industry allows having a comfortable life and passing on the skills and culture of our ancestors. 本题问黄小玲对在制瓷行业工作的看法，根据题干中的关键词 Huang Xiaoling 可以定位到最后一段，由黄小玲说的话可以得出答案。

Saturday【F 短文填空】

答案解析

（1）lucky。分析句子结构可知，空格处需填入一个形容词修饰后面的名词 symbol。上文提到携带四叶草会给人带来好运，所以四叶草是一个幸运符号，故填 lucky。

Week Eight 文化风俗

（2）from。come from 为固定搭配，意为"来自"，故填 from。

（3）leaving。空格后面提到夏娃摘了一朵四叶草作为天堂的纪念品，由此可知亚当和夏娃是要离开伊甸园了。由空格前的 were 可知，这里使用的是过去进行时表示"正要离开"，故填 leaving。

（4）that。It is/was believed+that... 为固定句型，意为"人们认为……"，故填 that。

（5）or。分析句子结构可知，空格前后是并列的动宾短语，由此可知空格处需填入一个连词。play terrible tricks 和 steal your children 是凯尔特精灵可能会做出的两种危险性举动，但并不一定会两样都做，所以空格处的连词应表示选择，or 意为"或，或者"，故填 or。

（6）action。分析句子结构可知，空格处需填入一个名词，作 take 的宾语。take action 为固定搭配，意为"采取行动"，故填 action。

（7）Another。分析句子结构可知，空格处所填词修饰后面的名词 story。本文主要讲了两种关于四叶草被视为幸运符号的说法，且上文提到 One story，表示"一种说法"，所以空格处应表示"另一种"，故填 Another。

（8）third。空格前有 one leaf、the next 等表示顺序的词，所以空格处应为表示"第三"的序数词，故填 third。

（9）However。空格上文提到圣帕特里克用三叶草来解释"圣三位一体"，空格下文提到凯尔特人可能早就有了四叶草能带来好运这一信念，前后句意有转折，且空格位于句首，与主句用逗号隔开，故填 However。

（10）leaves。分析句子结构可知，空格处需填入一个名词。空格所在部分意为：这可能是因为很难找到一朵有四片_____的三叶草。leaf（叶子）符合句意，且空格前为 four，应填 leaf 的复数形式，故填 leaves。

Week Nine
Monday【A 完形填空】
● 答案解析

1. B。考查代词辨析。A项意为"我们"，B项意为"它"，C项意为"他"，D项意为"他们"。根据句子结构可知，空格所在句缺少主语，空格所在句的意思是"_____能够杀死……10多种致病菌和病毒"，空格前一句指出"工程师们开发出了一种尖端的空气消毒机"。由此可知空格处指代的是空气消毒机，故选B。

2. C。考查介词辨析和上下文语义。空格前指出"它能够杀死10多种致病菌和病毒"。空格后指出"导致新冠肺炎疫情的新型冠状病毒"。由下文第三段首句可知空格后提到的新型冠状病毒是包括在10多种致病菌和病毒中的，including 表示"包括"，符合上下文语义，故选C。

3. A。考查名词辨析和上下文语义。A项意为"产品"，B项意为"游戏"，C项意为"信息"，D项意为"电话"。空格所在句的意思是"_____得到了一批医学专家和病毒学家的认可"。上文围绕空气消毒机展开，由此可知空格处指的就是空气消毒机，将四个选项代入文中，只有A项符合文意，故选A。

4. C。考查介词辨析。空格后是 Friday，表示具体的某一天应使用介词 on。at 表示"在某一时刻"，in 表示"在世纪、年、季度、月、周"，of 表示所属关系，均不符合此处语境，故均排除。故选C。

5. A。考查形容词辨析和上下文语义。A项意为"新的"，B项意为"简单的"，C项意为"古老的；旧的"，D项意为"漂亮的"。空格所在句的意思是"超过10万台_____产品已被运往河北省张家口市"。结合全文可知，这款空气消毒机是新开发出来的，所以是新产品，A项符合文意，故选A。

6. C。考查动词辨析。A项意为"拿走"，B项意为"出售"，C项意为"使用"，D项意为"持有"。空格所在句的主语是"超过10万台新产品"，即"空气消毒机"。结合上下文可知，这款空气消毒机是被用于防控新冠肺炎疫情的。将四个选项代入文中，只有C项符合文意，表示"在公共场所投入使用"，故选C。

7. D。考查短语辨析。A项意为"特别是"，B项意为"即使"，C项意为"偶然地"，D项意为"此外"。空格所在句的意思是"_____，……人口密集城市的政府大楼、医院、火车站和其他拥挤场所也部署了消毒机"。将四个选项代入文中，只有D项符合文意，指的是除了张家口市，这些地方也都部署了消毒机，故选D。

8. A。考查短语辨析。A项和B项都意为"例如"，C项意为"因为"，D项意为"根据"。空格后的 Beijing, Chongqing and Chengdu 是对前面 densely populated cities（人口密集城市）的举例，由此可知A项和B项符合此处语义，空格位于句中，且后面没有逗号，因此只能用 such as，故选A。

9. B。考查名词辨析。A项意为"选择"，B项意为"测试"，C项意为"决定"，D项意为"发明"。空格所在句的意思是"设计师和疾病控制专家的_____……该设备能够在短短15分钟内杀死其有效工作半径内的几乎所有新型冠状病毒病原体"。将四个选项代入文中，只有B项符合文意，表示"设计师和疾病控制专家的测试"，故选B。

10. B。考查动词辨析。A项意为"使得；制作"，B项意为"显示，表明"，C项意为"说"，D项意为"分享"。空格所在句的意思是"设计师和疾病控制专家的测试_____该设备能够……"。将四个选项代入文中，只有B项符合文意，故选B。

11. D。考查形容词辨析。A项意为"危险的"，B项意为"坏的"，C项意为"活跃的"，D项意为"安全的"。空格所在部分的意思是"并强调它对人类和动物绝对_____"。根据上文可知，空气消毒机能在多个地方投入使用，说明它是安全的，D项符合上下文语义，故选D。

12. B。考查动词辨析。A项意为"忘记"，B项意为"比较"，C项意为"停止"，D项意为"覆盖"。空格所在句的意思是"与化学制剂和紫外线灯等其他消毒方法_____，我们的产品具有零健康危害……"。根据句意可知，这里是将"我们的产品"与其他消毒方法做比较，B项符合文意，故选B。

13. A。考查形容词辨析。A项意为"更高的"，B项意为"更低的"，C项意为"更差的"，D项意为"更轻的"。空格所在句的意思是"与化学制剂和紫外线灯等其他消毒方法相比，我们的产品具有零健康危害、消毒过程更快、有效性_____和运行时间更长的特点"。空格前后都在描述该新产品的优点，所以其有效性肯定比其他方法更高，A项符合文意，故选A。

14. C。考查形容词辨析。A项意为"困难的"，B项意为"不可能的"，C项意为"容易的"，D项意为"流行的"。空格所在句的意思是"它_____使用，不需要额外的成本，而且适合有很多人的室内场所"。结合上下文可知，这款空气消毒机是一项好的发明，且空格后面也在描述其优点，由此可知它是很容易使用的，故选C。

15. A。考查名词辨析。A项意为"过程"，B项意为"结果"，C项意为"历史"，D项意为"目标"。空格所在句的意思是"产品经理们表示，他们已经在开发_____中获得了13项技术和工艺专利"。将四个选项代入文中，只有A项符合文意，故选A。

Tuesday【B 阅读理解】

● 答案解析

1. B。细节理解题。根据题干关键词 developed the driverless car 定位到第一段第二句。该句指出 The driverless car, developed by Chinese information technology company Baidu...（由中国信息技术公司百度开发的无人驾驶汽车……）。由此可知，该无人驾驶汽车是由百度开发的，故选B。A项和C项利用文中的部分信息作干扰，D项在文中未提及，故均排除。

2. D。细节理解题。A项"中国曾在一些重要赛事中使用过无人驾驶汽车"在文中未提及，故错误；B项"无人驾驶汽车载着一名司机行驶了约800米"与文意不符，文中说的是 torch（火炬），故错误；C项"无人驾驶汽车在中国很常见"在文中未提及，故错误；D项"无人驾驶汽车是由一家中国公司发明的"符合文意，第一段指出"由中国信息技术公司百度开发的无人驾驶汽车"，故选D。

3. A。语篇理解题。根据题干关键词 automobile industry's future 定位到第二段第一句。该句指出"百度智能驾驶事业群副总裁魏东说：'我们更愿意称它为机器人，因为我们将在日常生活中越来越多地接触到移动机器人。'他补充说，这辆汽车代表着汽车行业的未来"。由此可知，人们未来的生活中一定会有更多的移动机器人，所以这款汽车代表着汽车行业的未来，A项符合文意，故选A。

4. C。细节理解题。根据题干关键词 commercialized autonomous driving project 定位到第三段最后一句。该句指出 It's the first commercialized autonomous driving project in China（这是中国第一个商业化的自动驾驶项目）。该句中的 It 指代上一句中的 robot taxis，由此可知C项正确，故选C。

5. C。细节理解题。A项"在机器人出租车上，必须有一名安全员坐在驾驶座上"与第四段第二句相符；B项"机器人出租车沿着预先设定好的路线行驶"、D项"机器人出租车会在变道时使用转向灯"与第四段第三句相符；C项"机器人出租车不能在整段行程中自动运行"与第四段第三句中的 can operate automatically throughout the whole trip（能在整段行程中自动运行）不符，故选C。

Wednesday【C 阅读理解】

● 答案解析

1. B。细节理解题。根据题干关键词 traffic jams 定位到第一段第一句。该句指出"交通拥堵在世界各地的城市都是一个普遍问题"，接下来的第二句表明"司机希望自己能从挡道的车辆上方飞过去"，第三句又指出 Such goals may be achieved sooner than many expect, with "flying cars"... fast becoming a reality（随着"飞行汽车"……迅速成为现实，这样的目标可能会比许多人预期的更早实现）。由此可知，飞行汽车可以解决交通拥堵的问题，故选B。

2. A。细节理解题。根据题干关键词 HT Aero 和 introduce 定位到第二段。该段指出 HT Aero, an affiliate of Chinese electric vehicle maker Xpeng, showed a flying car late last month, saying it plans to introduce these vehicles in 2024（上个月月末，中国电动汽车制造商小鹏汽车的子公司HT Aero展示了一款飞行汽车，并表示计划在2024年推出这种汽车）。由此可知，A项符合文意，故选A。

3. C。细节理解题。根据题干关键词cost定位到第三段第二句。该句指出 ...each vehicle will cost less than 1 million yuan（每辆车……将花费不到100万人民币），由此可知每辆飞行汽车将花费不到100万人民币，C项符合原文，故选C。

4. A。细节理解题。根据题干关键词 led to increased interest 定位到第三段最后一句。该句指出"'几种趋势的趋同'导致人们增加了对它的兴趣"。接着第四段里德尔指出 First, on-demand services... Second, there's a focus... Third, there's a lot of funding...（第一，按需服务……第二，关注……第三，……大量资金）。由此可知里德尔提到了3个原因，故选A。

5. D。细节理解题。根据题干关键词 flying vehicles 和 ordinary vehicles 定位到最后一段第三句 Flying vehicles are typically about the size of ordinary ones, or slightly larger（飞

行汽车的大小通常和普通汽车差不多，或者稍微大一些）。D项是对原文的同义改写，符合文意。C项与原文不符，可排除。根据最后一段最后一句可知，A项中的400错误，B项中的ordinary vehicles错误，故均排除，故选D。

Thursday【D 阅读理解】

答案解析

1. C。细节理解题。根据题干关键词the robotic shark 和displayed 定位到第一段第二句 The robotic shark has been on display in an aquarium at Shanghai Haichang Ocean Park in the city's Pudong New Area since January（自1月以来，这条机器鲨鱼一直在上海浦东新区的上海海昌海洋公园的一个水族馆里展出）。由此可知，这条机器鲨鱼是在上海被展览，故选C。

2. B。细节理解题。A项"它是由沈阳——一厂的工程师设计和制造的"、C项"它每分钟可移动42米"对应原文第二段第一句的内容。B项中的4.2 meters与文中的4.7 meters不符，故错误。D项"它可以像真正的鲨鱼一样游动、转弯、上浮和下潜"对应原文第二段第二句的内容。故选B。

3. A。词义猜测题。preset 所在句的意思是"他说，这条鲨鱼可以被远程控制，也可以根据_____程序或自身传感器游动"。将四个选项代入文中，只有A项符合上下文语义，故选A。

4. C。细节理解题。根据题干关键词expertise 和develop robotic aquatic animals 定位到第四段第一句。该句指出the factory decided several years ago to take advantage of its expertise in space propulsion systems to develop robotic aquatic animals（该工厂几年前决定利用其在航天推进系统方面的专长来开发水生机器动物）。由此可知，C项属于原词复现。其余选项均利用文中的碎片信息进行干扰，均可排除。故选C。

5. D。推理判断题。题干问的是"沈阳——一厂最有可能会向以下哪家公司推广其产品"。第四段最后一句指出 It will also promote the products to businesses engaged in fields such as underwater salvage and mineral prospecting（该工厂还将向水下打捞和矿产勘探等领域的企业推广其产品）。在四个选项中，只有D项与文中所述的水下打捞领域相关，故选D。

Friday【E 短文填空】

答案解析

（1）completely。根据句子结构可知，空格所在句不缺成分，空格所在句的意思是"自20世纪中叶以来，科学家们认为月球是_____干旱的"。由此可知，空格处应填入一个副词，修饰形容词dry。选项中的completely符合要求，且代入原文后符合语义，故填completely。

（2）showed。根据句子结构可知，空格所在句缺少谓语，且后面是that引导的宾语从句。空格所在句的意思是"2020年12月嫦娥五号取回的月球样本_____，其着陆点一带的土壤水含量不到百万分之120，即每公吨120克以下"。选项中的show为动词，且代入原文后符合语义，又根据前面的 in December 2020 可知，时态为一般过去时，故填showed。

（3）drier。空格位于much和than中间，由此可知空格处应填入一个形容词的比较级形式，选项中的dry、clear、different为形容词，将其一一代入文中，只有dry符合文意，表示"该地区的一块岩石被发现含有百万分之180的水，比在地球上发现的岩石要干燥得多"。dry的比较级为drier，故填drier。

（4）because。根据句子结构可知，空格所在句不缺成分。空格所在句的意思是"有趣的是，_____月球上的岩石因某种不明原因比其周围的土壤更潮湿，这表明月球上可能有其他的水源，比如来自月球内部的水"。由此可知，"月球上的岩石比其周围的土壤更潮湿"是"表明月球上可能有其他的水源"的原因，故填because。

（5）different。空格所在句去掉同位语和例子，可将其简化为 Lin Honglei said detecting water signals is _____ from finding actual liquid water（林红磊表示，探测水信号与发现真正的液态水是_____）。空格位于系动词后面，故需填入一个能作表语的词，选项中只剩clear 和different 符合要求，将其一一代入文中，只有different 符合文意，故填different。

Saturday【F 短文填空】

答案解析

（1）technology。空格所在句的意思是"虽然3D打印并不新奇，但该_____是如何发展到能应对更极端的太空条件的呢"。空格处需填入一个名词，空格前出现了定冠词 the，故空格处指代的是上文出现过的名词，即 3D printing，3D 打印是一种技术，空格首字母为 t，由此可知 technology 符合文意，故填 technology。

（2）first。空格所在句的意思是"《生活科学》称，_____，这项技术相对来说不为人知，但在 21 世纪得到了普及"。根据句子结构可知，空格所在句结构完整，故空格处应该是一个表示时间的固定短语，首字母为 f，at first 表示"最初"，代入文中符合文意，故填 first。

（3）used。根据句子结构可知，空格所在句缺少谓语，根据句意"在 3D 打印的早期，它主要_____快速原型制作"可知，3D 打印是用于快速原型制作的，空格处首字母为 u，use 符合文意，而空格前出现了 was，此处为被动语态，故填 used。

（4）However。空格所在句的意思是"_____，这正是今天的机器所允许的"。空格前一句指出"在室温下，金属本身并不能变成液态用于印刷"。由此可知，前后为转折关系，而空格处首字母为 H，且后面有逗号，故填 However。

（5）method。空格所在句的意思是"与金属切割相比，3D 打印是一种更快速地制作小型金属模型的_____"。空格处应填入一个名词，金属切割和 3D 打印都可以用于制作金属模型，即都属于制作金属模型的方法，空格处首字母为 m，method 符合文意，故填 method。

（6）book。空格所在句的意思是"《塑料工程概论》（2018年）_____解释说，金属切割是一种'减法'工艺，成本极高且耗时"。由此可知，空格处需填入一个能指代《塑料工程概论》的名词，空格后的内容为斜体，且空格首字母为 b，由此可推知《塑料工程概论》是一本书，故填 book。

（7）an。根据句子结构可知，空格所在句不缺成分，主句是 3D printing is _____ additive process，为主系表结构，空格处应填入不定冠词，而后面的 additive 以元音音素开头，故填 an。

（8）than。根据空格前的 more steps 可知，此处为比较级结构，空格所在句的意思是"在印刷方法上，某些金属印刷方法_____其他金属印刷方法的步骤要多"。空格首字母为 t，故填 than。

（9）similar。空格所在句的意思是"这使得印刷过程_____塑料印刷"。空格前一句指出"选择性金属烧结通过将金属与塑料结合来打印金属"。由此可知，空格处应填入一个表示"类似的"意思的词，空格首字母为 s，similar 符合文意，故填 similar。

（10）difference。空格所在句的意思是"_____在于，从机器中取出时，它还不是一个纯金属的部件"。上文提到了金属印刷和塑料印刷的相似之处，由此可知，此处描述的是二者的不同之处，空格首字母为 d，故填 difference。

Week Ten

Monday【A 完形填空】

答案解析

1. C。考查动词辨析。A项意为"照顾",B项意为"分开",C项意为"给……留下深刻印象",D项意为"拿着"。将各选项代入原文中,只有C项符合逻辑,意为《少林寺》这部电影给张美丽留下了深刻印象,故选C。

2. A。考查固定搭配。at the age of... 为固定搭配,意为"在……年纪",故选A。

3. B。考查动词辨析。A项意为"走",B项意为"去",C项意为"游泳",D项意为"准备"。结合文意可知,张美丽走着或者游去上大学都是不合理的,因此A项和C项均错误。D项 prepared 与 to 搭配,通常以 prepare to do sth. 的形式出现,因此D项也错误。B项代入原文符合文意,故选B。

4. B。考查动词辨析。A项意为"提供;主动提出",B项意为"选择",C项意为"害怕",D项意为"憎恨"。根据上文可知,张美丽从小就对武术有浓厚的兴趣,因此在毕业后,她应该是选择当一名保镖,A、C、D三项均不符合文意,故选B。

5. D。考查动词辨析。A项意为"打斗",B项意为"给予",C项意为"支付",D项意为"经历"。将各选项代入原文,只有D项符合逻辑和文意,意为张美丽经历了多个科目的训练,故选D。

6. C。考查固定搭配。A项意为"步伐",B项意为"车站",C项意为"标准",D项意为"暴风雨"。up to standard 为固定搭配,意为"达到标准",因此C项代入原文符合文意,故选C。

7. A。考查名词辨析。A项意为"优势",B项意为"任务",C项意为"味道",D项意为"练习"。根据原文冒号后面的内容可知,此处列举的都是女保镖相较于男保镖的优势,因此A项符合文意,故选A。

8. D。考查动词辨析。A项意为"隐藏",B项意为"完成",C项意为"清除",D项意为"感觉到,觉察出"。将各选项代入原文,只有D项符合逻辑和文意,意为女保镖能够很容易地察觉他人的情绪,故选D。

9. D。考查形容词辨析。A项意为"轻的",B项意为"容易的",C项意为"缓慢的",D项意为"严格的"。根据下文可知,只有20%的人能最终成为保镖,所以考核是十分严格的,因此D项符合文意,故选D。

10. C。考查介词辨析。A项意为"直到……",B项意为"在……之前",C项意为"比",D项意为"(被看)作;作为"。根据空格前的 more 可知,此处是把女保镖和男保镖进行比较,more... than... 意为"比……更……",因此C项符合文意,故选C。

Tuesday【B 阅读理解】

答案解析

1. D。细节理解题。根据表格右栏的 modern, inclusive and diversified 可知王逢陈的作品具有现代化、包容和多元化的特点,D项描述正确。其他三项都是陈鹏作品的特点和设计理念。故选D。

2. C。细节理解题。综合比较两位设计师的设计特点和理念可知,左右两栏分别提到了 offering the best wishes for the international viewers(向全世界观众传递最美好的祝愿)和 building a bridge between Chinese culture and western culture and thus to express the idea of international togetherness(在中西文化之间搭建桥梁,表达国际团结的理念)。因此两位设计师的作品都具有国际化的特点。故选C。

3. A。推理判断题。这篇文章主要介绍了为2022年北京冬奥会开幕式设计服装的两位设计师,因此这篇文章的内容与人物或者时尚有关,只有A项符合条件,故选A。

Wednesday【C 阅读理解】

答案解析

1. C。推理判断题。由原文第六段可知,打树花表演在古代只有富人和社会地位高的人才消费得起,C项"富人家的儿子"符合文意,故选C。

2. C。细节理解题。由原文第四段可知王德和其助手每年在春节期间为当地人和游客表演打树花,故选C。

3. B。推理判断题。由原文倒数第四段可知,打树花这一表演具有风险性,表演者容易受伤,紧接着下一段就描述了王德因表演而受伤的经历,因此该表演是危险的。A、C、D三项原文中均未提及,故均排除。故选B。

Thursday【D 阅读理解】

答案解析

1. D。细节理解题。根据题干中的 inherited the craft of making blue calico 定位到第二段的 he has become a city-level

inheritor of the craft, following the steps of his father-in-law Wu Yuanxin and his wife Wu Lingshu（他跟随岳父吴元新和妻子吴灵姝的脚步，成了这门手艺的市级传承人），由此可知他是从岳父和妻子那里继承这门手艺的，故选D。

2. C。细节理解题。根据原文第五段倪沈键所说的话it's difficult to make much money in a short time（做这行在短时间内赚不了多少钱）可知，凭这门手艺短时间内是赚不到什么钱的，故C项说法错误，故选C。

3. D。细节理解题。根据原文第七段和第九段可知，倪沈键在大学开设了相关课程，并在多所大学和中小学开展了活动，且一直在尝试对这项工艺做出改变，因此A、B、C三项都是倪沈键为传承这门手艺所做的事，故选D。

4. B。推理判断题。这篇文章所描述的蓝印花布染色工艺是一门艺术，并且整篇文章介绍的是倪沈键及其家人作为这门艺术的传承人的经历，所以这篇文章应该是被刊登在艺术杂志上，故选B。

Friday【E 阅读理解】
● 答案解析

1. A。细节理解题。由原文第一段和第二段可知，开幕式表演结束两天后，王媛媛仍然很兴奋。由原文第四段可知，B、C两项描述的都是其表演之前的感受，D项文中未提及。故选A。

2. B。细节理解题。由原文第四段可知，表演之前，王媛媛和她的团队非常紧张和担心，不知道观众是否会喜欢这个节目，并且担心会在表演中出错，因此B项描述正确。由原文内容可知，在开幕式之前，张艺谋已经邀请了她们进行表演，因此A项不正确。由原文倒数第二段可知，张艺谋是信任她们的，因此C项错误。A、C两项错误，所以D项也是错误的。故选B。

3. B。细节理解题。由原文第八段可知，《大红灯笼高高挂》这部作品由张艺谋导演执导，王媛媛只是为其芭蕾舞剧编舞，所以B项不是王媛媛所做过的事，故选B。

4. D。细节理解题。原文倒数第二、三段为王媛媛对本次开幕式和张艺谋的评价。works day and night 意为"夜以继日地工作"，为B项的同义表达；A项为原句复现；C项为原文中 he trusted us 的同义表达，因此A、B、C三项都是正确的。故选D。

Saturday【F 任务型阅读】
● 答案解析

1. He knew more about craftsmanship in an activity of introducing intangible cultural heritage in his high school. 根据原文第五段 Huang did not know much about craftsmanship until he was in high school, when local authorities organized an activity to introduce intangible cultural heritage to the school in 2016（直到2016年黄杨伟上高中，当地政府在学校里组织了一场介绍非物质文化遗产的活动，他才对手工艺有了更多的了解）可知，黄杨伟是在高中的一次活动中对手工艺有了更多的了解。

2. Because they think weaving is a girl's thing. 根据原文第七段 "I developed a deep love for the ethnic craft, but some villagers cannot understand why a man loves weaving so much," he says. "They think it's a girl's thing."（"我深深地爱上了织锦这项民族技艺，但一些村民无法理解为什么一个男人如此爱编织。"他说，"他们认为这是女孩做的事。"）可知，村民们不理解黄杨伟的爱好，是因为他们觉得编织是女孩才会做的事。

3. He hopes he can bring Li ethnic culture to more parts of the world by weaving brocade. 在文章的最后，黄杨伟表达了自己对织锦的愿望，他希望能通过织锦面向全世界传播黎族文化。

Week Eleven

Monday【A 完形填空】

答案解析

1. B。考查动词辨析。A 项意为"知道",B 项意为"预计",C 项意为"同意",D 项意为"相信;认为"。四个选项代入后分别表示"众所周知""预计""达成共识""人们认为"。空格后面句子的时态是将来时,因此"预计"最符合语义和逻辑,故选 B。

2. A。考查固定搭配。A 项可与 sale 构成搭配,意为"出售";B 项可与 sale 构成搭配,意为"待售";C、D 项不能与 sale 构成合理搭配,故排除 C、D 项。A、B 项分别代入文中意为"此外,除夕当天的火车票从周一开始正式发售/待售",A 项符合语义和逻辑,故选 A。

3. C。考查动词辨析。A 项意为"开始",B 项意为"继续",C 项意为"结束",D 项意为"完成"。第一段第一句介绍了春运开始的时间是 January 17(1 月 17 日),由此可知 February 25(2 月 25 日)是春运结束的时间,A、B 项排除。D 项是及物动词,空格后无宾语,故排除。故选 C。

4. B。考查动词辨析。A 项意为"分享",B 项意为"改善",C 项意为"影响",D 项意为"改变"。空格所在句意为:为了更好地确保春运管理的顺利,有关部门还采取了措施_____乘客体验。只有 B 项代入后符合语义和逻辑,故选 B。

5. B。考查名词辨析。A 项意为"保护",B 项意为"控制",C 项意为"报告",D 项意为"研究"。空格前是并列连词 and,因此空格所填词和 prevention 并列。四个选项中,只有 B 项代入后符合语义和逻辑,而且 prevention and control 是惯用表达,表示"防控",故选 B。

6. C。考查副词辨析。A 项意为"缓慢地",B 项意为"安静地",C 项意为"快速地",D 项意为"完全地"。根据常识可知,发生疫情,应尽快采取措施,做出调整,C 项代入后符合语义和逻辑,故选 C。

7. D。考查副词辨析。A 项意为"反而;却",表示对比或转折关系;B 项意为"因此",表示因果关系;C 项意为"然而",表示转折关系;D 项意为"而且,也",表示递进关系。上一段讲述了第一条措施,用了 First,空格所在句提出第二条措施,属于递进关系,故选 D。

8. A。考查介词短语辨析。A 项意为"比如",表示列举;B 项意为"此外",表示递进关系;C 项意为"同时",表示时间先后关系;D 项意为"相比之下",表示对比。空格前一句引出 Contactless services(非接触式服务),空格后面是具体的做法 the number of self-service equipment at the stations will be increased, and fast channels for entering the station will be added(增加车站自助服务设备的数量,增设进站快速通道),后面是对前面的举例说明,故选 A。

9. A。考查形容词辨析。A 项意为"线上的;网上的",B 项意为"线下的;离线的",C 项意为"基础的",D 项意为"标准的"。空格所在句也是对 Contactless services(非接触式服务)的举例说明,只有 A 项代入后符合语义和逻辑,故选 A。

10. D。考查形容词辨析。A 项意为"重要的",B 项意为"公共的",C 项意为"感人的;移动的",D 项意为"结尾的"。空格所填词与 and 前面的 opening 并列,D 项 closing 与 opening 相对,代入文中表示"开闭幕式",符合语义和逻辑,故选 D。

Tuesday【B 阅读理解】

答案解析

1. D。细节理解题。根据题干中的 mysterious 定位到表格第一行第二列。其中,第二段第一句指出,What makes the lake more mysterious is the possibility that an ancient city lived under its quiet and calm surface(使这个湖更加神秘的是,在它平静的表面下可能存在着一座古城)。由此可知,玉溪抚仙湖变得更加神秘是因为湖中可能存在一座古城,故选 D。

2. C。细节理解题。根据题干中的 historical and natural resources 定位到表格第二行第二列。其中,第一段第二句介绍了普洱市的历史意义,Back in ancient China, the region served as an important stop along the trade route Tea Horse Road(在中国古代,这个地区是商贸通道茶马古道的重要一站)。第二段指出,Apart from its tea, Pu'er holds rich natural resources(除了茶叶,普洱还有丰富的自然资源)。由此可知,普洱市既有厚重的历史,又有丰富的自然资源,故选 C。

3. C。推理判断题。表格第三行第二列第二句指出,For those wishing to communicate with the giant creatures themselves, the Wild Elephant Valley is a must-visit(对于

那些希望与这种巨型生物交流的人来说，野象谷是必游之地）。题干中的 huge animals 是文中 giant creatures 的同义表达，故选 C。

Wednesday【C 阅读理解】
● 答案解析

1. C。细节理解题。根据题干中的 new vacation choices 定位到第一段第二句。该句指出，New vacation choices, including ice and snow tourism, short-distance travel and cultural tourism, not only brought people...（冰雪旅游、短途旅游和文化旅游等新的度假选择，不仅给人们带来了……）。由此可知，Long-distance travel（长途旅行）不包含在内，故选 C。

2. A。细节理解题。根据题干中的 the list of popular tourist attractions for ice and snow travel 定位到第四段。该段指出，According to online news, cities with many ice and snow sports activities in the south, such as Shanghai and Guangzhou, have also joined the list of popular destinations for ice and snow travel（据线上消息称，南方许多举办冰雪活动的城市，如上海和广州，也加入了冰雪旅游热门目的地的名单）。题干中的 have been on the list 是文中 have also joined the list 的同义表达，tourist attractions 是文中 destinations 的同义表达，popular 和 ice and snow travel 是原词复现，故选 A。

3. D。细节理解题。根据题干中的 more than two cultural activities 定位到倒数第二段第一句。该句指出，...81.8 percent took part in more than two cultural activities（……81.8% 的游客参加了两次以上的文化活动）。题干中的 attended 是文中 took part in 的同义表达，more than two cultural activities 是原词复现，故选 D。

4. A。主旨大意题。本文主要介绍春节期间三种新的度假选择，包括冰雪旅游、短途旅游和文化旅游。由此可知这篇文章旨在介绍几种新的度假选择，故选 A。

Thursday【D 阅读理解】
● 答案解析

1. B。细节理解题。根据题干中的 Shenzhen 和 for the first time 定位到第二段第一句。该句指出，It all started in 2014 when I arrived in Shenzhen for the first time（这一切都是从 2014 年我第一次来到深圳开始的），故选 B。

2. C。词义猜测题。根据题干中的 occupies 和 Paragraph 3 定位到第三段第一句。该句指出，The park occupies a 13-kilometer-long stretch of reclaimed land...（该公园_____了一段 13 千米长的填海地……）。后面 along the southern coast of Shenzhen on the north shore of Shenzhen Bay, starting at the west near Shenzhen Bay Bridge and ending at the Hongshulin Nature Reserve（深圳南部沿海，毗邻深圳湾北岸，西起深圳湾大桥西侧，东至红树林自然保护区）都是对公园范围的描述，由此推测画线单词跟占地面积有关，只有 C 项代入后符合语境，故选 C。

3. B。细节理解题。根据题干中的 recommend 和 shoot the sunrise 定位到第四段最后一句。该句指出，Recommended places to shoot the sunrise are where Dasha River Park Road meets Shenzhen Bay Park and the park entry point near the Shenzhen Bay Park Metro Station（推荐拍摄日出的地点是大沙河公园路与深圳湾公园的交叉路口，以及深圳湾公园地铁站附近的公园入口）。由此可知推荐的地点有两个，故选 B。

4. C。细节理解题。根据题干中的 gather 和 during winter 定位到倒数第二段。该段第二句指出，Many bird photography enthusiasts gather at this time of the year to photograph birds（许多鸟类摄影爱好者在每年的这个时候聚集在一起拍摄鸟类）。题干中的 Many people 是对文中 Many bird photography enthusiasts 的概括；gather 是原词复现；during winter 对应文中的 at this time of the year；take photos 是文中 photograph 的同义表达，故选 C。

Friday【E 任务型阅读】
● 答案解析

1. 2.2. 根据题干中的 phase II 定位到第一段第二句和第三段第一句。第一段第二句指出，Another 2.2 square kilometers of attractions and five hotels are planned for the phase II of the Universal resort（该环球度假区二期还有 2.2 平方千米的景点和 5 家酒店正在筹划建设中）。第三段第一句指出，According to Cui, construction is planned on another 2.2 square kilometers, part of phase II（据崔述强介绍，二期工程还有 2.2 平方千米正在筹划建设中）。由此可知，二期工程占地 2.2 平方千米，故答案为 2.2。

2. Because only two hotels have been built. 根据题干中的 the number of rooms 和 limited 定位到第三段第三句。该句

117

指出，But only two hotels have been built, so the number of rooms is limited（但是目前只建了2家酒店，所以房间数量有限）。故答案为Because only two hotels have been built。

3. **On September 20, 2021.** 根据题干中的the Universal Beijing Resort officially open定位到第四段第一句。该句指出，The Universal Beijing Resort officially opened on September 20, 2021, after nearly 20 years of planning（经过近20年的规划，北京环球度假区于2021年9月20日正式开放）。故答案为On September 20, 2021。

4. **They should make an appointment.** 根据题干中的Paragraph 4定位到第四段。该段最后一句指出，The resort has taken strict epidemic control measures and adopted the reservation system（度假区实施了严格的疫情控制措施，并采用了预约制）。环球度假区采取了预约制，因此游客需要提前预约。故答案为They should make an appointment。

Saturday【F 短文填空】

● 答案解析

（1）**before。** 空格所在句意为：在2022年冬奥会和冬残奥会开幕三周_____，主办方北京市政府详细介绍了冬奥会期间的交通管理措施……。句子的主干完整，空格所在部分为时间状语，根据常识可知，一般是在冬奥会开幕之前开一系列发布会介绍相关情况，故填before。

（2）**past。** 空格所在句意为：借鉴_____奥运会的经验，北京准备为2022年冬奥会设立一段交通服务期。空格前是定冠词the，空格后是名词短语Olympic Games，由此可知空格处填形容词。根据常识可知，经验是从过去的事件中得出的，故填past。previous、former等表示"以往的"的词也可。

（3）**up。** 空格所在句意为：在这55天里将采取的措施包括_____奥林匹克专用车道。空格前是动名词setting，空格后是名词短语an Olympic lane，set不能直接跟lane

搭配，因此空格处应填介词。set up意为"建起，设立"，代入后符合语义和逻辑，故填up。

（4）**from。** 空格所在句意为：禁止载有危险化学品和建筑垃圾的车辆上路行驶。prevent sb. from doing sth. 是固定搭配，意为"禁止某人做某事"，因此空格处填from。

（5）**pressure。** 空格所在句意为：此外，他们还鼓励北京居民在家办公，并采用弹性工作制，以减少通勤，缓解奥运场馆附近地区的交通_____。空格所在部分位于and之后，与reduce commuting并列，reduce commuting是动宾结构，因此空格处应填名词，作relieve的宾语。根据句意可知，在家办公、减少通勤等都可以缓解交通压力，故填pressure。

（6）**Therefore。** 空格所在句意为：_____，北京市将提倡绿色低碳出行，优先考虑公共交通。空格前一句说，预计部分时段、部分路段将出现交通拥堵现象；空格后是北京市提出的解决办法，由此可知，空格前后是因果关系，且句子主干完整，故填Therefore，首字母要大写。Consequently、Thus等表示因果关系的副词也可。

（7）**obey。** 空格所在句意为：_____奥林匹克专用车道管理规则，优先保障冬奥交通。空格前是并列连词and，_____ rules与空格前面的encourage green and low-carbon travel和prioritize public transport并列，因此空格处应填动词原形。根据常识可知，应遵守交通规则，故填obey。follow、observe等表示"遵守"的动词也可。

（8）**open。** 空格所在句意为：吴世江说，北京市的地铁和公交服务将延长运营时间，并可能根据情况_____额外的线路，以确保居民在春节假期期间的出行。空格前是情态动词may，空格后是名词短语additional routes，因此空格处应填动词原形。空格前讲的是延长运营时间，空格所在部分与其并列，因此空格所在部分应表示"开通额外的线路"，故填open。

Week Twelve
Monday【A 完形填空】
答案解析

1. D。考查名词辨析和上下文语义。A项意为"节日",B项意为"舞蹈",C项意为"歌曲",D项意为"传统"。下文提到 According to this tradition（根据这一传统）,由此可知 jingrwai iawbei 是一项特殊的传统,故选 D。

2. D。考查形容词辨析。A项意为"重要的",B项意为"有名的",C项意为"严厉的",D项意为"常规的,普通的"。空格所在的短语与后面的 a special melodious tune 为并列结构,且根据下文可知他们的名字仅限正式场合使用,但是曲调会成为他们一生的身份,由此可知,官方名字是常规的,而不是特殊的,故选 D。

3. A。考查固定搭配。at birth 为固定短语,意为"在出生时"。根据上文的 newborn baby（新生儿）可知"在出生时"符合句意,故选 A。

4. B。考查介词辨析。A项意为"与……一起",B项意为"为了（用途、目的）",C项意为"通过（某种手段、方式）",D项意为"从;来自"。be used for 为固定搭配,意为"用于……",符合句意,故选 B。

5. C。考查状语从句。A项意为"虽然",引导让步状语从句;B项意为"因为",引导原因状语从句;C项意为"一旦",引导条件状语从句;D项意为"直到",引导时间状语从句。空格所在部分意为:_____一个人死了,他们的曲调就会随他们而去。根据句意可知空格所在句应该是一个条件状语从句,故选 C。

6. C。考查动词辨析。A项意为"拒绝",B项意为"强迫",C项意为"重复",D项意为"后悔"。空格所在部分意为:永远不会再被其他人_____。将各选项代入句中可知"重复"符合句意,故选 C。

7. B。考查形容词辨析。A项意为"疯狂的",B项意为"强烈的;强壮的",C项意为"坚硬的",D项意为"有趣的"。空格所在句意为:它表达了母亲在孩子出生时_____爱和喜悦。将各选项代入句中可知"强烈的"符合句意,故选 B。

8. C。考查动词短语辨析。A项意为"放弃",B项意为"起床",C项意为"属于",D项意为"到达"。空格所在部分意为:_____卡西部落的一位女性诗狄阿普·孔西说。将各选项代入句中可知"属于"符合句意,故选 C。

9. D。考查名词辨析。A项意为"农场",B项意为"河流",C项意为"村庄",D项意为"森林"。下文提到 hunting（打猎）以及 bad spirits that live in the forests（生活在森林里的恶灵）,由此可知"森林"符合句意,故选 D。

10. A。考查宾语从句。分析句子结构可知空格前面主谓完整,缺少宾语,空格后面为从句,从句成分完整,所以宾语从句的引导词在从句中不充当任何成分,故用 that,故选 A。

11. D。考查名词辨析。A项意为"规则",B项意为"希望",C项意为"举止",D项意为"危险"。本段介绍了曲调在当地村民生活中的作用,即可以驱赶恶灵。空格所在部分意为:当你在森林里被呼唤你的曲调时,不会有任何_____能够靠近你。所以,"危险"符合句意,故选 D。

12. B。考查形容词辨析。A项意为"更长的",B项意为"更短的",C项意为"更重的",D项意为"更老的"。空格所在部分意为:长调也有一个_____版本。与长调对应的应为短调,所以"更短的"符合句意,故选 B。

13. B。考查固定搭配。A项意为"不同的",B项意为"相似的",C项意为"简单的",D项意为"奇怪的"。be similar to 为固定搭配,意为"与……类似",符合句意,故选 B。

14. A。考查形容词辨析。A项意为"特殊的",B项意为"自信的",C项意为"自豪的",D项意为"无聊的"。空格所在句意为:这些曲调从远处听起来像口哨,这就是孔通村被赋予"口哨村"这一_____名称的原因。将各选项代入句中,可知"特殊的"符合句意,故选 A。

15. C。考查上下文语义。A项意为"顶部",B项意为"末端",C项意为"开始",D项意为"底部"。由下文可知本段主要在推测孔通村这一特殊传统的开始时间,所以"开始"符合句意,故选 C。

Tuesday【B 阅读理解】
答案解析

1. A。细节理解题。根据题干中的 Gaelic had been the main language 定位到第一段,第二句中提到 It began to be canceled from the early 17th century（从17世纪初开始,盖尔语被取消）,可知从17世纪初开始,盖尔语逐渐在苏格兰失去主要语言的地位,故选 A。

2. D。词义猜测题。画线单词位于第三段,下文主要讲述了当地人为重新发展盖尔语所做的努力以及盖尔语在当地的发展现状——精通盖尔语的人遍布当地各行业。画线单词所在句意为：自20世纪70年代以来，艾琳伊阿尔曼镇一直处于苏格兰盖尔语_____的中心。所以只有"复兴"符合语境，故选D。

3. B。推理判断题。根据题干中的关键词the last two paragraphs定位到本文最后两段，最后一段的主旨句提到Decades on, Noble's idea has slowly been proven（几十年过去了，诺布尔的想法已经慢慢得到了证实），倒数第二段提到了诺布尔的想法，即the Gaelic language could be used to stop population decline in Skye and actually become an economic driver in its own right（盖尔语可以用于阻止斯凯岛的人口下降，而且实际上盖尔语本身就可以成为一种经济驱动力）。由此可以推测诺布尔关于盖尔语的用处的两个想法都得以成真，故选B。

Wednesday【C 阅读理解】

答案解析

1. B。细节理解题。根据题干中的strangers定位到表格第一行，由Small talk with strangers第二列的内容可知挪威人很少会与陌生人闲聊，故选B。

2. A。细节理解题。根据题干中的winter和wearing shoes定位到表格第二行，由第二行第二列的Your host won't be pleased if you wear shoes with snow into their house可知如果你穿着带雪的鞋子进入挪威人的房子，主人会不高兴。A项意为"不开心的"，B项意为"满意的"，C项意为"友好的"，D项意为"奇怪的"。unhappy是won't be pleased的同义表达，故选A。

3. D。细节理解题。根据表格第一行第二列However, this isn't the case in Norway, where casually greeting strangers is just not the done thing（然而在挪威，情况并非如此，随便跟陌生人打招呼并不是理所应当的事）可知A项表述错误；根据表格第二行第二列Wearing shoes indoors is considered impolite... And this is especially true in Norway during the winter months（……在室内穿鞋被认为是不礼貌的。这在挪威的冬季尤其如此）可知B项表述错误；根据表格第三行第二列splitting the bill is pretty standard whatever the occasion is in Norway（在挪威，无论是什么场合，分摊账单都是相当标准的做法）可知C项表述错误；根据表格第四行第二列they think that it is a lot more polite to grab what they want（他们认为，自己拿想

要的东西要有礼貌得多）可知D项表述正确，故选D。

4. C。主旨大意题。本文主要介绍了挪威的一些社交准则，即在挪威的社交场合中哪些是可以做的，哪些可能会被认为不礼貌，C项符合文意，故选C。

Thursday【D 阅读理解】

答案解析

1. B。细节理解题。根据第一段第二句It's a simple mixture of strong black tea, condensed milk and enough sugar可知拉茶是由浓红茶、炼乳和足够的糖组成的简单混合物，里面没有巧克力，故选B。

2. C。细节理解题。根据题干中的关键词The quality of teh tarik定位到第二段第一句，由the quality of teh tarik is measured by its "pull"可知拉茶的质量主要在于"拉"的技术高低，故选C。

3. C。细节理解题。根据第五段中Malaysia is a cultural melting pot of indigenous Malay, Chinese, British and South Indian可知马来西亚人口主要由本地马来人、中国人、英国人和南印度人组成，所以A项中的"日本人"表述错误；根据Black tea was first introduced by the Chinese in the 1830s可知红茶最初是在19世纪30年代由中国人引进马来西亚的，所以B项中的"20世纪30年代"表述错误；根据the skill of pulling was developed by South Indian street cooks after 1850可知拉茶的技巧是在1850年后由南印度的街头厨师开发的，所以C项表述正确；根据milk and sugar were introduced nearly 100 years later during the end of British colonialism可知牛奶和糖是在英国殖民主义结束时被引进的，并不是本土马来西亚人发明的，所以D项表述错误。故选C。

4. B。主旨大意题。本文第一段和第二段介绍马来西亚人对拉茶的喜爱和拉茶的制作技艺；第三段介绍拉茶受欢迎的原因；最后三段介绍拉茶背后的文化意义和历史。综合以上分析可知，本文主要介绍了马来西亚的一种国民饮料——拉茶，故选B。

Friday【E 任务型阅读】

答案解析

1. A。空格所在段落的首句提到夏威夷花环是夏威夷海岛上的一种庆祝传统，段落最后一句又提到羽毛花环留存了过去几代人的记忆，由此可知空格所在句引出了羽毛

花环，且空格后面有转折连词but，表示语义发生转折。将提到羽毛花环的句子代入句中可知A项符合语义，故选A。

2. E。空格前面提到羽毛服装和饰品长期以来一直代表着皇室和尊重，空格后面提到一些在夏威夷能够体现某些特定阶层身份的物品。在所给选项中，只有E项提到了羽毛在夏威夷和身份象征之间的联系，故选E。

3. D。空格位于句首，所以空格处需填入的句子可能为空格所在段落的主旨句。空格后面提到夏威夷一个国王的黄色披风，这种颜色的羽毛最能彰显威望又十分罕见。在所给选项中，只有D项提到了颜色，且能概括本段大意，故选D。

4. B。空格位于句首，所以空格处需填入的句子可能为空格所在段落的主旨句。空格后面提到制作羽毛花环耗时长、工序繁杂。在所给选项中，B项符合语境，且能概括本段大意，故选B。

5. F。空格后面为but加上现在分词短语，意为"而是提醒人们要延续这段文化"，在语义上有递进，且上文提到羽毛花环的意义。在所给选项中，F项符合语境，故选F。

Saturday【F 短文填空】

● 答案解析

（1）second。空格前面是不定冠词a，后面是名词living room，所以空格处的单词需变为序数词，a second表示"又一，再一"。故填second。

（2）latest。空格前面为定冠词the，后面为名词news，且括号内所给的单词是形容词，空格后为news，latest表示"最近的，最新的"，latest news可看作固定搭配，意为"最近的新闻"。故填latest。

（3）ordering。空格所在的句子已有动词hear，hear sb. doing sth. 为hear的固定用法，意为"听见某人做某事"，故将括号内所给单词order改成现在分词形式，故填ordering。

（4）reasons。空格前面有many，many后常接可数名词复数，reason为可数名词，故填reasons。

（5）different。be different from为固定搭配，意为"与……不同"，故填different。

（6）surprised。空格前面有情态动词和be动词，后面是to do 不定式短语，所以需将括号内所给的名词surprise改成形容词，因主语是人，故填surprised。

（7）companies。company意为"公司"时为可数名词，由dozens of可知，这里应填其复数形式，故填companies。

（8）over/around。all over/around the world为固定搭配，意为"全世界"，故填over/around。

（9）moved。根据空格所在句子的时间状语20 years ago（20年前）可知，这里的时态为一般过去时，故填moved。

（10）down。sit down为固定搭配，意为"坐下"，故填down。

Week Thirteen

Monday【A 完形填空】

● 答案解析

1. B。考查名词辨析。A项意为"重量"，B项意为"数量"，C项意为"质量"。空格所在句的意思是"中国海洋大学的张沛东教授在过去的15年里致力于一件事：在'海底大草原'上种植'草'，以恢复郁郁葱葱的栖息地，保护海岸，增加野生动物的_____和储存碳"。将三个选项代入文中，只有B项符合文意，故选B。

2. A。考查上下文语义。空格所在句的意思是"这个'大草原'就是海草（生态系统），被公认为世界_____典型的海岸带生态系统之一"，后面接着指出"与红树林、珊瑚礁一起"，由此可知海草生态系统是三大典型的海岸带生态系统之一，故选A。

3. C。考查短语辨析。A项意为"除了……"，B项意为"即使"，C项意为"因为"。空格所在句的意思是"生长在沿海海湾的海草曾经非常丰富，但_____沿海开发以及污水和人工海产养殖造成的污染，海草床变得贫瘠"。but后的内容指出海草床变得贫瘠，而空格后的内容均是破坏海洋生态的人类行为，由此可知空格后指出了海草床变得贫瘠的原因，C项符合逻辑，故选C。

4. A。考查上下文语义。A项意为"牛"，B项意为"狗"，C项意为"猫"。空格所在句的意思是"海草对海洋生物的意义就像草原对_____羊一样重要"。由and可知，空格处的内容与sheep为并列关系，应属于同一类，根据常识可知，草原对牛和羊是非常重要的，故选A。

5. C。考查固定搭配。空格位于play an important _____ in 结构中，将三个选项代入文中，只有role能与其构成固定搭配，play an important role in 表示"在……中发挥重要作用"，符合文意，故选C。

6. B。考查形容词辨析。A项意为"简单的"，B项意为"普遍的"，C项意为"乐观的"。空格所在句的意思是"海草的减少是世界范围内的一个_____问题"。结合全文可知，A项和C项代入文中均不符合文意，B项符合文意，故选B。

7. A。考查名词辨析和上下文语义。A项意为"城市"，B项意为"国家"，C项意为"乡村"。空格所在句的意思是"在山东青岛、烟台和威海等沿海_____的海湾地区，鳗草是海草床的主要植物之一……"。空格后的such as 表示举例，由此可知空格处所填词应能概括Qingdao, Yantai and Weihai in Shandong Province，根据常识可知这几个地方都是城市，故选A。

8. C。考查动词辨析。A项意为"分享"，B项意为"谈论"，C项意为"找到"。空格所在句的意思是"该团队开发了培育鳗草的技术，并_____修复海草床的方法"。下文提到海草的增多大大地改善了水质，由此可知这里是找到了修复海草床的方法，C项符合文意，故选C。

9. A。考查名词辨析。A项意为"研究"，B项意为"能力"，C项意为"危险"。空格所在句的意思是"威海市荣成（一个县级市）的天鹅湖是该团队开展_____的第一个地点"。将三个选项代入文中，只有A项符合文意，故选A。

10. C。考查动词辨析。A项意为"来"，B项意为"离开"，C项意为"度过；花费"。空格所在句的意思是"据中国中央电视台报道，每年有近1万只天鹅在那里_____冬，为游客和摄影师创造了令人惊叹的场景"。将三个选项代入文中，只有C项符合文意，故选C。

Tuesday【B 阅读理解】

● 答案解析

1. C。细节理解题。根据题干关键词bats and humans have in common 定位到第一段。第一段第四句指出However, our two species share a common feature about learning how to speak: babbling（然而，我们这两个物种在学习如何说话这方面有一个共同的特点：咿呀学语）。由此可知，人类和蝙蝠的共同特点是在学习如何说话的时候会咿呀学语，C项符合文意，故选C。A项利用第二段第一句作干扰，B项在文中未提及，故均排除。

2. A。词义猜测题。根据题干关键词biologist 定位到第二段最后一句。该句指出"These findings suggest that humans and baby bats have a lot in common in how they learn to control their vocal apparatus," said Tecumseh Fitch, a cognitive biologist at the University of Vienna（维也纳大学的认知_____特库姆塞·费奇说："这些发现表明，人类和幼年蝙蝠学习控制发声器官的方式有很大的相似之处"）。由此可知，biologist 是特库姆塞·费奇的同位语，而且他来自维也纳大学。根据特库姆塞·费奇所说的话可知，他应该是研究生物的，故选A。

3. A。细节理解题。根据题干关键词analysts 和over 216 babbling bouts of 20 bat pups 定位到第三段第五句。该句

指出 Analysts recorded over 216 babbling bouts of 20 bat pups in Costa Rica and Panama（分析人员在哥斯达黎加和巴拿马记录了20只蝙蝠幼崽超过216次的咿呀学语）。A 项符合文意，B 项中的 Canada 和 C 项中的 Las Vegas 在文中未提及，故选 A。

4. C。细节理解题。C 项中的"大象"与最后一段提到的"鼹鼠、巨獭和海豚"不符，所以 C 项错误，故选 C。

5. B。推理判断题。本文讲述的是研究人员发现蝙蝠幼崽像人类婴儿一样咿呀学语，属于对自然的探索与发现，故选 B。

Wednesday【C 阅读理解】
答案解析

1. A。细节理解题。根据题干关键词 worker bees 和 a single hive 定位到第二段第一句。该句指出 A single hive can contain between 20,000 and 80,000 worker bees（一个蜂房可以容纳2万到8万只工蜂）。由此可知，A 项"5万只"属于这一范围，B 项"20万只"和 C 项"80万只"均不符合文意，故选 A。

2. A。细节理解题。A 项是第二段第三句的原句复现，故正确；第二段第二句指出 Colonies are also highly organized, with a queen, drones and workers caring for the hive（蜂群也是高度组织化的，有蜂王、雄蜂和打理蜂房的工蜂），B 项"每个蜂群里只有雄蜂和工蜂"与文意不符，故错误；C 项"它们的寿命大约是4到6个月"与第二段第四句"它们的寿命在夏天大约是4到6周"不符，故错误。故选 A。

3. C。细节理解题。根据题干关键词 pouches 和 hind legs 定位到第三段第三句。该句指出 The females' hind legs have pouches, which they use to carry pollen back to the hive（雌蜂的后腿上有囊袋，用来将花粉带回蜂房）。由此可知雌蜂后腿上的囊袋是用来将花粉带回蜂房的，C 项符合文意，故选 C。

4. B。细节理解题。题干问的是"所有蜜蜂都会离开它们的蜂房吗？"第三段最后一句指出 Honey bees take the nectar and pollen back to the colony where they produce honey—a source of food for those bees that never leave the hive（蜜蜂把花蜜和花粉带回蜂群，在那里生产蜂蜜——这是那些从不离开蜂房的蜜蜂的食物来源）。由此可知有一些蜜蜂从不离开蜂房，故选 B。

5. C。细节理解题。根据题干关键词 453-gram jars of honey 定位到第四段第二句。该句指出 Honey bees can visit up to 5,000 flowers in a single day, and they would have to visit about 2 million to make a 453-gram jar of honey [蜜蜂一天可以采多达5 000朵花（的花粉和花蜜），它们大约需要采200万朵花（的花粉和花蜜）才能制造出一罐453克的蜂蜜]。由此可知，制造出一罐453克的蜂蜜，蜜蜂大约需要采200万朵花的花粉和花蜜，题干问的是"制作三罐453克的蜂蜜，蜜蜂需要采多少朵花的花粉和花蜜"，故答案为大约600万朵花，故选 C。

Thursday【D 任务型阅读】
答案解析

1. B。空格前一句指出"近日，一个中国研究团队在中国东北部的大兴安岭地区发现了野生东北虎的足迹"。空格后一句又指出 The reappearance of these tigers was confirmed（这些老虎的再次出现被证实了）。六个选项中，B 项中出现了 appearance，与下一句的 reappearance 相呼应。B 项意为"这是50多年来在山区首次出现这一珍稀物种的足迹"，代入文中符合文意，故选 B。

2. C。空格前一句指出"2021年12月29日，由黑龙江省野生动物研究所的动物学家周绍春带领的研究小组在北极村国家级自然保护区的雪地上发现了脚印"。C 项 These footprints might be those of Siberian tigers（这些脚印可能是东北虎的）承接上文，符合上下文语义，故选 C。

3. F。空格前一句指出 Four feces samples were collected during footprint tracking（研究人员在足迹追踪过程中采集了4份粪便样本）。F 项中的 these feces samples 对应上一句中的 Four feces samples，F 项意为"后来，这些粪便样本被证实是东北虎的"，代入文中符合文意，故选 F。

4. E。空格后面指出 it still reveals the improvement of wildlife habitats in the region and the restoration of food chains（这仍然表明了该地区野生动物栖息地的改善和食物链的恢复），将剩余选项代入文中，只有 E 项 Although the recent finding does not mean the long-term living of Siberian tigers（虽然最近的发现并不意味着东北虎的长期生存）符合上下文语义，空格后的 it 指代该句中的 the recent finding，故选 E。

5. A。空格前指出"该物种在20世纪初广泛分布于中国东北部，大兴安岭是它们的主要栖息地之一"。剩余的 A

项和 D 项中，A 项意为"然而，1974 年至 1976 年进行的一项调查显示，由于一些原因，东北虎在山区消失了"；D 项意为"但是张明海说老虎将在中国得到适当保护"，与该段内容无关。由此可知，A 项符合文意，故选 A。

Friday【E 任务型阅读】
● 答案解析

（1）rich。根据最后一段中的 China is one of the countries with the richest orchid species in the world（中国是世界上兰科植物种类最丰富的国家之一）可知，中国有丰富的兰科植物，be rich in... 表示"富于……的"，故填 rich。

（2）Viewing。根据最后一段中的 The orchid family has important economic value and unique viewing value（兰科植物具有重要的经济价值和独特的观赏价值）可知，野生兰科植物也具有这两种价值，即 economic value 和 viewing value，故填 Viewing。

（3）died。根据第一段中的 Some varieties have even become extinct...（一些品种甚至……灭绝）可知，现在的问题是，一些野生兰科植物品种灭绝，空格后为介词 out，因此可判断此处考查的是动词短语 die out，表示"灭绝；消失"，时态为一般过去时，故填 died。

（4）Reason。根据第一段中的 Some varieties have even become extinct due to the exploitation and degradation of their native ecosystem（一些品种甚至由于当地生态系统的开发和退化而灭绝）可知，当地生态系统的开发和退化是一些野生兰科植物灭绝的原因，reason 符合语义，故填 Reason。

（5）protect。根据第一段中的 In order to strengthen the protection of orchids and establish a scientific management and monitoring system, the NFGA carried out a special investigation project aiming at the nation's wild orchid resources in 2018（为加强对兰科植物的保护，建立科学的管理和监测体系，2018 年，国家林业和草原局开展了一项针对全国野生兰科植物资源的专项调查项目）可知，国家林业和草原局开展此项目是为了保护野生兰科植物，故填 protect。

Saturday【F 短文填空】
● 答案解析

（1）food。空格前一句指出"近日，居住在不同地区的共 39 头野生亚洲象聚集在中国西南部云南省江城县进食"，空格所在句的意思是"由于冬天森林里的_____来源短缺，当村里种植的玉米逐渐收割时，成群的大象便带着它们的幼崽来到这里觅食"。空格处需填入一个名词，根据后面出现的 corn（玉米）可知，由于食物短缺，大象才来到这里觅食，故填 food。

（2）but。空格处位于 do nothing _____ eat 结构中，nothing but 为固定搭配，表示"只有；除了……什么都不……"，代入文中意为"它们每天除了吃什么都不做"，符合上下文语义，故填 but。

（3）belong。根据句子结构可知，空格所在句缺少谓语。根据句意"据该县野生动物保护站站长介绍，这 39 头大象_____两个族群"可知，belong 符合文意，且空格后出现了 to，故填 belong。

（4）looked。根据句子结构可知，空格处需填入一个动词，剩下的选项中只有 look、buy、grow、lead、provide 为动词。空格所在句的意思是"它们在康平镇和整董镇附近分批聚集，白天主要在农田上_____食……"。将动词分别代入文中，只有 look 符合文意，look for 意为"寻找"。空格处的谓语动词由 and 连接，由此可知时态应与前面的 gathered 保持一致，故填 looked。

（5）to。空格位于定语从句中，空格前是 has caused damage（造成了破坏），空格后是 villagers' agricultural facilities and crops（村民的农业设施和农作物），结合主句可知，应该是大象对村民的农业设施和农作物造成了破坏，空格前后为动宾关系，此处应填入表对象的介词，故填 to。

（6）lead。空格位于 try to do 结构中，由此可知空格处应填入一个动词原形。剩下的选项中，只有 buy、grow、lead、provide 为动词。空格所在部分的意思是"我们正试图将这些大象_____回山区"，将动词一一代入文中，只有 lead（带领）符合文意，故填 lead。

（7）providing。空格位于 by 介词短语中，由此可知空格处应填入一个动名词。剩下的选项中，只有 buy、grow、provide 为动词。空格所在句的意思是"我们正试图通过_____食物将这些大象带回山区"，只有 provide 符合文意，故填 providing。

（8）people。空格所在句的意思是"当地官方采取了加强监测和早期预警、交通控制、设置路障等措施，以确保_____和大象的安全"。空格处应填入一个名词，剩下的选项中，只有people和book为名词，将其一一代入文中，people符合文意，故填people。

（9）under。空格所在句的主干是Wild Asian elephants are _____ A-level state protection in China（野生亚洲象在中国_____国家一级保护），由此可知，野生亚洲象处于国家一级保护状态，应用介词under，under protection意为"受保护"，故填under。

（10）grown。空格所在句的意思是"由于加强了环境保护和野生动物保护工作，中国的野生亚洲象数量已经_____到大约300头"，由此可知，野生亚洲象的数量肯定是增加了，剩余的选项中只有grow有"增长"的意思，此处为现在完成时，故填grown。

Week Fourteen

Monday【A 完形填空】

答案解析

1. **A。**考查动词辨析。A项意为"开幕"，B项意为"继续"，C项意为"停止"，D项意为"结束"。根据常识可知，北京冬奥会在2月4日开幕，故选A。

2. **C。**考查介词辨析。A项意为"在……中"，B项意为"在……上"，C项意为"（用于速度、比率等）以，达"，D项意为"（数量、程度等）相差"。5 micrograms per cubic meter 是比率，故选C。

3. **B。**考查短语辨析。A项意为"因为"，B项意为"根据"，C项意为"除了"，D项意为"代表"。空格前是具体的数据"截至周四，冬奥会期间污染物的平均浓度为24微克/立方米"，空格后是数据发布单位"生态环境部"，由此可知此处表示数据来源，故选B。

4. **A。**考查定语从句。A项无义，B项表示人，C项表示"谁的"，D项表示物。空格前句子完整，且有最高级，因此引导词只能用that，故选A。

5. **D。**考查名词辨析。A项意为"成员"，B项意为"客人"，C项意为"志愿者"，D项意为"主办方"。根据常识可知，北京是"双奥之城"，举办了冬季和夏季奥运会，D项代入后符合语义和逻辑，故选D。

6. **B。**考查定语从句。A项无义，B项表示人，C项表示"谁的"，D项表示物。空格前有逗号，因此该定语从句是非限制性定语从句，又因先行词是人，故排除A、D项。由于空格在定语从句中作主语，因此排除C项，故选B。

7. **A。**考查固定搭配。A项 (so) far 意为"到目前为止"，B项 (so) that 意为"以便"，C项 (so) much 意为"如此多"，D项 (so) high 意为"如此高"。将四个选项一一代入文中可知，只有A项符合语义和逻辑，故选A。

8. **D。**考查形容词比较级的辨析。A项意为"更少的"，B项意为"更清晰的"，C项意为"更坏的"，D项意为"更好的"。空格所在句意为：到目前为止，冬奥会期间京津冀的空气质量比去年同期_____得多，PM 2.5 的平均浓度同比下降了40%。PM 2.5 浓度降低，说明空气质量变好，故选D。B项很具有迷惑性，但 clearer 修饰 air，而不修饰 air quality，故排除。

9. **B。**考查名词辨析。A项意为"原因"，B项意为"结果"，C项意为"记录"，D项意为"评论"。空格所在部分意为：这种巨大的改善是政府持续努力控制该地区空气污染的_____。政府努力为因，空气质量改善为果，故选B。

10. **C。**考查动词辨析。A项意为"失败"，B项意为"改变"，C项意为"帮助"，D项意为"发生"。空格所在部分意为：尽管有利于降低空气污染物浓度的气象条件也_____。有利的条件会起到积极作用，C项代入后符合语义和逻辑，意为"尽管有利于降低空气污染物浓度的气象条件也有所帮助"，故选C。

Tuesday【B 阅读理解】

答案解析

1. **D。**细节理解题。第二段第一句指出 In 2013, I caught the Chinese merganser, an endangered bird species for the first time in the province's Shuangpai County（2013年，我在湖南省双牌县第一次拍到中华秋沙鸭，这是一种濒危鸟类）。由此可知曹建华第一次拍到中华秋沙鸭是在2013年，故A项正确；an endangered bird species 是原词复现，故B项正确。第三段第二句指出 So I was quite excited when experts told me they were one of the oldest species in the world（所以当专家告诉我它们是世界上最古老的物种之一时，我非常兴奋）。one of the oldest species 是原词复现，故C项正确。第一段最后一句指出 Every winter, I wait for them at a national wetland park in Hunan Province（每年冬天，我都会在湖南省的一个国家湿地公园等它们）。由此可知季节是冬天而非秋天，D项错误，故选D。

2. **B。**词义猜测题。根据题干中的 Paragraph 6 定位到第六段。第二句指出 Nets and other fishing gear were a huge threat to the birds along the Yangtze River, but the threat is vanishing as the country has put a complete 10-year fishing ban in the key waters of the Yangtze since the beginning of 2020（渔网和其他渔具曾经对长江沿岸的鸟类构成了巨大的威胁，但这种威胁正在_____，因为中国自2020年年初以来在长江重点水域实施了为期10年的全面禁渔计划）。根据常识可知，实施禁渔计划之后，对鸟类的威胁会减少或消失。A项意为"发生"，B项意为"消失"，C项意为"继续存在"，D项意为"发挥作用"。只有B项代入后符合语义和逻辑，故选B。

3. **D。**主旨大意题。本题考查主旨大意，应从全文的角度考虑。由第一段的 I'm Cao Jianjun, a photography

Week Fourteen 环境保护

enthusiast 和第二段的 Since then, my camera lens has caught more and more of the beautiful birds 可知 A 项正确，不过这只是片面信息；由第二段的 an endangered bird species 和第三段的 one of the oldest species in the world 可知 B 项正确，不过这也是片面信息；由第五段的 With the improving environment, the county is not only a habitat for migratory birds but a hot tourist destination featuring bird watching and leisure activities 可知 C 项正确，但其概括不全面；D 项出现在最后一段，是对全文的总结，故选 D。

Wednesday【C 阅读理解】

答案解析

1. D。细节理解题。根据题干中的 the fireworks above the National Stadium 定位到第一段，该段指出 The fireworks... not only presented beautiful images, but also showed state-of-the-art technologies and environmental awareness, industry insiders said（业内人士表示，……烟花不仅呈现出美丽的画面，还体现了最先进的技术和环保意识）。A 项 Beautiful images 是原词复现，B 项 High technologies 是文中 state-of-the-art technologies 的同义表达，C 项 Environmental awareness 是原词复现，故这三个选项内容正确；D 项在文中并未提及，故选 D。

2. C。细节理解题。根据题干中的 used for the opening ceremony 定位到第二段最后一句。该句指出 ...compared with normal fireworks, the ones used for the opening ceremony reduced pollutants by about 70 percent（……与普通烟花相比，开幕式上使用的烟花减少了大约 70% 的污染物）。题干中的 the fireworks used for the opening ceremony 对应文中的 the ones used for the opening ceremony，cut pollutants by 是文中 reduced pollutants by 的同义表达，故选 C。

3. C。词义猜测题。题目问的是"下列哪一个空格不能填入带下划线的单词 green"。将 green 代入句子中，A 项意为"我们需要开发绿色清洁产品"，符合逻辑；B 项意为"等绿灯亮了再走"，符合逻辑；C 项意为"她的眼睛哭绿了"，不符合常识，所以错误；D 项意为"几场雨过后，大地绿油油的，生机盎然"，符合逻辑。故选 C。

4. B。细节理解题。根据题干中的 no residue left 定位到第三段。第三句指出 The reason why no residue was produced was that we adopted the technology of 'slight-smoke fireworks', which produce less smoke and waste while burning（之所以没有产生残留物，是因为我们采用了"微烟烟花"技术，"微烟烟花"燃放时产生的烟雾和废物更少）。B 项中的 the technology of "slight-smoke fireworks" 为原词复现，故选 B。

5. D。细节理解题。根据题干中的 3D technology 定位到最后一段。第二、三句指出 "We tried countless times to finally decide the layout and the angles to show the patterns perfectly." The research team used 3D technology to design drafts on a computer, and then improved the drafts through many experiments so that the height and inclination of the fireworks presented the best show without pollution（"我们尝试了无数次，最终确定了烟花的布局和摆放角度，以完美地展示图案。"研究小组利用 3D 技术在电脑上设计出草稿，然后通过大量实验改进草稿，使烟花的高度和倾斜度呈现出最佳效果，而不造成污染）。A 项 Deciding the layout、B 项 Designing drafts 和 C 项中的 the height 为原词复现，故这三个选项内容正确；D 项 Changing the shape 原文未提及，故选 D。

Thursday【D 任务型阅读】

答案解析

（1）protection。第一段第一句介绍了该法律的主题 China passed a new law on wetlands protection...（中国通过了一部新的湿地保护法……），故空格处应填 protection。

（2）first。第一段第一句指明了该法律的地位 ...establishing the country's first specialized law on the problem（……确立了中国第一部关于该问题的专门法律），题干中的 specialized law 为原词复现，on this problem 是文中 on the problem 的同义表达，故空格处应填 first。

（3）June。第一段第二句指出 The law will take effect on June 1, 2022（该法律将于 2022 年 6 月 1 日生效）。题干中的 come into force 是文中 take effect 的同义表达，故空格处应填 June。

（4）public。第二段第一句指出 Governments at all levels should raise public awareness of protecting wetlands through various activities...（各级政府应通过各种活动提高公众保护湿地的意识……），故空格处应填 public。

127

（5）students。第二段第二句指出 Education authorities and schools are also asked to increase the awareness of students on the protection of wetlands（教育主管部门和学校也被要求提高学生保护湿地的意识）。题干中的 Education departments and schools 是文中 Education authorities and schools 的同义表达，increase 是原词复现，故空格处应填 students。

（6）different。第三段第一句指出 According to the law, the country will manage wetlands at different levels...（根据该法律的要求，国家将对湿地实行分级管理……），故空格处应填 different。

（7）list。第三段第二句指出 A national list of important wetlands will be released by forestry and grassland authorities and other related departments of the State Council...（国务院林业草原主管部门将会同其他有关部门发布国家重要湿地名录……）。题干中的 make...public 是文中 released 的同义表达，important wetlands 是原词复现，故空格处应填 list。

（8）individuals。第四段指出 The law prohibits any organization or individual from destroying the habitat of birds and aquatic life in wetlands（该法律禁止任何组织或个人破坏湿地中鸟类和水生生物的生存环境）。题干中的 are not allowed to destroy the habitat 是文中 prohibits...from destroying the habitat 的被动表达，故空格处应填 individual，又由题干中 and 前的 organizations 可知，此处需要用复数形式，故填 individuals。

（9）exploit。倒数第二段第二句指出 It is forbidden to exploit peat from peat swamp wetlands or to exploit their groundwater without authorization, according to the law（该法律规定，禁止在泥炭沼泽湿地开采泥炭或者擅自开采地下水）。题干中的 It's not allowed 是文中 It is forbidden 的同义表达，without permission 是文中 without authorization 的同义表达，groundwater 是原词复现，故空格处应填 exploit。

（10）established/set up。最后一段指出 The law includes rules on setting up a system of compensation for ecological conservation...（该法律包括建立生态保护补偿制度的规定……）。故空格处应填入 set up 或其近义词 establish，而且此处为被动语态，空格位于 be 动词之后，因此空格处应填动词的过去分词形式，即 established/set up。

Friday【E 短文填空】

● 答案解析

（1）reached。空格所在部分意为：空气质量指数为"优"或"良"的天数比例_____91.6%。空格位于 and 连接的第二个并列分句中，空格前是主语 the percentage，介词短语 of days with "excellent" or "good" air quality index (AQI) 作后置定语修饰 percentage，空格后是百分比 91.6 percent，由此可知空格处应填谓语动词，而且根据前一个并列分句的谓语动词 was 可知，时态为过去时，polluted、reached、focused on 符合语法规则，但代入后符合语义和逻辑的只有 reached，故空格处应填 reached。

（2）below。空格所在部分意为：提出的目标是到2025年，上海 PM 2.5 的年均浓度_____每立方米35微克。空格位于不定式短语中，作 an annual average concentration of PM 2.5 的宾语补足语，空格后为 35 micrograms per cubic meter。根据常识可知，PM 2.5 浓度越低越好，故空格处应填 below。

（3）focused on。空格所在句意为：此外，上海_____使水变得更加清洁。be focused on 是固定搭配，意为"集中精力于"，代入后符合语义和逻辑，意为"上海还致力于使水变得更加清洁"，故空格处应填 focused on。

（4）pollution。空格所在部分意为：上海市水_____防治工作取得成效。空格前是动词 prevent and control，所以空格处应填名词作为动词的承受者。五个选项中只有 pollution 是名词，故空格处应填 pollution。

（5）polluted。空格所在句意为：自2018年年底以来，上海已经消除了被严重_____的水体。该句的谓语动词是 has eliminated，空格所在部分是其宾语。空格前是副词 heavily，空格后是名词短语 bodies of water，由此可知，空格处应填形容词，五个选项中只有 polluted 符合要求，而且代入后符合语义和逻辑，意为"被严重污染的水体"，故空格处应填 polluted。

Saturday【F 短文填空】

答案解析

（1）including。空格所在部分意为：探讨了如何应对＿＿＿可再生能源储备、碳汇以及……的平衡……多方面问题。空格前是名词 problems，空格后是三个并列的名词短语 renewable energy storage, carbon sink and the balance，举例说明 problems，故空格处应填 including。

（2）between。空格所在部分意为：处理气候变化和经济增长＿＿＿的平衡。该题考查固定表达，表示"……和……的平衡"用短语 balance between... and...，故空格处应填 between。

（3）risk。空格所在部分意为：气温上升是主要的环境＿＿＿。根据常识可知，气温上升对环境不利，会造成严重后果，是一种危险，r 开头表示"危险"的词有 risk（风险），故空格处应填 risk。

（4）cutting。空格所在句意为：最好的解决办法是通过开发可再生能源来＿＿＿温室气体排放。根据常识可知，要解决气温上升的问题，需要减少温室气体排放，c 开头表示"减少"的词有 cut（削减），空格前是 is，空格所在部分作表语，cut 应用动名词形式，故空格处填 cutting。

（5）countries。空格所在句意为：他说，中国和其他＿＿＿可以"共同努力，分享最佳做法……"。空格前有 and，表明空格所在部分与 and 之前的 China 并列，China 是一个国家，由此推测空格处填 country，空格前的修饰词是 other，因此应填名词的复数形式，故空格处应填 countries。

（6）transmission。空格所在部分意为：我们如何协调配电和＿＿＿系统。空格所在部分与该段开头呼应，开头提到 clean energy transmission and distribution（清洁能源输送和分配），因此空格处应填 transmission。

（7）member。空格所在部分意为：中国科学院＿＿＿周成虎表示，中国一直在建设碳汇生态系统。结合全文可知，文中出现的人物都是世界顶尖的科学家，由此推测周成虎是中国科学院院士，即中国科学院的成员，故空格处应填 member。

（8）put。空格所在部分意为：中国一直在建设碳汇生态系统，并在加强畜牧业碳排放管理方面＿＿＿许多努力。本题考查固定表达，put efforts into 表示"为……付出努力"。由空格前的 has 可知，此处的时态为现在完成时，put 的过去分词还是 put，故空格处应填 put。

（9）believes。空格所在句意为：他＿＿＿技术可以显著提高未来清洁能源应用的可能性。分析句子结构可知，本句是一个复合句，主句缺谓语，空格后面的 technology can... in the future 是一个宾语从句，因此空格处应填一个谓语动词。由句意可知，空格后是杨培东教授的一种看法、观点，因此空格处表达的应该是"认为；觉得"之意。由首字母 b 可知，此处可以填 believe，表示"认为；相信"。又由主语 He 可知，此处应使用第三人称单数形式，故空格处应填 believes。

（10）produce。空格所在部分意为：这样就可以＿＿＿无限的清洁能源。空格前是情态动词 can，空格后是名词短语 infinite clean energy（无限的清洁能源），因此空格处应填动词原形。本文的主旨是减少碳排放，开发清洁能源，produce（产生；制造）符合要求，故空格处应填 produce。